Is God Invisible?

In this volume, Charles Taliaferro and Jil Evans promote aesthetic personalism by examining three domains of aesthetics – the philosophy of beauty, aesthetic experience, and philosophy of art – through the lens of Judaism, Christianity, Islam, theistic Hinduism, and the all-seeing Compassionate Buddha. These religious traditions assume an inclusive, overarching God's-eye, or ideal point of view, that can create an emancipatory appreciation of beauty and goodness. This appreciation also recognizes the reality and value of the aesthetic experience of persons and deepens the experience of artworks. Taliaferro and Evans also explore and contrast the invisibility of persons and God. The belief that God or the sacred is invisible does not mean God or the sacred cannot be experienced through visual and other sensory or unique modes. Conversely, the assumption that human persons are thoroughly visible, or observable in all respects, ignores how racism and other forms of bias render persons invisible to others.

Readers can find color figures at: www.cambridge.org/taliaferroevans images

Charles Taliaferro is Professor of Philosophy and the Oscar and Gertrude Boe Distinguished Chair at St. Olaf College.

Jil Evans is an American painter and author, and member of the Traffic Zone Center for Visual Art cooperative in Minneapolis, Minnesota.

Cambridge Studies in Religion, Philosophy, and Society

Series Editors
Paul K. Moser, *Loyola University, Chicago*
Chad Meister, *Bethel College, Indiana*

This is a series of interdisciplinary texts devoted to major-level courses in religion, philosophy, and related fields. It includes original, current, and wide-spanning contributions by leading scholars from various disciplines that (a) focus on the central academic topics in religion and philosophy, (b) are seminal and up-to-date regarding recent developments in scholarship on the various key topics, and (c) incorporate, with needed precision and depth, the major differing perspectives and backgrounds – the central voices on the major religions and the religious, philosophical, and sociological viewpoints that cover the intellectual landscape today. Cambridge Studies in Religion, Philosophy, and Society is a direct response to this recent and widespread interest and need.

Recent Books in the Series
Roger Trigg *Religious Diversity: Philosophical and Political Dimensions*
John Cottingham *Philosophy of Religion: Towards a More Humane Approach*
William J. Wainwright *Reason, Revelation, and Devotion: Inference and Argument in Religion*
Harry J. Gensler *Ethics and Religion*
Fraser Watts *Psychology, Religion, and Spirituality: Concepts and Applications*
Gordon Graham *Philosophy, Art, and Religion: Understanding Faith and Creativity*
Keith Ward *The Christian Idea of God: A Philosophical Foundation for Faith*
Timothy Samuel Shah and Jack Friedman *Homo Religiosus? Exploring the Roots of Religion and Religious Freedom in Human Experience*
Sylvia Walsh *Kierkegaard and Religion: Personality, Character, and Virtue*
Roger S. Gottlieb *Morality and the Environmental Crisis*
J. L. Schellenberg *Religion after Science: The Cultural Consequences of Religious Immaturity*
Clifford Williams *Religion and the Meaning of Life: An Existential Approach*
Allen W. Wood *Kant and Religion*
Michael McGhee *Spirituality for the Godless: Buddhism, Humanism, and Religion*

Is God Invisible?

An Essay on Religion and Aesthetics

CHARLES TALIAFERRO
St. Olaf College

JIL EVANS
Traffic Zone Center for Visual Art

CAMBRIDGE
UNIVERSITY PRESS

University Printing House, Cambridge CB2 8BS, United Kingdom

One Liberty Plaza, 20th Floor, New York, NY 10006, USA

477 Williamstown Road, Port Melbourne, VIC 3207, Australia

314–321, 3rd Floor, Plot 3, Splendor Forum, Jasola District Centre, New Delhi – 110025, India

79 Anson Road, #06–04/06, Singapore 079906

Cambridge University Press is part of the University of Cambridge.

It furthers the University's mission by disseminating knowledge in the pursuit of education, learning, and research at the highest international levels of excellence.

www.cambridge.org
Information on this title: www.cambridge.org/9781108470742
DOI: 10.1017/9781108681001

© Charles Taliaferro and Jil Evans 2021

This publication is in copyright. Subject to statutory exception and to the provisions of relevant collective licensing agreements, no reproduction of any part may take place without the written permission of Cambridge University Press.

First published 2021

A catalogue record for this publication is available from the British Library.

Library of Congress Cataloging-in-Publication Data
NAMES: Taliaferro, Charles, author. | Evans, Jil, 1958– author.
TITLE: Is God invisible? : an essay on religion and aesthetics / Charles Taliaferro, St. Olaf College, Jil Evans, Traffic Zone Center for Visual Art.
DESCRIPTION: Cambridge, United Kingdom ; New York, NY, USA : Cambridge University Press, 2020. | Series: Cambridge studies in religion, philosophy, and society | Includes bibliographical references and index.
IDENTIFIERS: LCCN 2020043471 (print) | LCCN 2020043472 (ebook) | ISBN 9781108470742 (hardback) | ISBN 9781108456517 (paperback) | ISBN 9781108681001 (ebook)
SUBJECTS: LCSH: Aesthetics – Religious aspects.
CLASSIFICATION: LCC BL65.A4 T35 2020 (print) | LCC BL65.A4 (ebook) | DDC 211–dc23
LC record available at https://lccn.loc.gov/2020043471
LC ebook record available at https://lccn.loc.gov/2020043472

ISBN 978-1-108-47074-2 Hardback
ISBN 978-1-108-45651-7 Paperback

Cambridge University Press has no responsibility for the persistence or accuracy of URLs for external or third-party internet websites referred to in this publication and does not guarantee that any content on such websites is, or will remain, accurate or appropriate.

Contents

List of Figures	*page* vi
List of Web Figures	vii
Acknowledgments	viii
Introduction: The View from Everywhere	1
1 Aesthetic Personalism	6
2 Is God Invisible?	16
3 The Gates of Perception	40
4 The Perception of Gates	63
5 The Beautiful Gate	90
6 Revealing and Concealing	113
7 Public Perception of Religious and Art Objects	139
8 A Personal Guide to the Aesthetic Experience of Works of Art	153
Epilogue	171
Index	172

Figures

2.1 Photograph of Mt. Sinai.	page 17
2.2 Saint Catherine's Monastery, Sinai, Egypt.	39
5.1 Juichimen Kannon, early eighteenth century CE, solid woodblock construction with traces of polychrome.	105
6.1 Melchior d'Hondecoeter, *The Menagerie*.	115
6.2 Ad Reinhardt, *Abstract Painting no. 4*.	117
6.3 Antonio Vivarini, *Virgin and Child Blessing*.	120
6.4 Giovanni Battista Tiepolo, *Discovery of the True Cross*.	121
6.5 Ca' d'Oro, Entrance Hall corner on the Grand Canal, Venice, Italy.	122
6.6 Carlo Crivelli, *Madonna and Child*.	123
6.7 Giovanni Bellini, San Giobbe altarpiece.	125
6.8 Titian, *Assumption of the Virgin*.	126
6.9 Titian, *The Punishment of Marsyas*.	128
6.10 Titian, *Pietà*.	129
6.11 Tintoretto, *Presentation of the Virgin*.	130
6.12 Tintoretto, *The Massacre of the Innocents*.	131
6.13 Giovanni Battista Tiepolo, *The Apotheosis of the Spanish Monarchy*.	133
6.14 Pieter de Hooch, *The Asparagus Vendor 1675–80*.	134
8.1 Nicolas Poussin, *Landscape with a Calm*.	160
8.2 Nicolas Poussin, *Landscape with a Man Killed by a Snake*.	161
8.3 J. Evans, *After Landscape with Man Killed by a Snake by Nicolas Poussin*.	164
8.4 Andrea Pozzo, fresco ceiling painting at Church of St. Ignatius.	166
8.5 J. Evans, *St. Ignazio no. 2*.	167
8.6 Jan Weenix, *A Vase of Flowers*.	168
8.7 J. Evans, *After Van Aelst no. 3*.	169

Web Figures

Web Figure 1. Melchior d'Hondecoeter, *The Menagerie*.
Web Figure 2. Antonio Vivarini, *Virgin and Child Blessing*.
Web Figure 3. Giovanni Battista Tiepolo, *Discovery of the True Cross*.
Web Figure 4. Giovanni Bellini, San Giobbe altarpiece.
Web Figure 5. Titian, *Assumption of the Virgin*.
Web Figure 6. Tintoretto, *The Massacre of the Innocents*.
Web Figure 7. Giovanni Battista Tiepolo, *The Apotheosis of the Spanish Monarchy*.
Web Figure 8. Pieter de Hooch, *The Asparagus Vendor*, 1675–80.
Web Figure 9. Jan Weenix, *A Vase of Flowers*.

Web figures can be found at: www.cambridge.org/taliaferroevansimages

Acknowledgments

We thank Chad Meister and Paul Moser for inviting us to write a book on religion and aesthetics for their series Cambridge Studies in Religion, Philosophy, and Society. Their encouragement and advice have been brilliant. We thank all those who have commented on earlier drafts of this book or engaged in helpful conversations, including Keith Ward, Tim Crane, Fiona Ellis, Tim Mawson, Mario DeCaro, David Macarthur, Paul Reasoner, Katherine Solomonson, Owen Sandercox, Ed Langerak, and the members of the philosophy departments at St. Olaf and Carleton colleges. A special thank-you to Ed and Nancy Polich of Dover Street. We are especially grateful to Kathleen Weflen for her expert editing. Thanks to Mattias Kostov, our research assistant. We are indebted to Bret D. Workman, Mary Bongiovi, Akash Datchinamurthy, Jessica McCurdy Crooks, Zoe Plewa, and G. E. Patterson for preparing the manuscript for publication. Above all, we are grateful for the support and kindness of Beatrice Rehl of Cambridge University Press.

Part of an earlier version of Chapter 2 was presented at Heythrop College, University of London in 2018, and part of Chapter 4 at Harvard University in 2019. Both occasions provided us with insightful feedback. With thanks to Anastasia Faunce, some of Chapter 6 on Venetian painting was presented in our course, "Reflecting Venice," March 2017, Minnesota Lifelong Learning Center, University of Minnesota.

This book extends the philosophy of imagination, aesthetics, and phenomenology developed in our first coauthored book, *The Image in Mind: Theism, Naturalism, and the Imagination*, though we do not presuppose the reader has any familiarity with that work.[1] If you find *Is God Invisible? An*

---

[1] See *The Image in Mind: Theism, Naturalism, and the Imagination* by C. Taliaferro and J. Evans (London: Continuum, 2010). See also our coedited book *Turning Images in Philosophy, Science, and Religion; A New Book of Nature* (Oxford: Oxford University Press, 2011).

Acknowledgments

Essay on Religion and Aesthetics engaging, we hope you will explore our earlier book as well as our contributions on the visual representation of evil in the six-volume *The History of Evil*.[2]

---

[2] We have coauthored philosophical reflections of the visual representations of evil in volume 3, *The History of Evil in the Early Modern Age: 1450–1700*, chapter 21, and in volume 4, *The History of Evil in the Eighteenth and Nineteenth Centuries*, chapter 22, both published by Routledge, 2018.

Introduction

The View from Everywhere

> Value ... is the very substance of exaltation, or more exactly it is the reality we have to evoke when we try to understand how exaltation can change into creative force.
>
> Gabriel Marcel[1]

Exaltation is at the heart of all religions. The aesthetics of religions disclose the values of the practitioners who shape the religion, and who, in turn, are further shaped in their practice and aesthetic experience. Religious life involves all the dimensions of aesthetics: beauty and ugliness, aesthetic emotions such as awe and love and hate, feelings of guilt and shame as well as joy and ecstasy, and a staggering range of artistic works. The field of aesthetics raises an array of religious concerns: Can we have aesthetically charged experiences of the divine? What is the relationship between beauty and divinity? In *Is God Invisible? An Essay on Religion and Aesthetics*, we investigate the aesthetics of religious life and values.

A major theme in this book involves bringing to light the relationship between the visibility and invisibility of persons and God. We are not always visible to each other. Due to racism, sexism, economic destitution, and other forms of oppression and divisiveness, some of us are ignored or shunned by society and deemed ugly and unworthy of attention. Moreover, each of us has a subjective life of aesthetically complex experiences of anguish, longing, and desire, which are elusive and often hidden from others. In this book we measure this invisibility in light of the belief in an all-seeing God, an ideal aesthetic observer and subject to whom all things are known and from whom no secrets are hid.[2] Divine omniscience may be described as *the view from everywhere*

---

[1] Cited by Kenneth Gallagher in *The Philosophy of Gabriel Marcel* (New York: Fordham University Press, 1975), p. 93.
[2] Language borrowed from *The Book of Common Prayer* as used in the Anglican communion, various editions. We develop the God's-eye point of view, drawing not just on Christian tradition, but also from Judaism, Islam, theistic Hinduism, and forms of Buddhism that highlight the eyes of the Buddha.

insofar as it encompasses all actual and possible points of view.[3] Given the unideal point of view that defines our human condition, we experience each other only episodically: Sometimes a face becomes visible for the first time simply because a flash of reflected light brings your eyes to see another. Or, fraught with urgency, a voice breaks through the noise and we hear an emotional vulnerability we had been ignoring. In so many of our interactions, it takes intentional attention, perception, and imagination to truly acknowledge the reality of others' subjective hopes, desires, fears, love, and hate. And our vices of vanity, envy, jealousy, self-serving rage, and contempt can easily lead to the willful concealment of others, banning them from our attention and concern. Just as it takes virtuous attunement to see each other, it may take a related attunement or openness to appreciate the importance of a God's-eye point of view (which affirms the reality of other persons' lives) and even an openness to the reality of a sacred, transcendent being (God, Allah, Brahman).[4]

The idea of a God's-eye point of view in aesthetics and value theory has been criticized as incoherent, a projection of male philosophers, and potentially exploitative. We respond to such charges, contending that an allegiance to a God's-eye point of view (or the view from everywhere) can be emancipatory and form an important ground for pursuing justice. We propose a God's-eye point of view in which *nothing is hidden*. Such a view provides vital support for grounding realism in aesthetics and ethics, as well as in making sense of the very idea of truth (there being truths that are not dependent upon human perception or language).

Our overall aim is to engage the religious dimension in all three areas of aesthetics: the affective nature of experience, the philosophy of beauty and ugliness, and the philosophy of art. Because each area involves experience, our methodology is *phenomenological*. In phenomenology (from the Greek for "that which appears"), philosophy is grounded in experience, so much so that *experientialism* would be a fitting synonym. *Experience* here is meant to be broader than relying only on the five senses plus memory and reason; in addition, there are aesthetic, ethical, and religious experiences; the experience of using the imagination; and experiencing the emotions and desires that

---

[3] Divine omniscience has been defined as "God knows everything" and "every property and every individual is such that if the individual has the property then God knows of that individual and property that the former has the latter," A. N. Prior, "Formalities of Omniscience," *Philosophy* 37 (140), 1962, pp. 114–129. For a further account, see "Divine Cognitive Power" by Charles Taliaferro, *International Journal for Philosophy of Religion*, 18, 1985, pp. 133–140. For accounts of omniscience that explicitly address God's knowing the affective experience of others, see *Omnisubjectivity* by Linda Zagzebski (Milwaukee: Marquette University, 2013) and "God and Concept Empiricism" by Michael Beaty and Charles Taliaferro, *Southwest Philosophy Review* 6:2, July 1990.

[4] It is possible to accept the validity of a God's-eye point of view, essentially what is known as an ideal observer theory, without believing there is a God or ideal observer. We address the ideal observer theory in Chapter 5.

contribute meaning in our lives. Typically, phenomenology is distinguished from *analytical philosophy* with its stress on *analysis* (from the Greek for "to cut apart, divide") of concepts and language. We do not see this as an either/or matter: while our principal methodology is phenomenological, we also draw on the resources of analytical philosophy. With the help of some analytical philosophy, we engage in a phenomenological inquiry into the aesthetic experience of persons with each other and the experience of a divine transcendent reality. We uphold what we are calling *aesthetic personalism*, the view that recognizes the central importance of the phenomenologically evident reality of persons. Persons of all ages, genders, ethnic, economic, social, sexual, religious, and political identities are valuable, self-aware subjects with aesthetic lives.

We also engage in the philosophy of the meaning of life in light of an aesthetic study of five great world religions and an alternative, secular naturalism. The topic of the meaning of life is receiving fresh attention after much neglect in the mid twentieth century. We believe that investigating the meaning of life must take religion and aesthetics seriously. Nearly all people throughout history have practiced some form of religion, and all people everywhere experience the aesthetic dimension of being alive in conscious and subconscious ways.

Our aim is not just to write about abstract theoretical matters, but to critically evaluate some museum practices and thus to contribute to the philosophy of museums (or museology). Philosophical and religious principles can enhance the perception of religious objects. We think that some religious artifacts should be approached personally, both respecting the persons or groups that made the objects as well as appreciating how some artifacts have a character or personality that invites us to view them as persons. We propose that some works of art should be recognized as possessing agency; sometimes works of art *do things*. A statue of the Buddha can invite you to meditate. We will critically consider cases when the personhoods of some religious art objects are respected and when they are not. An important qualification: we are not assigning personhood to some art objects the way some treat corporations as persons (with accompanying legal rights).[5] We will, rather, be making a phenomenological point about how our experience of some religious objects can be akin to our experience of a healthy, embodied person who integrates desires and purposes.

A final chapter offers a personal guide in pursuing the study of religion and aesthetics. This chapter builds on some practical exercises Evans introduced to

---

[5] We have reservations about treating corporations as persons legally and ethically, though we think that corporations can be experienced as having a character or personality. For a critical approach to corporations as persons see *On Caring* by Milton Mayeroff (New York: Harper Perennial, 1971), p. 7.

European curators and philosophers at the University of Glasgow. The exercises involve drawing from the observation of works of art.[6]

We remind readers that this book is *an essay*, not a treatise or encyclopedia. We do not address every philosophically and theologically interesting dimension of the relationship between religion and aesthetics.

Putting our book in the context of the current literature, we have sympathy with why some philosophers and theologians disparage philosophy of religion today. We believe this is largely because they do not appreciate its power to phenomenologically engage in the rich aesthetic dimensions of religious life and values. We seek both to engage these elements as well as to challenge what we believe are highly misleading caricatures of the concept of God and the sacred. Since the mid twentieth century, some philosophers have assumed that the God of the Abrahamic faiths is a nonnatural, disembodied person akin to a spooky but supremely powerful poltergeist. We have set out to reset the stage for a sounder, philosophically articulate religious understanding of the sacred in the Abrahamic faiths, Hinduism, and Buddhism. We are especially critical of the way in which critics of theism (David Hume, Bertrand Russell, A. J. Ayer, and others) depict God as an aesthetically anemic specter.

The disparagement by some people of mainstream philosophy of religion reminds us of a time when we witnessed a salvage operation in the midst of a disaster. On the afternoon of December 20, 1992, we arrived at a conference on science and religion held in Windsor Castle, England. A fire had broken out in the late morning. Despite the presence of 35 fire engines and over 200 firefighters, a constable welcomed us onto the grounds where firefighters were rescuing what they could as the fire gradually got under control. Today some philosophers and theologians seem to treat traditional philosophy or, more specifically, philosophy of religion, like a burning building, as depicted in "Burning Down the House? D. Z. Phillips and the Metaphysics of Theism" in which Phillips is described as seeking to undermine the metaphysics of classical theism.[7] There are ample voices calling for the reform, re-visioning, or renewing of philosophy of religion, and some calling for the end of the field and even of philosophy itself. An article in the *Times Literary Supplement* has the title "Philosophy Is Dead."[8] We do not think this proclamation is accurate. (Perhaps we are somewhat battle hardened as one of us is also a painter who continues to paint through periodic pronouncements of the death of painting.) While we are not alarmed about the destitution of contemporary philosophy

---

[6] This took place at a conference, "Philosophy and Museums: Ethics, Aesthetics, and Ontology," in 2013. The conference was part of the international *Abstracta in Concreta* project that focuses on how abstract religious and philosophical ideas are represented (and sometimes misrepresented) in museum collections. Evans led participants to engage works of art by sketching them.

[7] *Philosophia Christi* 9 (2), 261–270, 2007.

[8] *Times Literary Supplement*, "Philosophy Is Dead" by Jonathan Ree, June 20, 2018. Interestingly, this review article of a book by Raymond Geuss concludes that Geuss's case against traditional philosophy is itself philosophical and thus demonstrates that there is still life in philosophy.

Introduction: The View from Everywhere

and philosophy of religion, we are committed in this book to fresh, constructive work that challenges the philosophical arsonists of our day. We do so, in part, by focusing on *what it's like to be religious* and its panoply of rich, aesthetically charged experiences and values.

Rather than picturing the chief task of philosophy of religion as salvaging objects from a burning castle, we commend seeing philosophy of religion more in line with the life and work of Al-Biruni (973–1050), one of the greatest of all scholars and scientists, known for his combination of impartiality and a passion for cross-cultural and especially cross-religious understanding. Fluent in Arabic, Farsi, Greek, Hebrew, and Sanskrit, Al-Biruni studied Islam, Judaism, Christianity, Zoroastrianism, Hinduism, and Buddhism. While he was a devout Muslim, his reputation for fairness in addressing religious traditions other than his own is monumental; he is a model for us all today. Rather than burning down religious worldviews and their secular alternatives (metaphorically or literally), he sought to exalt – in the sense of lift up for us to see and assess – a multitude of religious worldviews and practices.[9]

While the medieval scholar Al-Biruni is our role model, closer to home we acknowledge our indebtedness to David Brown, Victoria Harrison, Douglas Hedley, Gordon Graham, Gwen Griffith-Dickens, Anthony O'Hear, Margaret Miles, Anthony Rudd, Nicholas Wolterstorff, and Mark Wynn, among others, who have done groundbreaking work in philosophy of religion in the context of art and philosophical aesthetics.

---

[9] As a scientist, Al-Biruni was also extraordinary, sketching an evolutionary account of life and geology. He measured the radius of the Earth and was off by only 200 miles (an error of less than 1 percent).

I

Aesthetic Personalism

> One thing now seems reasonably clear: being cannot ... be indifferent to value: it could only be so if one were to identify it as a crude datum considered as existing in its own right, and that we are not justified in doing.
>
> Gabriel Marcel[1]

In the current intellectual climate, there is a monolithic assumption that the natural sciences are our best guide to reality. While there is little doubt about the titanic significance and the *necessity* of physics, chemistry, and biology informing our understanding of reality, there is some doubt about the *sufficiency* of the natural sciences in helping us identify and explain values (what is good or evil, beautiful or ugly) in society and politics, our personal choices, our religious or secular life, and even the very existence of conscious, subjective experience. A growing range of philosophers has argued that to fully address the reality of consciousness and values we need to expand our inquiry beyond the confines of the natural sciences.[2] In this book we undertake such an expanded exploration, looking into the aesthetic dimension of religious worldviews and their secular alternatives, including those that limit inquiry to the natural sciences.

---

[1] Cited by Kenneth Gallagher in *The Philosophy of Gabriel Marcel*, p. 92.
[2] Objections to the sufficiency of the natural sciences to address values, meaning, and even the very nature of consciousness, come not only from advocates of religion, but also from secular philosophers such as Thomas Nagel, Tim Crane, and Peter Unger. See Unger's *All The Power in the World* (Oxford: Oxford University Press, 2005). We especially recommend chapter 1, "The Mystery of the Physical." The view that the natural sciences are both necessary and sufficient to address all domains of life is sometimes called *scientism*. Unger calls it *scientificalism*. For a critical overview, see *Scientism: The New Orthodoxy*, edited by Daniel N. Robinson and R. N. Williams (London: Bloomsbury, 2015).

Preliminary Matters 7

A book on aesthetics and religion invites three questions: What is meant by *aesthetics?* What is meant by *religion?* And what is the relationship between the two? In the first section of this chapter, we briefly address these questions and then, in the second section, articulate the position we advance in this book: *aesthetic personalism.* The third section initiates our investigation into the aesthetic experience of the divine and human persons: Are human persons and the divine best thought of as completely visible or invisible, natural or nonnatural?

PRELIMINARY MATTERS

Aesthetics today in English often refers to three concerns: the philosophy of beauty and ugliness, the philosophy of art, and the affective aspects of experience, such as when we experience an intimate enclosure within a circle of apple trees, shrink back from the austerity of a prison cell, are held pinned by a sideways glance, or lose interest in a bloodless, stale abstraction.[3] What we are referring to as affective experience is akin to what some Indian philosophers refer to as rasa or aesthetic emotions.[4]

We use the term *aesthetics* in this broad sense to include all three concerns, investigating religion from the standpoint of beauty and ugliness, in the context of the philosophy of art, and in terms of affective experience. Each of these elements is involved in the religious work entitled *Ramayana*. This epic includes beauty (the beauty of friendship, marriage, fidelity, courage, compassion, forgiveness, joy, love) and ugliness (the ugliness of betrayal, envy, jealousy, greed). The epic is itself a work of art, an aesthetically rich creation of imagination, inspired by the heroic-folk tradition. And the work involves affective experience. In one telling passage, Rama (an avatar or incarnation of God) describes the saintly response to violence in aromatic terms:

The conduct of the saint and the sinner is analogous to that of the sandal tree and the axe: the axe cuts down the tree, but the fragrant sandal imparts the perfume to the very axe that fells it.[5]

---

[3] Our reference to aesthetic properties is (roughly) in accord with Gary Iseminger's *The Aesthetic Function of Art* (Ithaca, NY: Cornell University Press, 2004) and Frank Sibley's classic work: see his papers "Aesthetic Concepts," *Philosophical Review* 68, 1959, pp. 421–450, and "Aesthetic and Non-aesthetic," *Philosophical Review* 75, 1965, pp. 135–159. We employ the term *aesthetic* to refer to affective, cognitive emotions, avoiding a dichotomy between cognition and the emotive. See Nelson Goodman's *Languages of Art: An Approach to a Theory of Symbols*, 2nd ed. (Indianapolis: Bobbs-Merrill, 1976), pp. 247–248.

[4] See *A Rasa Reader: Classical Indian Aesthetics: Historical Sourcebook in Classical Indian Thought*, edited by Sheldon Pollock (New York: Columbia University Press, 2018).

[5] *Wisdom Teachings from the Hindu Ramayana*, by Anantanand Rambachan (West Conshohocken, PA: Infinity Publishing, 2013), p. 11. Mahatma Gandhi thought of the *Ramayana* (or *Ramacharitamanas*, as translated by the poet Tulsidas) as the greatest book in the history of religious literature. See *A Survey of Hinduism*, by Klaus Klostermaier (Albany: State

This passage is particularly evocative, as it aligns with Gandhi's practice of *satyagraha* (holding on to truth), nonviolent resistance.

We are not using the term *aesthetic* so broadly that it encompasses some other meanings of *aesthetics*. *Aesthetic* has been used to refer to the values or lives of aesthetes who give themselves over to a life of immediate, sensuous satisfaction (e.g., Don Juan, the seventeenth-century fictional lover) in contrast to those devoted to self-mastery or asceticism. We do not employ Søren Kierkegaard's identification of the aesthetic life as distinct from ethical and religious lives. Nor do we use the term *aesthetic* meaning detached, dispassionate, or not engaged in practical matters (as when, in the philosophy of art, there is sometimes an appeal to *the aesthetic point of view* conceived of as a disinterested vantage point). We propose instead that the aesthetic dimension of lived experience is inextricable in the meaning of embodied life, both in passionate religious engagement as well as in the affective aridity religious practitioners refer to as "the dark night of the soul" (*la noche oscura del alma*) when God feels hidden or obscured (*Deus absconditus*). After all, the feeling that God is absent has an aesthetic dimension, a feeling of vacuity, abandonment, or emptiness.[6]

Our book addresses Judaism, Christianity, Islam, Hinduism, and Buddhism as significant world religions. Our focus on these five religions is not because we do not recognize other traditions as religious and of enormous value but because, in terms of the world population, these five together make up the majority of religious practitioners. Because of our desire to not be any more diffuse than we are due to limitations on space, we have not been able to address each of the important different strands within each of the five traditions. The exception to our focus on these world religions is in Chapter 7 when we address the perception of religious objects. In that chapter we offer a philosophical analysis of two major art exhibits involving Native American experience and Native American art.[7]

In defining religion, we explicitly do not require religion be defined in terms of the nonnatural, the supernatural, or theism. One of us has elsewhere advanced a definition of religion, though our project in this book does not rest on the acceptability of the following:

University of New York Press, 1989), p. 83. The *Ramayana* has been altered over time with recension and rewriting.

[6] For a further treatment of aesthetics, see *Aesthetics: A Beginner's Guide*, by Charles Taliaferro (Oxford: Oneworld Press, 2011) and our coauthored *The Image in Mind* and coedited *Turning Images*.

[7] While we address these exhibits in our chapter on the creation and perception of *religious* artifacts and works of art, it is more common to reference Native American *spirituality* rather than Native American religion(s). Still, Native American spirituality would be covered by our definition of religion in this chapter and so should (in our view) receive the legal protection (e.g., laws against religious discrimination) and rights (e.g., laws prohibiting the infringement of the freedom to exercise one's religion) of traditions currently recognized as religions (e.g., Christianity).

Aesthetics from a Personalist Perspective

A religion involves a communal, transmittable body of teaching and prescribed practices about an ultimate reality or state of being that calls for reverence or awe, a body which guides its practitioners into what it describes as a saving, illuminating, or emancipatory relation to this reality through a life of prayers, meditation, rites and/or worship and/or moral practices like repentance, reconciliation, and personal transformation.[8]

We believe that this definition would apply both to the five traditions we address in this book as well as to Native American spirituality, Zoroastrianism, Confucianism, Daoism, Shintoism, Sikhism, African religions, and communities that combine non-Christian and Roman Catholic ways of life in Latin America, among others.[9]

In addressing our question about the relationship of religion and aesthetics, we do not use the terms *aesthetics* and *religion* as contraries. Some have charged that these are contrary terms, on the grounds that religion involves commitment and passion while aesthetics involves detachment. Because we believe there is an aesthetic dimension to all experience, we cannot make sense of religious experience void of an aesthetic dimension. Nor do we understand what is meant by an aesthetic experience void of values and the particular histories of embodied persons. Even when aesthetic experience seems to transport us to remote lands (in epic fairy tales like Tolkien's Middle Earth or science fiction as in the Star Wars imaginarium), we remain *embodied* readers and viewers, creatures of imagination. We stress our historical lives as each of us has a history, a past, even if society has suppressed all records and imposed false narratives about the past.

AESTHETICS FROM A PERSONALIST PERSPECTIVE

What we are calling *aesthetic personalism* has its roots in the personalist movement in philosophy beginning in the late nineteenth century and flourishing during the twentieth century, mostly after World War II. Personalists treat persons as irreducibly real, conscious, self-aware individuals, enduring over time as free agents who are responsible for living a valuable life in a world that is permeated with meaning.[10] Persons are not

---

[8] See *A Dictionary of Philosophy of Religion*, coedited by Charles Taliaferro and Elsa Marty (New York: Bloomsbury, 2017), 2nd ed.
[9] We believe our understanding of religion would also count as religious the many non-Christian and non-Islamic traditions of Africa. We appeal to African religious concepts of God as all-seeing and all-knowing in Chapter 5, drawing on recent work by Abdulai Iddrisu. Taliaferro has done some work on Roman Catholic and indigenous religions in "Latin American Perspectives on Religion," edited by Charles Taliaferro, Marciano Spica, and Agnaldo Portugal, *Open Theology* 2018 (4), 685–686.
[10] Some of the main personalists are Bordon Parker Bowne (1847–1910), Edgar Shefield Brightman (1884–1953), and Peter Bertocci (1910–89), whom Taliaferro studied under in 1979. Because of their academic positions at Boston University, they are sometimes referred to as the *Boston Personalists*. Martin Luther King Jr. (1929–68), a student of Brightman's, is probably the most

reduced to social relations, as in some forms of Marxism. Nor are we to be valued, as in some forms of utilitarianism, because of our states of pleasure or happiness, which would be to value people for their state of being rather than being valued as persons themselves. Most importantly, personalists believe that there are compelling, phenomenological grounds for resisting philosophies that seek to eliminate persons and our conscious experiences from their account of what is fundamentally real.[11] These philosophers contend that any full explanation of our subjective, conscious states must, ultimately, be in exclusively physical factors that are nonsubjective and not conscious. We believe this flies in the face of the evident experience that we ourselves are conscious agents who act for reasons and desires.

Our view is the opposite of those who treat the self as fiction.[12] A prominent twentieth-century personalist, Peter Bertocci aptly summarizes personalism's stress on conscious subjectivity: "Whatever else personal existence is, as lived, it consists in a unity of activities – sensory, memorial, perceptual, reasoning, emotive, volitional, moral and appreciative *(aesthetic and religious)* [emphasis ours] ... It is an irreducible, active matrix."[13] Aesthetic personalism is a branch of personalism that gives special attention to aesthetic values and the cognitive nature of aesthetic experience.

Our commitment to inquiry that takes persons and their aesthetic experiences seriously will emerge as we challenge what we think are more narrow empiricist methods of inquiry. At the outset we suggest that aesthetic personalism is supported in our experience of ourselves and the world such that aesthetic personalism has some degree of initial, prima facie evidence in its favor. At least prior to the deployment of philosophical theories, we do not experience the world or ourselves as neutral things or facts to which we assign meaning. Rather, we experience reality as hostile or friendly, nurturing or destructive, desirable or repulsive, beautiful or ugly.[14] Perhaps this experience of a world of values and disvalues may be shown to be illusory, but its ostensible

---

well-known American adherent to a form of personalism. Understood broadly, Max Scheler (1874–1928), Martin Buber (1878–1965), Gabriel Marcel (1889–1973), Dietrich von Hildebrand (1889–1977), and Karol Wojtyła (Pope John Paul II 1920–2005), among others, are recognized for their contributions to personalism.

[11] Those who seek to eliminate consciousness (Paul and Patricia Churchland) are sometimes called *eliminativists*. For a critique of eliminativism, see *Consciousness and the Mind of God*, by Charles Taliaferro (Cambridge: Cambridge University Press, 1994). A literary exploration of the implications of one, rather severe form of eliminativism can be found in the 1946 Pulitzer prize–winning novel *All The King's Men*, by Robert Penn Warren, when the main character, Jack, embraces (for a time) a philosophy he calls "The Great Twitch" in which the conscious responsibility of persons is eviscerated.

[12] We take the opposite view of D. Dennett in "The Self as a Center of Narrative Gravity," *Philosophia* 15, 1992, pp. 275–288. See Chapter 7 for our response to Dennett's essay.

[13] Bertocci, *The Person God Is* (London: George Allen and Unwin, 1970), p. 212.

[14] See Dietrich von Hildebrand, *Aesthetics*, translated by Brian McNeil (Steubenville, OH: Hildebrand Project, 2016), vol. 1.

reality is philosophically significant. We propose that these responses form a revealing attunement between ourselves and the world, sometimes providing evidence of accord with our surroundings, sometimes revealing a hostile or even absurd relationship. Questions about the significance and value of our experience are central to questions about the meaning of life. Human experience is suffused and charged with evident, discoverable meaning. John Fischer suggests that the denial of such values is plausible only if we adopt a perspective that he calls "philosophical outer space," in which we "zoom-out" far away from the human condition:

> The arguments for nihilism are not compelling. The zoom-out argument takes us to a perspective akin to the view from outer space. But outer space has no gravity, and untethered objects and persons float away. Philosophical outer space is like that: when we abstract away from details that matter, we lose the proper perspective. From our more rooted, grounded perspective, life is a rich texture of meaning conferring activities and projects.[15]

In our view, Tim Crane is right in his recent book, *The Meaning of Belief: Religion from an Atheist's Point of View*, that one of the key driving forces behind religious life is the desire for meaning; we long to know whether our lives matter to those around us and even on a cosmic, transcendent scale. Does it matter whether we live or die? This is a question of deep aesthetic and religious significance. Thomas Nagel expressed the search for meaning with this question: "How can one bring into one's individual life a full recognition of one's relation to the universe as a whole?"[16] The existentialist Albert Camus stressed the importance of confronting the meaning of life.

> Galileo, who held a scientific truth of great importance [the truth about heliocentricity], abjured it with the greatest of ease as soon as it endangered his life. In a certain sense, he did right. That truth was not worth the stake. Whether the earth or the sun revolves around the other is a matter of profound indifference. To tell the truth, it is a futile question. On the other hand, I see many people die because they judge that life is not worth living. I see others paradoxically getting killed for the sake of ideas or illusions that give them a reason for living ... I therefore conclude that the meaning of life is the most urgent of questions.[17]

---

[15] John Fischer, *Death, Immortality, and Meaning in Life* (Oxford: Oxford University Press, 2020), p. 184.
[16] Thomas Nagel, *Secular Philosophy and the Religious Temperament* (Oxford: Oxford University Press, 2010), p. 5.
[17] Albert Camus, *The Myth of Sisyphus and Other Essays*, translated by Justin O'Brien (New York: Alfred A. Knopf, 1969), pp. 3–4. Questions about the meaning of life were abjured by some philosophers in the English-speaking world in the 1970s on the grounds that they were inappropriate conceptually (propositions have meaning, but life?). This has been largely overturned, as questions about life's meaning have been interpreted as questions about what is real and what is its significance. On this view, a famous anecdote about Bertrand Russell being apoplectic when a taxi driver asked him "What's it all about?" needs revisiting: Russell essentially could provide the answer in the form of his famous essay "A Free Man's Worship," which we address in

We only add that one of the reasons why Galileo's heliocentricity had the importance that it had for his contemporaries was its implications for the meaning of life. (Does Galileo's claim undermine the reliability of the Bible? Does it give reasons for thinking that humans are not at the center of creation?)[18] It should also be noted that most contributors to the revived interest in the meaning of (and in) life contend that a meaningful life involves being in contact with reality rather than having an utterly false or delusional world view. As John Fischer puts it, "a meaningful life requires that one be in suitable contact with reality."[19] If that is true, then those of us interested in the meaning of life have a reason to investigate promising religious and secular views of reality.

Setting up our project in the next three chapters, let us now turn to the philosophy of God today, especially its aesthetic dimension, and how philosophers deploy the concepts of visibility and what is natural.

GOD AS NATURAL OR NONNATURAL, PERSONS AS VISIBLE OR INVISIBLE

Some philosophers and theologians depict God in the Abrahamic traditions as an invisible, disembodied, supernatural, or nonnatural person. Thinking of God as a disembodied, invisible person is not limited to the critics of theism. One of the most gifted Christian philosophers working today describes a central Christian tenet as the belief that there is an invisible person.[20] Other philosophers and theologians think of God as wholly other, not at all like a person, visible or invisible, radically separate from the natural world and immune to human experience. To stress God's otherness, some theologians warn us to not think of God as a thing or an object that exists the way we might think of planets, stars, and galaxies existing. Herbert McCabe claims that "It is not possible that God and the universe should add up to two [things]."[21] "We address God as 'you,'" observes Nicholas Lash, "and speak of God as

---

Chapter 4: All life on Earth will eventually end, all human individuals are annihilated at their death, and we live in a Godless universe. For an excellent survey of new work on the meaning of life, see *Exploring the Meaning of Life; An Anthology and Guide*, edited by Joshua Searchris (Oxford: Wiley-Blackwell, 2013). See also Stewart Goetz's *The Purpose of Life* (London: Continuum Press, 2012).

[18] The meaning of life is an area to which multiple disciplines are now contributing, as evidenced in the conference *The Meaning of Life* held at Harvard University in 2019 when contributions were made by philosophers, psychologists, and different social scientists.

[19] John Fischer, *Death, Immortality, and Meaning in Life*, p. 183. Fischer defends this thesis over against thought experiments involving persons whose false views of the world due to deception are never discovered by the person deceived. See especially chapter 3.

[20] Michael Rea in his 2017 Gifford Lectures at St. Andrews University: *Though the Darkness Hide Thee: Seeking the Face of the Invisible God*. Available online. See his *The Hiddenness of God* (Oxford: Oxford University Press, 2018).

[21] Herbert McCabe, *God Matters* (London: Continuum Press, 1987), p. 6.

'him' rather than 'it,' not because God is 'a person' (which he certainly is not, for he is not anything)."[22] The way in which God is pictured or conceived has a direct bearing on how religion is pictured or conceived. For example, some who think the object of religious life is beyond nature, or nonnatural, create a picture of religion as a practice that is devoted to something that is nonnatural.

> Religions are passionate communal displays of costly commitments to the satisfaction of non-natural beings and/or the overcoming of non-natural regulative structures.[23]

We believe that the above images of God and religion are the result of a highly restrictive understanding of what counts as natural as well as an austere, constricted view of the nature of experience. In secular, modern philosophy, experience is often limited to what can be empirically described or measured. This reduction of what can count as "real" in human experience gives rise to a deep skepticism about claims coming from religion, aesthetics, ethics, and value theory. Some philosophers and theologians have also imposed religious constraints on experience; they define *God* and *experience* in ways that make a claim to experience God nonsensical. To some philosophers, the claim to experience God is the same as claiming to experience that which cannot be experienced. We shall argue that such constraints are unwarranted.[24]

We propose that many reported experiences of the divine found in the testimony of people across history and culture are natural.[25] Many of the religious concepts of God and claims about the experience of the divine should lead us to expand our concept of what is natural beyond the natural sciences. The phenomenology of experience, in perception, self-consciousness, the acknowledgement of others, memory, and behavior, all bear value in thinking about how the divine may be experienced or perceived.

We build a case for an expanded phenomenological point of view in Chapter 2 by raising and addressing those who charge that the idea of God as an invisible reality is philosophically preposterous. We will show that such critics – David

---

[22] Nicholas Lash, *Easter in Ordinary: Reflections on Human Experience and the Knowledge of God* (London: SCM Press, 1988), p. 276.
[23] Graham Oppy, *Naturalism and Religion* (London: Routledge, 2018), p. 36.
[24] We contend that such constraints involve what philosophers used to call *persuasive definitions*, cases of when terms are defined (sometimes illicitly) in evaluative ways that strategically rule out promising alternatives. For example, if one defines "selfish" as any act that is done because the agent desires to do it, then virtually all action will be classified as selfish. This rules out plausible counterexamples of nonselfish acts as when an agent helps others because they desire the well-being of others for their own sake.
[25] This is a major theme in the book *The Naturalness of Belief; New Essays on Theism's Rationality*, edited by Paul Copan and Charles Taliaferro (New York: Lexington Books, 2019). See especially chapter 5, "In what sense might religion be natural?" by A. Visala and J. L. Barrett, pp. 67–84. See also Barrett's other work: *Why Would Anyone Believe in God?* (Walnut Creek, CA: Altamira Press, 2004); *Cognitive Science, Religion, and Theology: From Human Minds to Divine Minds* (West Conshohocken, PA: Templeton Press, 2011); and *Born Believers: The Science of Children's Religious Belief* (New York: The Free Press, 2012).

Hume, Bertrand Russell, A. J. Ayer, Antony Flew, and Gareth Moore – radically misconstrue the traditional belief that God is not a visible object and they do not recognize the multilayered ways in which we may be visible or invisible to each other. Our response to these critics involves challenging both their conceptual and aesthetic points of view.

As will be clear in Chapter 2, we believe that there is a philosophically interesting analogy between our visibility or invisibility to one another and the visibility or invisibility of God. The key lies in exposing and setting aside a behaviorist, materialist approach to minds and bodies. Thinking of God as not identical with a visual object does not preclude the idea that God is manifested in and through visual and other modes of experience. Analogously, we maintain that our own identity is not a simple equation of who we are and our manifest, visual life. We propose that our own identity as embodied persons admits of several senses in which we may be visible or invisible to each other. Under ideal, healthy, morally responsible conditions, we are accessible and responsive to each other in all our sensory modes. But this is not essentially so. The most obvious case of when we might be thought to be invisible to one another is when people refuse to see us. This is powerfully represented in Ralph Ellison's *Invisible Man*, a novel that exposes and confronts racism in America.

> I am an invisible man. No, I am not a spook like those who haunted Edgar Allan Poe; nor am I one of your Hollywood movie ectoplasms. I am a man of substance of flesh and bone, fiber and liquids – and I might even be said to possess a mind. I am invisible, understand, simply because people refuse to see me.[26]

Another case of invisibility is when we disguise our goals and ideas; we present ourselves to others as possessing the virtues of selflessness and grace, while all along we harbor resentment and malignant hatred for others. Crime fiction and tragic tales of betrayal would be impossible without persons having unobserved motives. Some philosophers go even further and propose that in addition to the above two forms of invisibility, there is a third: our mental life (our thinking, feeling, sensing, desiring, intending) is distinct from our bodies, including our brains and neural events. On this view, while the mental and physical are obviously in continuous causal interaction, there is more going on in our lives than bodily events. While we are normally available to each other through a spectrum of visual and other sensory modes, we contend that we are not, strictly speaking, identical with our bodies or bodily processes. On this expansive, nonmaterialist view, our own visibility and observability as persons rests on the proper functioning of our psychophysical, or mind–body, relationship.

In Chapter 2 we defend the plausibility of this mind–body relationship with what philosophers call *the knowledge argument*, which raises a classic problem in philosophy, *the problem of other minds*: How do you know that other people are as they seem – mindful, conscious individuals as opposed to automatons or

---

[26] *The Invisible Man*, opening lines. Published in 1952 by Random House.

some other mindless creatures?[27] We shall explore the philosophical worry that our mental lives are not directly observable to others. We may also be invisible to each other due to willful ignorance, absence of self-awareness, duplicity, or the breakdown of a harmonious union of mind and body leading us to not fully function as embodied persons. Severe impairments, involving social or mind–body breakdowns, can cut us off from each other.

Here is an overview of what follows: we consider the phenomenological, aesthetic dimension of experiencing the divine (Chapters 2 and 3), the aesthetic meaning of religious worldviews and their secular alternatives (Chapter 4), the philosophy of beauty (Chapter 5), the ways in which works of art can conceal or reveal our identity, the sacred, and the profane (Chapter 6), a case for recognizing some religious works of art as persons or person-like objects and philosophical reflections on the perception and public exhibition of religious objects (Chapter 7), and a personal guide to the aesthetic study of religious and secular works of art (Chapter 8).

---

[27] A classic treatment of the problem of other minds at the intersection of philosophy of mind and philosophy of religion is *God and Other Minds*, by Alvin Plantinga (Ithaca, NY: Cornell University Press, 1967), chapters 8–10. Taliaferro argues that personal embodiment involves a coordination of virtues (or good powers) in "The Virtues of Embodiment," *Philosophy* 76 (1), 2001, pp. 111–125.

2

Is God Invisible?

> Without phenomenology, philosophy is blind.
>
> Richard Fumerton[1]

In Bertrand Russell's *The Wisdom of the West*, the photograph (on page 17) is paired with the caption "Mt. Sinai, home of Yahweh, the Invisible God of the Jews."[2] Indeed, this photograph depicts what is believed to be the 7,500-foot-high, volcanic, granite mountain located on the Sinai Peninsula of Egypt, which the Hebrew Bible, Christian Old Testament, and the Qur'an identify as the site where Yahweh makes a covenant with Moses. The choice of this grey, out-of-focus, distant view is akin to Herman Melville's description in *The Encantadas* of the Galapagos Islands: "It is to be doubted whether any spot on earth can, in desolateness, furnish a parallel to this group … . In these isles rain never falls … Another feature in these isles is their emphatic uninhabitableness."[3] The juxtaposition of the title "home of Yahweh" with the black-and-white photograph of an inhospitable looking landscape invites the viewer to wonder: If there is a God, why would God choose to live there? There is no hint of what the Hebrew Bible describes as glory (*kabod*) or of the beauty of the Lord (Psalm 27:4; the Hebrew term *noam*, commonly translated as "beauty," also refers to "favor" and "sweetness") or God's splendor (Hebrew *tiphahrah*). Moreover, the label raises a philosophical question: Is it proper to think of the God of Abrahamic traditions as invisible?

---

[1] Richard Fumerton, *Knowledge, Thought, and the Case for Dualism* (Cambridge: Cambridge University Press, 2014), p. 241.
[2] Bertrand Russell, *Wisdom of the West: A Historical Survey of Western Philosophy in Its Social and Political Setting*, edited by Paul Foulkes (London: Rathbone Books Limited, 1959), p. 127.
[3] Herman Melville, *The Encantadas*, published in *Putnam's Magazine*, 1854.

Is God Invisible?

FIGURE 2.1 Photograph of Mt. Sinai provided by Matson Photography Service for Bertrand Russell's *The Wisdom of the West*.

Some of the critics of theism certainly think so. In *The Natural History of Religion*, David Hume refers to gods/God as "invisible, intelligent power" at least six times. Hume locates the origin of belief in an invisible intelligent power, not in any desire for truth based on evidence, but in a passionate desire for happiness and a desire for revenge, seeking a refuge from the dread of misery and death.

It must necessarily, indeed, be allowed, that in order to carry men's attention beyond the present course of things, or lead them into any inference concerning *invisible intelligent power* [emphasis ours], they must be actuated by some passion which prompts their thought and reflection; some motive which urges their first inquiry. But what passion shall we here have recourse to, for explaining an effect of such mighty consequence? Not speculative curiosity surely, or the pure love of truth. That motive is too refined for such gross apprehensions, and would lead men into inquiries concerning the frame of nature; a subject too large and comprehensive for their narrow capacities. No passions, therefore, can be supposed to work upon such barbarians, but the ordinary affections of human life; the anxious concern for happiness, the dread of future misery, the terror of death, the thirst of revenge, the appetite for food and other necessaries. Agitated by hopes and fears of this nature, especially the latter, men scrutinize, with a trembling curiosity, the course of future causes, and examine the various and contrary events of human life. And in this disordered scene, with eyes still more disordered and astonished, they see the first obscure traces of divinity.[4]

---

[4] David Hume, *The Natural History of Religion*, Section II: The Origin of Polytheism, 1889, pp. 9–10.

Hume's disdain for this form of reasoning is evident in his describing religious persons as barbarians with disordered passions and eyes.[5] For Hume the claim that God is invisible is not *ipso facto* incoherent. Hume is committed to the view that persons and some nonhuman animals have sensory experiences (what he sometimes refers to as "mental operations") that are not visible to other persons. Even so, his analysis of the motive behind believing in an invisible, divine power is (to use a modest term) unflattering.[6] If you are not being providentially looked after by a visible, powerful, benign agent, he says, perhaps your craving for safety will lead you to think that there are one or more invisible powers who might come to your aid.

More recently, Antony Flew, A. J. Ayer, and Gareth Moore, among others, go further than Hume by casting doubt on the coherence of an invisible, intelligent agent. They propose that belief in God in the Abrahamic faith as an invisible person does not make sense. If these critics are correct, then the idea of God has something in common with the depictions in the *Carceri* series (*Imaginary Prisons*) by the Italian artist Giovanni Battista Piranesi (1720–78). In these etchings, immense interior structures appear at first glance to make sense as scenes of complex and intricate architectural spaces. However, once you begin to follow any path in detail, say a staircase or a high wooden crosswalk, you find yourself on stairs leading to nowhere, ending abruptly at a stone wall, or crossing over to an incoherent, physically impossible structure.

We reply to the critique of God as invisible and articulate the positive, aesthetically charged ways in which the God of Abrahamic faith, while not a visual object, may be seen as manifested in sensory, perceptual experiences. This more-open phenomenology will allow for a richer aesthetic of God and of religious experience.[7] The renewed interest in aesthetics in philosophy of religion recognizes that our emotions function cognitively, embedded in sensations and reactions: "I feel it in my bones."

---

[5] There is an interesting, relevant parallel between Hume's dismissal of reports of miracles and his dismissal of reports of nonwhite intelligence. For an analysis of the relationship between Hume's racism and his view on miracles, see Charles Taliaferro's *Evidence and Faith* (Cambridge: Cambridge University Press, 2005), chapter 4. Hume dismisses reports that black people are as intelligent and creative as whites on the grounds that such reports are by uneducated barbarians.

[6] In the *Treatise of Human Nature*, Hume articulates the problem of other minds in the context of knowing whether some animals have minds (sensations, use reason, and so on). He explicitly contends that we know nonhuman animals undertake "mental operations," not by direct observation but as an inference based on our observing how animal behavior is analogous to our own behavior (Book 1, Part 3, section 16). For earlier classic cases of the argument for other minds based on reasoning by analogy (ostensible persons act the way they do analogous to the way you act when you have mental states), see Descartes' *Discourse on Method,* Part 5 and John Locke's *An Essay Concerning Human Understanding,* Book 4, chapter 3, par. 27.

[7] Part of the renewed interest in aesthetics in the philosophy of religion looks at how our embodied emotions function in bodily sensations and reactions. See Mark Wynn's *Faith and Place: An Essay in Embodied Religious Epistemology* (Oxford: Oxford University Press, 2009) and *Renewing the Senses: A Study of the Philosophy and Theology of the Spiritual Life* (Oxford: Oxford University Press, 2013).

We challenge other depictions of the God of Abrahamic faiths – as nonnatural, disembodied, and supernatural – which we propose are not fitting and imply misconceptions of God (the technical Latin term is *suggesti falsi*, suggesting that which is false).

AN INVISIBLE GOD

On June 13, 1949, the BBC broadcast a debate that would become famous between the Christian philosopher Frederick Copleston and the prominent secular philosopher A. J. Ayer, who was teaching philosophy at the University of London. Ayer:

Suppose I suggest 'There is a drogulus over there,' and you say 'What?' and I say 'Drogulus,' and you say 'What is a drogulus?' 'Well,' I say, 'I can't describe what a drogulus is, because it is not the sort of thing you can see or touch, it has no physical effects of any kind, but it's a disembodied being.' And you say, 'Well, how am I to tell if it's there or not?' and I say, 'There is no way of telling. Everything's just the same if it's there or it's not there. But the fact is it's there. There's a drogulus there standing behind you, spiritually behind you.' Does that make sense?[8]

Ayer implies that such a claim does not make sense. He seems to hold that an essential condition for something to be identified or described as having a location is that it must be able to have physical effects (allowing it to be seen or touched) and either be a body or be physically embodied.

At the time of the broadcast, Ayer was the foremost popular advocate of logical positivism. That philosophy only allowed propositions of logic, mathematics, or statements that are empirically verifiable as meaningful, the latter being statements that can be confirmed by sense experience or the sciences. Logical positivism was a radical position that ruled out as nonsense propositions about God as well as propositions about what is ethical or unethical, beautiful or ugly. Regardless of the overall status of logical positivism (which was severely criticized in the 1970s), Ayer's position receives some support from common sense.[9] For example, his drogulus seems even more elusive than dementors in J. R. Rowling's Harry Potter imaginarium, which at least have a vaporous, observable presence. Ayer's position is that if the religious concept of God is like his drogulus, the concept of God does not make sense.

Consider Antony Flew's parable about an invisible, undetectable gardener.[10]

---

[8] "Logical Positivism – A Debate," published in *A Modern Introduction to Philosophy*, 2nd edition, edited by Paul Edwards and Arthur Pap (New York: Free Press, 1965), pp. 726–756.
[9] See Alvin Plantinga's *God and Other Minds* on verificationism for a critique of logical positivism.
[10] Flew adopted his parable from one introduced by John Wisdom, "Gods," Proceedings of the Aristotelian Society, 1944–5. Wisdom has amusing reflections on invisible leprechauns in chapter 1 of his *Other Minds* (Berkeley: University of California Press, 1968).

Once upon a time two explorers came upon a clearing in the jungle. In the clearing were growing many flowers and many weeds. One explorer says, "Some gardener must tend this plot." The other disagrees, "There is no gardener." So they pitch their tents and set a watch. No gardener is ever seen. "But perhaps he is an invisible gardener." So they set up a barbed-wire fence. They electrify it. They patrol with bloodhounds. (For they remember how H. G. Wells' "Invisible Man" could be both smelled and touched though he could not be seen.) But no shrieks ever suggest that some intruder has received a shock. No movements of the wire ever betray an invisible climber. The bloodhounds never give cry. Yet still the Believer is not convinced. "But there is a gardener, invisible, intangible, insensitive to electric shocks, a gardener who has no scent and makes no sound, a gardener who comes secretly to look after the garden which he loves." At last the sceptic despairs, "But what remains of your original assertion? Just how does what you call an invisible, intangible, eternally elusive gardener differ from an imaginary gardener or even from no gardener at all?"[11]

Flew's parable extends the critique of an invisible God further than Ayer's does insofar as it depicts the believer and unbeliever disputing about a physical site, a garden, with the believer claiming the site is best explained by an agent, who turns out to not be otherwise detectable, and the unbeliever not only denying this, but also questioning the coherence of an agent who cannot be sensed or detected through empirical means. (As an aside, note the aesthetics of the parable: violent tools employed, setting up a barbed-wire fence, patrolling with bloodhounds, listening for shrieks.)

In *Believing in God*, Gareth Moore offers an extensive attack on the concept of God as an invisible person and, ultimately, on an *invisible anything*. Moore is a very interesting contributor to the critique of God as invisible, as Moore was a member of the Dominican Roman Catholic religious order, and thus presumed to be a practicing Christian. At times he writes as though he is merely offering an exposition of what is involved in believing that there is an invisible God:

The one Christians speak of, the one they speak to and reverence, is in fact there all the time, only you cannot see him. God is invisible. And not just that; you cannot bump into him or touch him, for he is intangible, neither does he make any sound. And he doesn't smell, either. In fact, he is absolutely undetectable by any of our senses, and cannot be found even by our most sophisticated scientific instruments. ... The invisibility, the intangibility of God, these are not a matter of our cognitive limitations; they are actual properties of God. If you like, God has no body.[12]

But rather than limit his thesis to the affirmation that the invisible God whom Christians pray to has *no body,* Moore goes on to claim that when Christians pray there is *nobody* there.

---

[11] "Theology and Falsification" in *New Essays in Philosophical Theology*, edited by A. Flew and A. MacIntyre (New York: Macmillan, 1955), p. 96.

[12] Gareth Moore, *Believing in God, A Philosophical Essay* (London: Bloomsbury T & T Clark, 1996), pp. 8–9.

An Invisible God

They [Christians] speak of God doing things when [they] can see nobody doing anything. In their churches they say they are speaking to God, but there is obviously nobody there to speak to; they speak into thin air. They kneel, but they kneel before nobody.[13]

Moore maintains that to defend the coherence of the view that there is an invisible God would be "a kind of joke, like saying 'There is a green, three-legged, ten-foot tall woman in the middle of the road, only you can't detect her because she is invisible, intangible, etc.'"[14] He offers a puzzling analogy: He compares the concept of the equator with the concept of God. "And yet of course the equator exists and it is invisible."[15] But what we call the equator is a creation of cartography. The equator is not a mind-independent reality of any kind. If the existence of the equator rests on mapmaking, does Moore believe that the reality of God depends on God-making? Because this analogy seems to render the concept of God as merely an idea that we humans cultivate, rather than the concept of the creator and sustainer of the cosmos, some of Moore's commentators wonder how Moore's position differs from simply denying the existence of God as a real, mind-independent reality.[16] Moore seems to affirm that there is something that can be referred to as *the presence of God* but only with respect to observable, material religious practitioners: "We can establish the presence of the heavenly, spiritual God ... by seeing an earthly, material man saying his prayers, *and nothing else*."[17] We assume that "nothing else" means no further fact or being such as God, as found in the Abrahamic traditions, who is thought of as the creator and sustainer of the cosmos and of all people, whether they pray or not.

Sadly, Moore died young (in 2002 at 54 years old) and so was unable to further clarify his position. In this context, we interpret his published work as advancing a third critique of the idea that God is a mind-independent, real, yet invisible being.

---

[13] Ibid., 4–5. See also pp. 9, 38, 44, 46, 51, 114, 117, 121, 187, 190, 239. Moore also claims that the term "God" is not a name for something or someone: 18, 44–46, 61–62, 280, 284.
[14] Ibid., p. 17.   [15] Ibid., p. 36.
[16] See *Eighteen Takes on God*, by Leslie Stevenson (Oxford: Oxford University Press, 2019). Stevenson is puzzled how Moore's view is compatible with a Christian belief in God. Mark Wynn describes Moore as maintaining a "minimalist reading of the import of religious language," noting that he, Wynn, prefers "a more metaphysically engaged" account of religious language. See Wynn's *Renewing the Senses: A Study of the Philosophy and Theology of the Spiritual Life*, p. 14. It is interesting that Moore's last book, published posthumously, *A Question of Truth: Christianity and Homosexuality* extolls a passionate portrait of a God who welcomes gay Christians (London: Continuum, 2003). We appeal to this significant work in Chapter 4.
[17] Ibid., p. 62. The denial that God plays a role as an agent is evident when Moore writes that to say "God has helped me" is "not an explanation of how you got through; it is an expression of the *mystery* of how you ... got through, *without help*" (p. 133).

THE PERCEIVABILITY OF THE GOD OF ABRAHAMIC TRADITIONS

Is God invisible? We think yes and no. The God of Abrahamic traditions is properly thought of as not identical with a visual object, and in that way God is not visible, but this God is also understood as manifested through visual and other sensory and perceptual experiences. The declarations "Out of Zion, the perfection of beauty [Hebrew *yuphee*, akin to *hah-dahr* and *tiphahrah*], God shines forth" (Psalm 50:2), and "One thing I have asked ... that I may dwell in the house of the Lord all the days of my life, to behold the beauty of the Lord" (Psalm 27:4) make little sense unless it is possible to behold, perceive, sense, or experience such divine beauty. In *Song of Songs*, the experiential encounter between God and the soul has been historically interpreted as an intimate love affair in which the soul seeks to be kissed by her divine lover, and the soul in turn advances through stages of love through kissing.[18] But instead of engaging in such classic and entrancing, intimate, sensory imagery, some of the critics of theism (as we have seen) focus on a far more sparse, austere, and isolated view of God. We believe that the case against an invisible God by these philosophers ignores and even excludes a broad phenomenology of religious experience as well as overlooking the fact that even our own visibility as persons is a complex, nuanced matter. Our visibility rests on our openness to see or, more broadly, to recognize and experience each other, which is not easily achieved because persons of a certain gender, race, class, or even species are routinely treated as invisible by others. Our own visibility rests on matters of virtue and vice; typically, vicious persons keep their true intentions disguised or invisible until they can act opportunistically. And, very importantly, our visibility is a function of proper mental–physical causal interaction in which a person's thoughts, feelings, emotions, and intentions are embodied. If we lose control of all our actions, our bodies will remain visible, but you will not see our healthy embodiment as persons. The rich literature recording religious experience provides a related idea of how proper attunement to the divine can reveal the presence of God both externally and internally as when Augustine writes: "Late have I loved Thee, O Beauty so ancient and so new! For behold Thou wert within me."[19]

There are scriptural sources (Hebrew and Christian Bibles and the Qur'an) for thinking of God as invisible. Consider a sampling of references to sacred

---

[18] The best known commentary on the erotic imagery in *Song of Songs* is the *Sermons on the Song of Songs* by St. Bernard of Clairvaux (1090–1153). At one point, we were so moved by kissing as a motif for the encounter with God that we were going to title this book *The Kiss: An Essay on Religion and Aesthetics*, but too many readers wondered how we might be addressing Rodin's sculpture *The Kiss*! In addition to St. Bernard's sermons, see Origen's *Homilies on the Song of Songs*.

[19] Augustine, *Confessions* 10:27. Some theologians distinguish between the experience of God as a reality within one as *enstasy* as distinct from experiencing the divine as outside oneself, *ecstasy*. Sometimes both are in play, as we find in Augustine's *Confessions*.

texts in Judaism and Christianity: "You cannot see my face, for no one may see me and live" (Exodus 33:20). "Were He to pass by me, I would not see Him. Were He to move past me, I would not perceive Him" (Job 19:11). "No one has seen God at any time, the only one who is in the bosom of the Father. He has explained Him" (John 1:18). "By faith Moses left Egypt, not afraid of the King's anger; for he endured as if seeing the invisible one" (Hebrews 11:27). God is said to be the one "who alone possesses unapproachable light, whom no man has seen or can see" (I Timothy 6:16). We read about "the King, eternal, immortal, invisible" (I Timothy 1:17), "seeing Him who is unseen" (Hebrews 11:27). There is a reference to "His invisible attributes" (Romans 1:20). "No one has beheld God at any time; if we love one another, God abides in us, and His love is perfected in us" (I John 4:12). "He is the image of the invisible God, the firstborn of all creatures" (I Timothy 1:17).

The Nicene Creed contains a reference to believing in things "visible and invisible." A famous Christian hymn refers to God as "immortal, invisible."[20]

Apart from their sacred texts, some Jewish, Christian, and Islamic philosophers have been led by Plato and Neoplatonists to think of God and the soul as invisible. In Plato's *Phaedo* there is this succinct exchange:

Then what do we say about the soul? Is it visible or invisible?
Not visible.[21]

And yet there are biblical passages and narratives suggesting that God can be seen in some sense. "So Jacob called the place Peniel, saying, 'For I have seen God face to face, and yet my life is preserved'" (Genesis 32:30). The Lord used to speak to Moses, "face to face" (Exodus 33:11); "But my servant Moses is not such a prophet: he alone is faithful of all my household. With him I speak face to face, openly and not in riddles. He shall see the very form of the Lord" (Numbers 12:7–8); and "Thou, O Lord, art seen eye to eye" (Numbers 14:4); "I saw the Lord sitting on His throne" (I King 22:19–23); "I saw the Lord, sitting on a throne ... for my eyes have seen the King, the Lord of hosts" (Isaiah 6:15); "I knew of thee then only by report, but now I see thee with my own eyes" (Job 42:5). New Testament texts reference God being seen in and through Jesus of Nazareth (I John 1: 1–3; Colossians 1:15; 2:9; John 14:9). As Gregory Nazianzus writes: "I too will proclaim the greatness of this day [the incarnation]: the immaterial becomes incarnate, the Word is made flesh, the invisible makes itself seen, the intangible can be touched."[22] And there are abundant accounts in many contexts of people claiming to perceive (sense or experience) God, sometimes through visually mediated experiences and

---

[20] "Immortal, Invisible, God Only Wise" by Walter Chalmers Smith (1824–1908).
[21] *Phaedo* 79b, translated by G. Grube. In *Plato; Complete Works*, edited by J. M. Cooper (Indianapolis: Hackett Publishing Company, 1997). See also the many places Plato refers to the forms as invisible, e.g., *Sophist* 245e–249d.
[22] Cited by Oliver Clement, *The Roots of Christian Mysticism: A Text and Commentary* (New York: New City Press, 1982), p. 41.

sometimes through nonvisually mediated perceiving (auditions, tastes, smells, touching). These experiential modes have been identified by some philosophers and theologians as that through which (*objectum quo*) persons are aware of God's presence.[23]

The Qur'an has a spectrum of verses similar to the Hebrew and Christian Bibles. The term for *invisible* does not appear, but there are references to the unseen: "These are accounts from the Unseen" (3:44; 2:3); "God is knower of the Unseen" (9:78; 34:3; 64:18; 81:24). These may be interpreted as God knowing what might be unseen by, and thus invisible to, us: the truth about people's souls, beliefs, fidelity. After all, "Nothing is hidden from God, on earth or in heaven" (93:5): "God is All-Hearing, All-Seeing" (4:134). As for whether humans may see God: "Vision cannot grasp Him, but His grasp is over all vision" (6:103). There is this account of Moses' petition to see God (Allah):

> Moses: "My Lord allow me to look and see you." He said: "You will not see Me, but look at the mountain; if it stays in its place, you will see me." But when the Lord manifested Himself to the mountain, He turned it into dust. Moses fell down unconscious. Then, when he recovered, he said, "Glory be to You, I repent to You, and I am the first of the believers." (7:143)

While Moses may not visually see God directly, this passage does speak of God being "manifest." And perhaps, through the disintegration of the mountain, God is experienced as a powerful, glorious presence. There are other passages that suggest some experiential contact with God. "God spoke to Moses directly" (4:164). We are told that we can see God at work in the created order (35:27), and in the afterlife we will not only see rewards and punishment, we will see the throne of God: "And you will see the angels hovering around the Throne, Glorifying God with praise" (39:75). "On that day some faces will be bright, looking at their Lord" (75:22–23).

Before considering the extent to which the Abrahamic faiths allow for sensory, religious experiences, we offer some further observations about divine invisibility. Note that invisibility is not traditionally thought of as a divine attribute along with omnipotence, omniscience, and perfect goodness. When in Romans 1:20 there is a reference to God's "invisible attributes," this is not the same thing as claiming that invisibility is an attribute. We propose that when divine invisibility or God's being (prior to an afterlife) unseen or invisible is invoked theologically, this is often a matter of advancing four factors:

- Securing the idea of divine omnipresence; God is not a finite, spatially circumscribable object; there is nowhere where God is not. If God were wholly identical with some finite, observable object, God would not be omnipresent. The link between the thesis that God is not visible with God's ubiquity is explicit in the work of St. Irenaeus: "Although the

---

[23] See William Alston's *Perceiving God* (Ithaca: Cornell University Press, 1991), chapter 1, especially pp. 48–59.

power of God is invisible, it bestows upon all a profound mental intuition and perception of His most powerful and omnipotent presence."[24] In the Qur'an, see also Surah 2:115: "To Allah belong the East and the West: whithersoever ye turn, there is the presence of Allah. For Allah is the all-Pervading, all-Knowing."

- God's noncontingency; God is not identical with the contingent cosmos that God has created and sustains. The visual cosmos is itself contingent. God is distinct from the mortal, decomposable objects we see around us.
- God's eternity; unlike the visible, temporal world, God is timeless, everlasting, or eternal.[25]
- Perhaps most importantly, a warning about idolatry; God is unlike seductive, visible idols. "There is nothing like Him, but He is All-hearing, All-seeing" (Qur'an 42:4). In Exodus 20:4–6, the second of the Ten Commandments is "You shall not make for yourself an idol of any kind or an image of anything in the heavens above, the earth below, or the waters under the earth." On visual images and idolatry, see Qur'an 7:1: "And the people of Moses made in his absence, out of their own ornaments, the image of a calf. It had a sound [as if it were mooing]. Did they not see that it could neither speak to them nor guide them? They took it for worship and they were Zalimum [wrongdoers]." See also 21:51–54 and Hadith 3:428. Aniconism, the avoidance of images in Islam, also stems from the belief that only Allah creates living forms. While Christian tradition has fostered massive numbers of icons and images of the divine, at times there are Christian iconoclastic movements to depict and destroy such images as idols.[26]

These four theological positions are not claiming that the God of Abrahamic faiths cannot be experienced in and through the world, whether through vision or a broader, phenomenological appearance. In fact, these theological tenets may even give some reason to be especially open to the possibility of God being disclosed in experience: God being omnipresent, God is nowhere absent; God's existing necessarily means God cannot fail to exist; God is not bound by the temporal constraints of creatures; God does not have the vices we find in cultic deities/idols; conversely, the omnipresent God of Abrahamic traditions is understood to love creation and to desire relationships.[27]

---

[24] St. Irenaeus, *Against Heresies*, in *The Faith of the Early Fathers*, selected and translated by W. A. Jurgens (Collegeville, MN: The Liturgical Press, 1920), volume 1, p. 86.

[25] Taliaferro addresses the implications of believing God is eternal in *The Golden Cord: A Short Book on the Sacred and the Secular* (Notre Dame: University of Notre Dame Press, 2012).

[26] Moshe Halbertal and Avishai Margalit argue that that any representation of God would be unworthy of God; idolatry consists in substituting a representation of God for God. See their book *Idolatry* (Cambridge: Harvard University Press, 1992), pp. 45–48.

[27] There is an enormous literature on this nature of Abrahamic faith: To what extent is God hidden? For a good overview, see *The God Who Seeks But Seems to Hide*, by Francis Jonback (Leuven, Belgium: Peters, 2017). See also *Hidden Divinity and Religious Belief*, edited by E. Stump and A. Green (Cambridge: Cambridge University Press, 2015).

Consider some of the ways in which the Abrahamic traditions have included testimony of experientially apprehending or encountering the divine. We are highly selective here as we are not writing a book arguing for the truth of theism based on religious experience. We are, rather, defending a phenomenological approach to religious experience that gives center place to the aesthetic experience of persons. In future chapters, we discuss the ways in which works of art can shape religious perception. We suggest that this phenomenological approach will give reasons to accept some worldviews (those recognizing the full reality of persons, values, consciousness) and reject others (a narrow version of strict naturalism limited to the natural sciences), but our work falls slightly outside literature advancing an argument from religious experience for theism.[28] What we advance, however, may be of use to the further projects of arguing for theistic or nontheistic accounts of experiencing the sacred.

Here is an example of a report of God being apprehended through (or on the occasion of) liturgy:

> I attended service at a church in Uppsala. ... During both the Confession of Sin and the Prayer of Thanksgiving which followed Communion, I had a strong consciousness of the Holy Spirit as a person, and an equally strong consciousness of the existence of God, that God was present.[29]

In this report, the liturgy is that through which (*objectum quo*) God is experienced. While presented in the first person, it does not seem exclusively private but, in principle, could be a collective, public experience.[30]

Here is a reported experience of God without aid from the five senses:

> All at once I ... felt the presence of God – I tell of the thing just as I was conscious of it – as if his goodness and his power were penetrating me altogether. ... I asked myself if it were

---

[28] There are many books defending theism based on religious experience: *The Rainbow of Experiences, Critical Trust, and God*, by Kai-man Kwan (London: Continuum, 2011); the previously cited *Perceiving God*, by William Alston; *The Evidential Force of Religious Experience*, by Caroline Davis (Oxford: Clarendon Press, 1989); *Natural Signs and the Knowledge of God*, by C. S. Evans (Oxford: Oxford University Press, 2010); *Experience of God and the Rationality of Religious Belief*, by Jerome Gellman (Ithaca, NY: Cornell University Press, 1997); *Mystical Experience of God*, also by Gellman (Aldershot: Ashgate, 2001); *Religious Belief and Religious Skepticism*, by Gary Gutting (Notre Dame: University of Notre Dame Press, 1982); *The Epistemology of Religious Experience*, by Keith Yandell (Cambridge: Cambridge University Press, 1999); *Mysticism*, by William Wainwright (Madison: University of Wisconsin Press, 1981). See also "In Defense of the Numinous," by Charles Taliaferro in *Philosophy and the Christian Worldview*, edited by D. Werther and M. Linville (London: Continuum, 2012) pp. 95–108.

[29] Cited by Alston in *Perceiving God*, p. 14.

[30] See footnote 35 for an abundance of more reported religious experiences. For philosophical reflection on how liturgy may be a vehicle for religious experience, see Taliaferro's "Religious Rites" in *The Cambridge Companion to Christian Philosophical Theology*, edited by C. Meister and C. Taliaferro (Cambridge: Cambridge University Press, 2009), pp. 183–200. See also *Ritualized Faith: Essays on the Philosophy of Liturgy*, edited by T. Cuneo (Oxford: Oxford University Press, 2016).

possible that Moses on Sinai could have had a more intimate communication with God. I think it well to add that in this ecstasy of mine God had neither form, color, odor, or taste; moreover, that the feeling of his presence was accompanied with no determinate localization. ... What I felt is this: God was present, though invisible; he fell under no one of my senses, yet my consciousness perceived him.[31]

We cite two more reported experiences of the divine. From one of the leading French philosophers of the twentieth century, Simone Weil:

Christ himself came down and took possession of me. ... I had never foreseen the possibility of that, of a real contact, person, here below, between a human being and God ... in this sudden possession of me by Christ. ... I only felt in the midst of my suffering the presence of a love. ... God in his mercy had prevented me from reading the mystics, so that it should be evident to me that I had not invented this absolutely unexpected contact.[32]

And from the life of Harriet Tubman, we cite another report. She was an American abolitionist who was born into slavery in 1822, escaped, and then spent her life fighting slavery and campaigning for women's suffrage until her death in 1913. She saved seventy enslaved people. Raised a Christian, she rejected any Bible verses countenancing slavery. She reported a vivid personal experience of God calling her to free slaves.

She had great fears about her future course, and confided, "The Lord told me to do this. I said: 'Oh Lord, I can't – don't ask me – take somebody else.'" But Tubman also reported that God spoke directly to her. "'It's you I want, Harriet Tubman.'"[33]

In an ideal world, we would narrate the social and historical context of each person's experience and not simply cite the above accounts of ostensibly experiencing the divine. Grace Jantzen rightly cautions against focusing only on subjective experience: "The sort of reading [of mystics] that I think is needed focuses less on subjective states and more on the goodness and beauty of life and teaching in relation to the overriding concern of the mystics."[34] But here, we offer these sketches to counter the claim that the God of Abrahamic faith is beyond our subjective states, our sensory experience and conscious perception. To describe ostensible experiences of the divine, we shall use terms like *experience, perception, sensory experience, sense, see, conscious awareness*, or *conscious contact* interchangeably. These terms are used in this context to

---

[31] Anonymous report in William James' *The Varieties of Religious Experience: A Study of Human Nature*, pp. 67–68.
[32] Weil cited by Dean Overman, *A Case for the Existence of God* (Lanham, MD: Rowman and Littlefield, 2009), p. 135.
[33] Catherine Clinton, *Harriet Tubman: The Road to Freedom* (New York: Little Brown and Company, 2004), p. 83.
[34] Grace Jantzen, "For an engaged reading: William James and the varieties of postmodern religious significance" in *William James and the Varieties of Religious Experience*, edited by J. Carrette (London: Routledge, 2005), p. 104.

convey the apparent act/object structure of these experiences in which a subject's experience, an *act*, appears to have an *object* other than herself. What is also common to these testimonies are the unbidden nature of the experiences. They are not "willed" by the person experiencing them, and there isn't a question of being able to control the duration of the experience, or articulate more than being met somehow by a power that is felt to be intimate, loving, and personal.[35]

We propose that the above accounts of experiencing God or the divine are best understood as reports of phenomenological *appearings*. That is, they are experiential perceptions or sensing of the reality of God or the divine, which people have taken to be real as opposed to hallucinations or matters of illusion or delusion.[36]

In Ayer's example of the drogulus, there is a claim that a subject is located in space (it is standing behind you) and yet not detectable by vision or touch. The same is true in Moore's case of there being a green, three-legged, ten-foot-tall woman in the middle of the road, only you can't detect her because she is invisible and intangible; presumably you cannot have a color or legs or height without being embodied spatially. These cases then seem to be instances of when some disputed object is claimed to be both spatial and nonspatial at the same time.[37] These are not comparable to the experiences as disclosed in Abrahamic traditions. In Christianity God is experienced spatially and in space, as the incarnate Jesus Christ. But more broadly, when God is reported to be experienced in space, this is often a matter of God being made manifested

---

[35] For reports of contemporary religious experience, see the Alister Hardy Religious Experience Research Centre in Lambert, Wales. They have archived over 6,000 accounts. David Hay, former Director of the Centre when it was in Oxford, has published an important work on such reports: *Religious Experience Today: Studying the Facts* (London: Bloomsbury, 1990), see chapters 5, 6, and Appendix. See also Andrew Newberg and Mark Waldman's *How God Changes Your Brain* (New York: Ballantine Books, 2009). Their Online Survey of Spiritual Experience between 2005 and 2007 received 300 detailed accounts of religious experience: "At the time of the experience, 63 percent said it was more real than their normal experience of reality" (p. 74). Also see the classic work *Mysticism*, by Evelyn Underhill (Nelson South, New Zealand: Renaissance Classics, 2012); S. A. Harvey's *Sensing Salvation: Ancient Christianity and the Olfactory Imagination* (Berkeley, CA: University of California Press, 2006), and *The Spiritual Senses: Perceiving God in Western Christianity*, edited by P. Gavrilyuk and S. Coakley (Cambridge: Cambridge University Press, 2011).

[36] So, when Julian of Norwich had her experience of Christ's love as recorded in *The Revelations of Divine Love*, we believe these were experiences in which Julian believed she was truly shown truths about the love of God (Christ), whether or not God exists.

[37] As an aside, some philosophers deny the unity of space, contending that there can be spatial objects that exist at the same time but are not some spatial distance from each other. This sometimes arises in accounts of dreaming when (arguably) it appears that the dream of a tiger (the visual image with its orange and black stripes) is not some spatial distance from the dreamer's brain or body. See Richard Swinburne's *Mind, Brain, and Free Will* (Oxford: Oxford University Press, 2013), chapter 1. Also see Anthony Quinton's *The Nature of Things* (London: Routledge and Kegan Pau, 1973).

The Perceivability of the God of Abrahamic Traditions

or disclosed through space, rather than a report that God is the very same thing as a spatial object. Without being a spatial object, God is still felt to be close, even intimately so.

We sometimes feel the proximate closeness of other people when they are not near us or close by in shared space. This is experienced sometimes in the same way that divine presence has been described, as unbidden, and of uncontrollable duration.

We also suggest persons may be physically proximate, but due to ignorance, apathy, or lack of affective responsiveness, they may be utterly remote. Victimizers and abusers can be experienced as hauntingly present by those they have injured. The minds of authors, visual artists, musicians, and architects can be experienced through their works. Spouses, lovers, siblings, close friends, teachers, and students may rightly be experienced as close when they are not physically proximate. Of course, this feeling of the presence of others may be asymmetric: We feel your affective personal proximity, but you do not feel ours. A classic case of asymmetric felt personal presence is W. E. B. Dubois' (1868–1963) account of sitting with Shakespeare, moving arm and arm with Balzac and Dumas, and summoning Aristotle and Aurelius in *The Souls of Black Folk*.

But a sense of shared personal experience can be symmetrical as when two or more physically remote persons sense each other's affective proximity, perhaps with a vivid sense of shared joy or sorrow. And such a sensed affective proximity can be causally significant; it can inspire action, initiate shame, prompt joy. The Hindu philosopher Eknath Easwaran offers this vision of the ways in which ordinary people can be in reciprocal relationships with great teachers, such as Jesus, the Compassionate Buddha, and others:

> This [reciprocal presence] does not require a physical presence. Jesus, the Buddha, great sages and saints like Sri Ramakrishna, Mahatma Gandhi, Teresa of Avila, St. Francis of Assisi, all continue to guide us. They are not dead. Their bodies are gone, but their spirit moves about freely in the world, helping those who turn to them with a unified heart. ... Even for people like you and me, luminous figures like those in every religion can be living companions – much more real, much more influential than flesh and blood friends whose lives are scattered. By reading about them, thinking about them, meditating on their words, we can bring their presence into our daily lives.[38]

The ability we have for sensing symmetrical and reciprocal personal presence is a plausible ground or conduit for the widely reported experiences of God. In

---

[38] Eknath Easwaran, *Passage Meditation: A Complete Spiritual Practice* (Tomales, CA: Nilgiri Press, 2016), pp. 161–162. His guide to meditation is based on Hinduism, but it is also explicit in its lending itself to different religious traditions, especially Christianity and Buddhism. Using the terminology introduced earlier, Easwaran believed meditation is the *objectum quo* (that through which) one encounters the divine; the meditation, then, is not itself the object of the experience (the *objectum quo*). Consider this analogy: You may need glasses to see a landscape or another person, but in using your glasses, you are not so much seeing your glasses (usually, they are not the object of your observation).

the latter case, the reports take the form of persons apprehending a living force, vastly unlike the experience of a fiction, hallucination, or memory. In principle, these experiences may not be merely hypothetical (we feel *as if* we are in the presence of a personal reality), but concrete (we feel an *actual* personal presence).[39]

Ayer, Flew, and Moore can be challenged on their ruling out invisible beings or activities (agents or subjects or subjective experience) on the grounds that not everything about Ayer, Flew, and Moore (as well as the rest of us) is visible to others. Let's take just Ayer. We can hear his questions, comments, and so on, and ably observe his intelligence. But do we, strictly speaking, directly observe Ayer's thoughts, feelings, sensations, emotions? As noted in connection with our observations about Hume at the outset of this chapter, we infer these and see his expression of these, but we propose that this is not with the same immediacy we observe his visible features.[40] Here we are appealing to a version of what philosophers call *the knowledge argument* against a materialist view of persons.[41] Some philosophers have argued (we think

---

[39] On the experience of the closeness of persons who are physically remote, see Eleonore Stump's *Atonement* (Oxford: Oxford University Press, 2018), chapter 4. In technical philosophical terms, the personal closeness described in religious experience appears to be *de re* (that is, focused on the person encountered) rather than *de dicto* (that is, through a proposition). We know you as a person when we are experientially acquainted with you, whereas propositional knowledge may be quite abstract as when all we know about you is that, according to reliable reports, you are the tallest spy in London.

[40] Apparently, Bertrand Russell personally wrestled with the worry that his life in the world as observed by others was distinct from his true identity. See Raymond Monk's biography *Bertrand Russell: The Spirit of Solitude 1872–1921* (New York: The Free Press, 1996), especially chapter 1, "Ghosts."

[41] See especially *From the Knowledge Argument to Mental Substance*, by Howard Robinson (Cambridge: Cambridge University Press, 2016). This includes a reliable guide to the history of the argument, its many objections and defense. Two of the better-known defenders of the argument are Thomas Nagel and T. L. S. Sprigge. See Nagel's famous essay "What It Is Like to Be a Bat" in *Philosophical Review* 83:4, 1974, pp. 435–450 and Sprigge's *The Importance of Subjectivity* (Oxford: Clarendon Press, 2011). See also *The Conscious Self*, by D. Lund (New York, Humanity Books, 2005) and *The Mind and Machines: What It Means to Be Human and Why It Matters* by Matthew Dickerson (Ada, MI: Brazos Press, 2011). Taliaferro defends the knowledge argument in several publications including "Substance Dualism: A Defence" in *The Blackwell Companion to Substance Dualism*, edited by J. Loose, A. J. L. Menuge, and J. P. Moreland (Oxford: Wiley Blackwell, 2018). In their strongest form, knowledge arguments are based on the principle of the indiscernibility of identicals: If A is B, whatever is true of A is true of B. So, the argument avoids cases of when a person might have incomplete concepts of, say, the Morning Star and the Evening Star and think they are different on the basis that one is seen in the morning and one in the evening, whereas it turns out there is only one thing, the planet Venus, which was presumed to be two stars. In the case of the brain or body, one may observe all its physical characteristics and history without any awareness that there is any mental life involved. But you could not know all about what we call the Morning Star and the Evening Star without realizing they are just two names for the same thing, Venus. On the importance of reference in this argument, see Richard Swinburne's *Are We Bodies or Souls?* (Oxford: Oxford University Press, 2019).

rightly) that if persons (their thinking, subjective experiences) are the very same thing as their bodies and their parts or processes (brain and brain events), then to know about one would be to know about the other (for according to materialism there are not two things, but one). As Thomas Nagel and T. L. S. Sprigge have argued, we can know all about a human person's or other animal's body and have no idea about the thinking, feeling, and so on that is occurring. Here is Sprigge's succinct account of our predicament:

> The main reason for holding that [there is a distinction between the mental and the physical] is that it seems entirely possible that a scientist should have complete knowledge of a human organism as a physical system and yet be ignorant of the character of that individual's consciousness.[42]

Sprigge presses his point further in terms of our experience of other persons:

> For that matter, there is nothing physical about another person, which absolutely proves that he is conscious. His consciousness is not something which could be located in his brain for everything about the brain could be as it is without the individual being conscious.[43]

Based on human reports and inferences to explain behavior (a subject withdrawing his hand from a stove is good reason to infer the subject feels pain), speech, and our understanding of anatomy, we rightly correlate the mental and the physical. Moreover, our public language and ethics is grounded on a confident coordination that we as embodied persons function as unified beings. But this should not overshadow the fact that our visibility and interaction with each other requires integrated mental–physical interaction. Rejecting the possibility of an invisible personal presence amounts to rejecting something we have good reason to believe about ourselves.[44]

Moore is aware of the objection that while our mental life (such as conscious painful feelings) may be expressed visually, this mental life is not a visible process. He seeks to defuse this objection by appealing to grammar and behavior:

> There is another connection here between talk of God and talk of sensations. If we think of pains, for instance, as things people have internally, just as they have warts externally, then they can come to seem peculiar and strangely inaccessible things. All we can get at to establish is that somebody is in pain is his behavior, not the pain itself. But this is an illusory difficulty, a logical one. We do not count anything as getting at the pain itself. It

---

[42] Sprigge, p. 9.
[43] Ibid., p. 9. See also Markus Gabriel's book *I Am Not a Brain*, translated by C. Turner (Cambridge: Polity, 2018).
[44] In contemporary philosophy the thesis that there is more to us than our bodies is sometimes enhanced with thought experiments involving what has been called a philosophical zombie. Some argue that it is conceivable that an exact physical replica of you might be created but lack consciousness. The being would talk and act as if it were conscious when, in fact, it would not be conscious at all.

is part of the logic of the word "pain" that the way we establish when people have pain is mostly by looking at their behavior (not only by looking at their behavior)... It is only misconstruing the logic of the word that makes pains and other sensations seem such strange things.[45]

Moore goes so far as to suggest we might usefully dismiss any use of the term *pain* to refer to the sensations of others, and refer only to behavior, speech, and grammar.

> If I had another word for my own pain, so that I only used the word 'pain' to refer to other people's pain, then I could, if I wished, do without the word pain altogether; for it is only their behavior that I might want to record what they say; and some of their sentences using the word; they say, for example, 'I am in pain,' I cannot see other people's pain; and this is not just an unfortunate accident, or due to any defective senses. It is a matter of logic. Other people's pain, if they really have them, are, like all their sensations, logically inaccessible, invisible to me. It makes no sense to say "I see his pain" or "I feel his pain," since anything that I could see or feel would for that very reason, not be his pain. Sensations are, we might want to say in some sense private.[46]

In reply, we contend that Moore's acknowledgement that the mental states of other persons is invisible (another person's pain cannot be seen or felt) is not just a matter of grammar or logic. If we stipulate that once upon a time there was an invisible spirit in pain, we have created a fictional creature whose pain (by definition) cannot be seen. But in the case of one another, the reason why we cannot directly observe another person's pain is a fact of the matter, not a question of stipulation or the way we use the word *pain*. As H. D. Lewis observes:

> If I have a pain this is something which I personally feel, it just cannot be resolved into the physical factors which cause me to feel it, even when the physiological story is told in the greatest detail from any cut finger or the state of my brain. Nor is the tale completed when note is taken of my reaction to the pain or of my disposition to act in certain ways such as putting on a plaster or visiting the doctor. The pain itself is none of these things, whatever the significance of the further factors noted. ... No one directly observes my thoughts. Others may learn about them without delay, especially if I am talking, or they may judge what they are like with much closeness from my demeanor and their knowledge of me, and so on. But the thoughts themselves are not locatable in my body.[47]

While Moore grants that we want to say that sensations are "in some way private," he seems ready to fully discount this in favor of attending only to the language and behavior of those who speak of their pain. But the whole reason why we care about people's behavior and language is that these are reflections of the conscious, experiential states of persons.[48]

---

[45] Moore, p. 63. He appears to be inspired by a strategy developed by Wittgenstein in the *Philosophical Investigations*.
[46] Ibid., p. 63.
[47] H. D. Lewis, *The Elusive Mind* (Philadelphia: Westminster Press, 1982), p. 8.
[48] A. J. Ayer would not have sympathized with Moore's strategy; he once jested that materialistic/behaviorist philosophers must have been anesthetized to take their view of the mental seriously,

The ostensible fact that we cannot directly observe the subjective, conscious states of others is not just significant for the philosophy of mind and religion. It underlies a host of concerns: There is the challenge of determining when a human fetus begins to have experiences (how much brain activity is essential to enable experience?), determining when a person dies (how little, if any, brain activity is a reliable sign of the irreversible loss of consciousness?), measuring the mental life of nonhuman animals (which nonhuman animals have morally significant mental states such as suffering?), considering whether one day there might be supercomputers that (or who) have conscious, subjective experiences. These challenges are all fueled, in part, on the premise that the conscious experience of others is not directly visible or observable.

Russell, Ayer, Flew, and Moore have not done justice to those in the Abrahamic traditions who claim to experience God through visual and nonvisual, perceptual experiences. In the depiction of God as invisible by Hume, Russell, Ayer, Flew, and Moore, there is a philosophical and aesthetic failure to engage the aesthetic dimensions of experience in the Abrahamic traditions. In Russell's photograph there are no people present or even a solitary monk in meditation. Ayer's drogulus seems more like a mischievous poltergeist than the God of Abrahamic or other religious faiths. Flew's only literary allusion to an invisible person is a villain (the main character in H. G. Wells' 1897 novel, *The Invisible Man*, who is a murderer and terrorist). Plotinus developed a much different picture for securing a divine presence, one grounded in anticipatory awe and the desire to see divinity.

> I think, therefore, that those ancient sages who sought to secure the presence of divine beings by the erection of shrines and statues, showed insight into the nature of ALL; they perceived that, though this Soul is everywhere tractable, its presence will be secured all the more readily when an appropriate receptacle is elaborated, a place especially capable of receiving some portion or phase of it, something reproducing it or representing it, and seeming like a mirror to catch an image of it.[49]

Plotinus here points to the active search for ALL, in building a fitting place to meet its presence, in comparison with passive waiting to entrap the invisible gardener.

---

cited by David Lund, *The Conscious Self*, p. 11. See also Ayer's *The Problems of Knowledge* (London, 1956), chapter 2. Russell also repudiated trying to solve the problem of other minds by reducing or eliminating the subjectivity of others in light of behavioral analysis. Here is a slightly amusing passage from Russell's *Human Knowledge: Its Scope and Limits*: "We are not content to think that we know only the space-time structure of our friends' minds, or their capacity for initiating causal chains that end in sensations of our own. A philosopher might pretend to think he knows only this, but let him get cross with his wife and you will see that he does not regard her as a mere spatio-temporal edifice with not a glimmer of intrinsic character," viz. her subjective states (New York: George Allen and Unwin, 1948), see pp. 483–486.

[49] *The Enneads of Plotinus*, The Fourth Ennead: Third Tractate, Section 11.

Why not use actual mystical texts in which there are ostensible experiences of the divine?[50] The Ayer–Copleston debate could have focused on a challenge to the listeners about whether they can trust their own sense of God or a sacred presence. There is some reason to think that a vast majority of their listeners would have some religious experience to reflect on. About fifty years after the debate, when Britain is supposed to have become more secular, a BBC survey found that 76 percent of the population reported having had some kind of spiritual experience.[51] If the debates took place today, the "believer" and "skeptic" could have engaged a supermajority of the world's population. The statistics globally on belief today are quite staggering: In the *Cambridge Companion to Atheism*, Phil Zuckerman, a sociologist and atheist, estimates that 88 percent of the world population today believes in God.[52] Perhaps many do not claim to have had an experience of God, but this finding is some reason to think that listeners would be open to investigating more realistic accounts of religious experiences than Ayer's drogulus, who is described as an interloper in one of the BBC London sound studios.[53]

---

[50] Consider, for example, Julian of Norwich's *Revelations of Divine Love*, one of the oldest book recording a woman's religious experience in English. There are so many texts that Flew and Hume et al. could have drawn from, whether these be ostensible reports of actual experiences of the divine or fictionalized versions. Rather than draw on Wells, Flew might have considered Tolstoy's *The Death of Ivan Ilyich*. In testing the coherence of an idea, fictional works, from novels to fantasy, can function as elaborate thought experiments. *Star Maker*, by Olaf Stapleton, published in 1937, would have made an exquisite thought experiment well beyond H. G. Well's work. It might also be noted that Tolkien's *The Hobbit* with its invisibility ring was published in 1937, well before Flew's work went to press, and might have been an apt reference. As an aside, Flew came to rethink his rejection of theism. He eventually came to accept a form of theism (though this is more accurately described as deism) as recounted in the book *There Is a God*, by Flew and R. A. Varghese (San Francisco: HarperOne, 2008). Flew came to accept a version of the theistic fine-tuning argument, thus eventually siding (in terms of the parable) with the believer in the invisible gardener.

[51] Cited by John Hick, *The New Frontier of Religion and Science: Religious Experiences and the Transcendent* (New York: Palgrave, 2006), p. 17.

[52] See "Atheism: Contemporary Rates and Patterns," *The Cambridge Companion to Atheism*, edited by Michael Martin (Cambridge: Cambridge University Press, 2006), pp. 47–68. In fairness, we should note that at least one philosopher would offer a radically smaller figure than 88 percent. Georges Rey maintains that the truth of atheism is so obvious that there may not be a single, mature, well-educated person who believes theism is true. He proposes that those who profess to be theists are too young, self-deceived, or too unintelligent to know better. See his "Meta-Atheism: Religious Avowal as Self-Deception" in *Philosophers without Gods*, edited by L. Antony (Oxford: Oxford University Press, 2007). For a response, see *Reading Philosophy of Religion*, by Graham Oppy and Michael Scott (Oxford: Wiley-Blackwell, 2010), pp. 230–234.

[53] It is not uncommon for those who deny the evidential significance of religious experience to compare reports of sensing God to reports of seeing or experiencing something so preposterous almost no one believes it to be remotely plausible. In their critical review of the argument from religious experience, Beverly Clack and Brian Clack ask their readers whether the following report is credible: "A man reported having seen in the New Jersey Barnes, a humanoid alien resembling a giant stalk of broccoli. There were no other witnesses to the event, and the man's testimony was discounted, largely on account of his reputation of a hardened alcoholic." *The*

Is God Disembodied, Supernatural, or Nonnatural?

What about Moore's claim: "We can establish the presence of the heavenly, spiritual God ... by seeing an earthly, material man saying his prayers, *and nothing else*"? Some people engage in prayer without believing or hoping or trusting there is a reality, divine or otherwise, who hears prayers or is the object of worship or source of mercy.[54] But many in the Dominican order he belonged to (which included St. Thomas Aquinas and St. Catherine of Sienna) would urge observers to take seriously their ostensible communion with a reality that goes beyond them and their prayers.

Let us now, more briefly, question some other concepts of the God of Abrahamic traditions cited at the outset of this chapter.[55]

IS GOD DISEMBODIED, SUPERNATURAL, OR NONNATURAL?

What about describing the God of Abrahamic traditions as disembodied, supernatural, or nonnatural?

The term *disembodiment* suggests or hints at an impairment or loss of something that should otherwise be present. This is confirmed by *The Cambridge Dictionary of Philosophy*, third edition, in which *disembodiment* is defined as "the immaterial state of a person who previously had a body."[56] From a Christian point of view, the term *embodiment* may be used theologically in a positive light about Jesus of Nazareth as fully God and fully human, without implying that prior to the incarnation God should be described as disembodied.

We think it would be less misleading for Christians to refer to God as incarnate or non-incarnate. From a Christian point of view, Christ was wholly God (*totus Deus*) but not the whole of God (*totum Dei*); in the Trinity, God the second Person of the Trinity was incarnate, but not God the Father.

Terms like *immaterial, incorporeal,* or *nonphysical* may aptly be used to describe God or the divine nature without implying impairment, but the use of

---

Philosophy of Religion: A Critical Introduction (Cambridge: Polity Press, 2019), p. 58. Such cases may be amusing, and to their credit the Clacks do not present this as a decisive counter-example to those who give epistemic credit to reported experiences of the divine, but one wonders why one should spend very much time on reports so vastly dissimilar to those ostensible experiences of the divine.

[54] Don Cupitt comes to mind; see his *Taking Leave of God*.

[55] Many of the philosophers addressed in this chapter (Hume, Russell, Ayer) employed the argument from analogy to justify the belief in other minds. Today there are other accounts such as the theory-theory model. We believe that none of these other strategies can succeed in circumventing the phenomenologically evident importance of first-person subjectivity. Dan Zahavi rightly criticizes theory-theory models when they "ignore the first-personal givenness of experiential dimension." *Subjectivity and Selfhood: Investigating the First-Person Perspective* (Cambridge: Massachusetts Institute of Technology Press, 2005), p. 222.

[56] See " Disembodiment, " *The Cambridge Dictionary of Philosophy*, edited by Robert Audi (Cambridge: Cambridge University Press, 2015), pp. 277–278.

these terms implies or suggests that we have a clear understanding of what is material or corporeal or physical. This is not obvious to a range of philosophers.[57] Anthony Kenny, perhaps the greatest living historian of philosophy, takes note of how contemporary science has removed our commonsense view of the natural world:

> At one time it seemed as if a robust naturalism could be easily stated. This was a conception that thought of the world as being made of solid, inert, impenetrable and conserved matter – a matter that interacts deterministically and through contact. But twentieth-century physics posited entities and interactions that did not fit the materialistic characterization of reality, and which took science away from a world of solid, inert, messy material atoms.[58]

As Michel Bitbol observes: "Material bodies are no longer the basic objects of physics. Ironically, the notion of material body motivated the very research that dissolved it."[59] To begin one's philosophical account of reality with the assumption that we have a problem-free, clear understanding of the mind-independent physical world is an unwarranted first step (*proton pseudos*, first thing false). Giving philosophical privilege to the concept of mind-independent physical objects diminishes the likelihood that we have a clearer understanding and awareness of our own conscious and subjective states of mind. Arguably, all of the sciences require scientists who make observations, advance hypotheses, devise experiments, employ reason, have new ideas, and so on. We have great confidence in the trustworthiness of the physical sciences, but we would not have any physical science itself without a prior trust in scientists who have a wide spectrum of subjective experience. In brief, we would have no third-person, scientific view of nature without a prior first-person confidence in our experience, ideas, and reasoning. As S. Gallagher and Dan Zahavi point out, "Science is performed by somebody; it is a specific theoretical stance toward the world. ... Scientific objectivity is something we strive for, but it rests on the observations of individuals."[60]

For this reason, describing God as immaterial or incorporeal is acceptable (rather than describing God as being disembodied), provided we realize that we

---

[57] See Noam Chomsky's *Rules and Interpretations* (New York: Columbia University Press, 1980), R. Fumerton's *Knowledge, Thought, and the Case for Dualism* (Cambridge: Cambridge University Press, 2014), "There Is No Question of Physicalism," by T. Crane and D. H. Mellor, *Mind*, 99, 1990, pp. 185–206, and " A Defense of Experiential Realism," by S. Klein in *Psychology of Consciousness: Theory, Research and Practice*, 2015, 2:1, pp. 41–56.

[58] Anthony Kenny, "Mere C. S. Lewis," *Times Literary Supplement*, June 19, 2013. See also *The Matter Myth* by Paul Davies and John Gribbin (Penguin, 1992), especially chapter 1, "The Death of Materialism."

[59] Michel Bitbol, "A More Radical Critique of Materialism: A Dialogue with Bas van Fraassen about Matter, Empiricism and Transcendentalism," in *Images of Empiricism: Essays on Science and Stances, with a reply by Bas van Fraassen* (Oxford: Oxford University Press, 2007).

[60] *The Phenomenological Mind*, by S. Gallagher and Dan Zahavi (London: Routledge, 2008), p. 48.

do not currently have a clear, problem-free concept of what counts as material or corporeal or physical.

The terms *supernatural* and *nonnatural* for the God of Abrahamic traditions are problematic for a similar reason: Namely, the use of both terms assumes we have a clear, problem-free understanding of what is natural. But this is not the case. As Tim Crane points out:

> The appeal to the idea of the supernatural relies on a conception of nature according to which nature, an autonomous, law-governed whole, is opposed to God and the divine. This conception of nature is a product of the scientific revolution of the seventeenth century, and it would surely not have been acknowledged before that time.[61]

Crane cites the French sociologist Émile Durkheim (1858–1917) in support of this position, and the passage is worthy of reprinting here for emphasis:

> The idea of the supernatural is of recent vintage: it presupposes its opposite, which it negates and which is not at all primitive. In order to call certain phenomena supernatural, one must already have the sense that there is a natural order of things, in other words, that the phenomena of the universe are connected to one another according to certain necessary relationships and laws.[62]

We suggest Abrahamic theists should not embrace the idea that God is nonnatural or supernatural. The Abrahamic traditions hold that the whole cosmos is sustained in existence by the creative, conserving power of God. God is thereby understood to be distinct from the cosmos and thus, in a sense, transcendent, but also imminent in the natural world, which would not exist without God's conserving power. One might be tempted to use the term *nonnatural* of God and the experience of God on the grounds that neither is normal or, to use a phrase of Philip Kitcher, a matter of "the mundane physical world." But in a sense, while God should be thought of as extraordinary compared with the contingent cosmos, God is believed to be the ultimate constant of the cosmos, and for this reason some theists describe God as the *ens realissimum* (most real being).[63] And yet for all that,

---

[61] Tim Crane, *The Meaning of Belief Religion from an Atheist's Point of View* (Cambridge: Harvard University Press, 2017) p. 10. See also Terence Nichols' *The Sacred Cosmos: Christian Faith and the Challenge of Naturalism* (Ada, MI: Brazos, 2003), p. 9.

[62] Cited by Crane, p. 10.

[63] Philip Kitcher, *Life after Faith: The Case for Secular Humanism* (New Haven: Yale University Press, 2014), p. 2. There are places, however, where some Christian philosophers identify special divine acts in terms of the extraordinary. Thomas Aquinas wrote that "those things are properly called miracles which are done by divine agency beyond the order commonly observed in nature" (*Contra Gentiles*, III). Still, Aquinas thought that what we commonly and ordinarily observe in nature is itself the result of God's creative will. For Aquinas, miracles are not violations of the laws of nature (as David Hume supposed) but acts of divine agency different from God's ordinary agentive creative sustaining of the cosmos.

according to the testimony of many, God is experienced in ordinary life. As Abraham Maslow observed, "The sacred is *in* the ordinary."[64] Maslow aptly underscored how the sacred can be made visible in ordinary life:

> The eternal becomes visible in and through the particular, the symbolic and platonic can be experienced in and through the concrete instants ... and one can transcend the universe of time and space while being of it.[65]

Eknath Easwaran's *Passage Meditation: A Complete Spiritual Practice* is a contemporary example of how Maslow's reference to the eternal and visible may be given practical shape.[66]

The use of the term *supernatural* is also flawed insofar as, historically, it was, and sometimes is today, used to refer to witches, house ghosts, and items that were explicitly identified as superstitious (by Hobbes in *Leviathan*), in the company of fairies, goblins, elves, sprites, nymphs, hamadryads, and auguries (to use Hume's list from his *Natural History of Religion*).[67] We suggest that the more charitable philosophical term for the God of Abrahamic faith is *theism* – a term introduced by Ralph Cudworth in the seventeenth century. Cudworth and his fellow Cambridge Platonists were among the first persons to conduct philosophy in English. (It is from them that we get many of the terms used in philosophy today such as "philosophy of religion," "consciousness," and more.)

We think it would be best to represent the God of Abrahamic traditions in terms of what is believed to be God's power, knowledge, goodness, creativity, and manifestation in the world through sensory experience as well as through conscious perception not involving the five senses.

In contrast to Russell's black-and-white photograph, we offer a different photograph of what is believed to be Mount Sinai with the following alternative caption: "According to Abrahamic tradition, a covenant was made between God and Moses on Mt. Sinai."

---

[64] Abraham Maslow, *Religions, Values, and Peak Experiences* (New York: The Viking Press, 1970), p. xi.

[65] Ibid., p. 116. The notion that religious experiences are not normal, but ruptures in our ordinary experience may be traceable to William James' *The Varieties of Religious Experience* and Rudolf Otto's *The Idea of the Holy*. But there is also evidence of religious experience in the context of domestic, normal life, as in Brother Lawrence's *The Practice of the Presence of God*. See also *The Golden Cord* and the thesis that part of Christian teaching about the eternal involves recognizing the hallowed nature of the domestic.

[66] This work (cited earlier) is in the tradition of Evelyn Underhill's classic *Practical Mysticism*, published in 1914. The subtitle of the original publication is amusing but speaks to the way in which mystical experiences may be seen as natural: "A Little Book for Normal People."

[67] For a more sympathetic use of *supernatural*, see *Supernatural: Death, Meaning and the Power of the Invisible World*, by Clay Routledge (Oxford: Oxford University Press, 2018).

Is God Disembodied, Supernatural, or Nonnatural?

FIGURE 2.2 Saint Catherine's Monastery. By permission of Saint Catherine's Monastery, Sinai, Egypt. Photograph courtesy of Michigan-Princeton-Alexandria Expeditions to Mount Sinai.

The meaning of Mount Sinai is weighted with generations of people who understood then, and understand today, that the story of what took place at this specific site is part of a history weaving them together with the divine.

Origen offers this portrait of our observability and the experience of the divine:

> Can a [human] person, regarded in its solidity, avoid being seen when it comes before our eyes? The higher divine realities on the other hand, even when they are in front of us, can be perceived only with their own consent. It depends entirely on them whether they are seen or hidden. It was by grace that God revealed himself to Abraham and the other prophets. The eyes of the heart did not allow Abraham to see God, but the grace of God was offered spontaneously to the gaze of that righteous man.[68]

---

[68] Origen, *Homily 3 on Luke*, found in *The Roots of Christian Mysticism*, edited by Oliver Clément, p. 149.

3

The Gates of Perception

> If the doors of perception were cleansed every thing would appear to man as it is, Infinite. For man has closed himself up, till he sees all things through narrow clinks of his cavern.
>
> William Blake[1]

The Bhagavad Gita is part of the Hindu epic *Mahabharata*. The scripture narrates a dialogue between the warrior prince Arjuna and his charioteer Krishna, who is an avatar (a kind of incarnation or manifestation) of Vishnu, the cosmic force of goodness, the inner Lord who lives in the hearts of all beings. Their dialogue takes place prior to a monumental battle. Arjuna is downcast, despairing over the monstrosity of the imminent mass killings of family, friends, and former teachers, who are in the opposing army. The dialogue has many layers and teachings about choices, our duties, actions, intentions, the presence of good and evil, and reincarnation. It culminates in the revelation of the divine. Here is a section from the chapter Divine Splendor. Krishna addresses Arjuna:

> Listen further, Arjuna, to my supreme teaching
> which gives you such joy. Desiring your welfare,
> O strong-armed warrior I will tell you more.
> Neither god nor sages know my origin, for I
> am the source from which the gods and sages
> come. Whoever knows me as the Lord of all
> creation, without birth or beginning knows
> the truth and frees himself from all evil.
> Discrimination, wisdom, understanding,
> forgiveness, truth, self-control, and peace of
> mind, pleasure and pain, birth and death, fear

---

[1] William Blake, "The Marriage of Heaven and Hell," *The Poetry and Prose of William Blake*, edited by D. Erdman (New York: Doubleday & Co., 1970), p. 39.

The Gates of Perception

> and courage, honor and dishonor; nonviolence,
> charity, equanimity, contentment, and perseverance
> in spiritual disciplines – all the different qualities
> found in living creatures have their source in me. ...
> To those steadfast in love and devotion I give
> spiritual wisdom, so that they may come to me.
> Out of compassion I destroy the darkness of their
> ignorance. From within them I light the lamp of
> wisdom and dispel all darkness from their lives.[2]

With some modest background beliefs (such as an appreciation of the centrality of consciousness in reality) and dispositions (openness to making contact with the transcendent), might a person today have what one believes to be an authentic revelation of the divine through meditating on this text, responding, in the words of Arjuna: "You are Brahman supreme, the highest abode, the supreme purifier, the luminous, eternal spirit"?

The translator of the text just cited, Eknath Easwaran, had such a spiritual awakening, or conversion, based on his meditation on the Gita during a time of existential crisis. In his mid-thirties, he was well acquainted with the Gita but living a secular life as a university professor in central India. While his life appeared to be a happy one, he writes: "I was surprised to find myself feeling empty inside. Something deep could not be satisfied. Old, old questions began to come unbidden as I lay awake at night. Why am I here? What is life for? What happens when I die?"[3] Upon the death of Gandhi, whom he knew personally, and the death of others, he was desolate until he recalled passages from the Gita:

> The words must have taken me in because when I opened my eyes at last it had grown dark. Time had been suspended and the burden of sorrow was gone. I felt as if I had returned from another world – an inner realm beyond time and space where somehow I was at home.[4]

In his subsequent commentaries on the Gita and the Upanishads, Easwaran has underscored the aesthetic nature of finding his home as a Hindu, resonating with Sri, or Lord, Krishna's revelation: "I am the source of all the joy, all the love, all the wisdom, and all the beauty within you."[5]

---

[2] *The Bhagavad Gita*, translated by Eknath Easwaran (Tomales, CA: Nilgiri Press, 2007). We highly recommend Easwaran's other books: *The Bhagavad Gita for Daily Living* (in three volumes); *Essence of the Bhagavad Gita*; *Essence of the Upanishads*; *Gandhi the Man*. Easwaran is especially good in dispelling the idea that the Gita should be read primarily as a war poem.
[3] Eknath Easwaran, *Passage Meditation; A Complete Spiritual Practice* (Tomales, CA: Nilgiri Press, 2016), p. VIII.
[4] Ibid., p. IX.
[5] See his *The Bhagavad Gita for Daily Living*, volume 1, The End of Sorrow (Tomales, CA: Nilgiri Press, 1979), p. 118.

In Chapter 2, we compared the invisibility of God to the invisibility of human persons; both the love of God and of persons can be invisible (*amor invisibilis*). But that does not entail that God and persons cannot be disclosed in profound, aesthetically rich, symmetrical experiences. In this chapter we engage three philosophers who are skeptical of the concept of a transcendent God found in traditional theologies. Tim Crane and Roger Scruton believe traditional concepts of transcendence place God beyond the possibility of experience. Howard Wettstein believes that a transcendent God is beyond reasonable belief. They are principally concerned with Christianity and Judaism, but their critical point of view would also apply to the claims to experience the transcendent Brahman in and through the Gita.

Crane, Wettstein, and Scruton promote slightly different views on the relationship between religion and aesthetics. Each of these philosophers presents the view that the gates of perceiving the divine are closed. Our response is to invite a broader phenomenological approach to religious experience, including divine disclosures that may be pictured as profound face-to-face encounters. From the standpoint of aesthetic personalism we contend that persons are capable of experiencing the transcendent. At the very least we propose that there is good reason not to define experience, the transcendent, and persons so as to rule out the possibility of persons experiencing the transcendent. In a classic paper, Friedrich Waismann describes amusing cases in which the definition of our terms can be sorely tested. Would we still consider a creature a cat if

> [i]t showed some queer behavior usually not to be found with cats, say, if, under certain conditions, it could be revived from death whereas normal cats could not? Shall I, in such a case, say that a new species has come into being? Or that it was a cat with extraordinary properties? Again, suppose I say "There is my friend over there." What if on drawing closer in order to shake hands with him he suddenly disappeared? "Therefore it was not my friend but some delusion or other." But suppose a few seconds later I saw him again. Could grasp his hand, etc. What then? "Therefore my friend was nevertheless there and his disappearance was some delusion or other." But imagine after a while he disappeared again, or seemed to disappear – what shall I say now? Have we rules ready for all imaginable possibilities?[6]

Perhaps intentionally, Waismann's two cases hint at the way some religious concepts stretch ordinary language; Christians believe that Jesus of Nazareth died and rose from the dead and that his resurrected body was quite extraordinary (Acts 1:9, "as they were watching [Jesus] was lifted up, and a cloud took him out of their sight"). As it happens, we think it unwarranted to rule out as impossible such cases on grammatical or conceptual grounds, and we argue in this chapter that we should not rule out as conceptually (or logically or

---

[6] Friedrich Waissman, "Verifiability," in *Logic and Language*, edited by Antony Flew (Oxford: Blackwell, 1958), pp. 119–120.

The Gates Are Closed

grammatically or epistemically) absurd the possibility of persons experiencing the transcendent. Incidentally, Waismann's image of a being who dies and comes to life again and appears and disappears is a classic description of the character Love in ancient Greek philosophy. In Plato's *Symposium* we are told:

> [Love] is by nature neither immortal nor mortal. But now he springs to life when he gets his way; now he dies – all in the very same day ... he keeps coming back to life; but then he finds his way to always slips away, and for this reason Love is never completely without resources.[7]

What Crane, Wettstein, and Scruton share with the philosophers encountered in Chapter 2 is the belief that the God of Abrahamic traditions is not properly viewed as a hypothesis that could be tested in the world as observed and studied by the natural sciences. Scruton writes: "God is not a 'hypothesis' to be set beside the fundamental constants and the laws of quantum dynamics. Look for him in the world of objects and you will not find him."[8] We too think God (whether of Abrahamic faiths or other theistic tradition) should not be seen as a *scientific* hypothesis, though we think that we can look for God in the world and there is reason to be open to God being experienced.[9]

THE GATES ARE CLOSED

Tim Crane contends that the God of Abrahamic faiths, or at least of Christianity, involves an appeal to what is unseen. Following William James, he says religion is "belief in an unseen, normative order."[10] He is highly critical of the new atheists (Richard Dawkins and company), however, as they principally characterize religion in terms of adhering to a hypothesis. Rather, for Crane, religion involves how we live. Religion involves belonging to a community and finding meaning in terms of one's personal identity. Crane sees religion as a "unified system of beliefs and practices relative to sacred things."[11] God, on the other hand, is transcendent, which means beyond our experience. "The transcendent is something beyond or outside of experience."[12]

Crane's skepticism about experiencing a transcendent God begins with his skepticism about the very concept of transcendence. He writes:

> My own atheism is a consequence of my denial of the transcendent. I believe the world around us that we experience, together with the invisible world described by science, is all there is. Nothing transcends it. ... The transcendent is, by definition, something

---

[7] Plato's *Symposium*, 203e, translated by Alexander Nehamas and Paul Woodruff in *Plato; Complete Works*, edited by John Cooper (Indianapolis: Hackett Publishing Company, 1997).
[8] Roger Scruton, *The Face of God* (London: Bloomsbury, 2012), p. 165.
[9] While we do not think of theism as a scientific hypothesis, we have no objection to thinking of it as a hypothesis.
[10] *The Meaning of Belief*, chapter 2.   [11] Ibid., chapter 2.   [12] Ibid., p. 11.

beyond; beyond all this, everything we experience, everything we claim to fully understand.[13]

There may be a slight tension in this claim and his view (cited in Chapter 2) that religious belief and practice can be part of what is taken to be natural. But perhaps the key to his atheism is this: Theism *ipso facto*, or by definition, goes beyond the world of experience. If we were able to experience God, God would not be transcendent.

Crane believes religion is about belonging, meaning, and identity in part because the religious are not bothered by the question of God's very being: What explains God? This is not a worry to the religious because, according to Crane, religious believers do not embrace a hypothesis:

> The classic objection to [theism] as a hypothesis ... is that creation by God raises exactly the same question as it answers. If the existence of the universe is explained by God's creative action, then what explains the existence of God? In my experience, believers are typically not troubled by this question. If they were to take it seriously, then it ought to worry them. But although the question is often posed by skeptics and atheists, their opponents are not worried by it. Some critics might take this as yet another sign of the irrationality of believers: they postulate a creator to explain the world, and then they are unable to explain the creator – and what is worse, they are unworried by this. But there is another possible reading of this impasse: that the idea of God creating the world is not functioning as a hypothesis in the scientific sense at all.[14]

The relationship between religion, practice, and aesthetics, given Crane's position, is represented on a superficial level by the handsome reproduction of a detail portion of *The Seven Sacraments*, a fifteenth-century painting by Rogier van der Weyden, used for the cover of his book *The Meaning of Belief: Religion from an Atheist's Point of View*. The detail of this painting shows people engaged in personal interactions: a child is being baptized, there are blessings, confession, a community of religious practitioners. We do not see what might involve a more explicit representation of persons experiencing the transcendent as one finds in, for example, icons depicting the giving of the Holy Spirit at Pentecost. However, the central panel of the triptych painting is not shown as part of Crane's book cover. It depicts a crucified Christ on the cross lifted high above Saint John and the three Marys gathered beneath him in mourning. They are in the middle of the community that circulates around them participating in the seven sacraments. So, the totality of the triptych does include the transcendent. And thinking about this work in a historical context might allow us to think about how the concept of the transcendent was taking form at that time.

There were huge shifts in western European culture when van der Weyden was working in Brussels as an early Flemish painter. Artisans took part in, and probably led, the growing interest in the natural world as something to study

[13] Ibid., p. 88.   [14] Ibid., pp. 61–62.

and observe. In the early modern era, the rise of naturalism in the arts – the ability to represent what things look like (skin having a particular texture and luminosity, fabrics having particular weights and densities, metals reflecting light from different angles) through extreme attention to the physical world taken in by sight (and eventually microscopes and other lenses) – aligned with a growing desire to know God through the senses. Previously, devotion had often consisted of using an image to help create a divine image in the "inner eye" for contemplation, but now one's sensory experience of the material world was seen as a desirable place to know God's grace – in the body. This kind of knowledge that comes through attention and observation is not theoretical, but embodied knowledge. For many of those who lived and moved around Van der Weyden's paintings when he made them, the participation in the sacraments led to knowledge of God through the senses. Just as the new illusionism in painting and drawing lifted a veil between the viewer and what was depicted, the knowledge and enthusiasm for the natural world that was expanding at this time lifted the veil between the world and God. The transcendent was seen with the eyes and experienced through the other senses as immanent.

Returning to Crane, we agree with him that there is more to religion than belief. Religions can shape and be shaped by the full expanse of our experience of beauty and ugliness, our sense of meaning and significance. There is nonetheless the belief or hope or trust or faith that there is God, or Brahman, or Nirvana.[15] While we think Crane is right about the importance of belonging and identity, we believe he overstates this, especially in his observation about why believers are not troubled by the question of what explains God.

In the Abrahamic traditions, the very concept of God is the concept of an ultimate reality that, unlike ourselves and the world around us, is noncontingent and not explainable by any force or cosmic law independent of God. Philosophers in what is known as *the perfect being tradition* contend that God's unsurpassably great nature includes all great-making properties, including omniscience, omnipotence, essential goodness and beauty, and existing necessarily.[16] When a reality is necessary, it cannot but exist; its nonexistence is impossible. Philosophers have refined the belief in God as ultimate by claiming that *the essence of God* is *existence*: While our essence and the essence of our cosmos is not existence (our cosmos might never have existed), God – if there is a God – could not fail to exist. Theistic theologians

---

[15] Today there are multiple models of what may count as religious belief. See the entry "Faith" by John Bishop in the *Stanford Encyclopedia of Philosophy* and *The Concept of Faith*, by Lad Sessions (Ithaca, NY: Cornell University Press, 1994). In the past, faith was often treated as a straightforward form of propositional belief (the belief that there is a God, for example), but faith is now viewed as having multiple dimensions (e.g., someone may have faith in God insofar as she hopes God exists, but she is agnostic whether God exists).

[16] See Yujin Nagasawa's *Maximal God: A New Defense of Perfect Being Theology* (Oxford: Oxford University Press, 2017). See his replies to the classic objections to the ontological argument.

have gone on to characterize God as deriving God's existence from God's own being (God exists *a se*) as opposed to deriving existence from some other thing (*ab alio*).[17] So, for some theists, God's existence is self-explaining. This is not the same as claiming that God is self-created (God created God), but that God's existence stems from God's maximal, unsurpassably great nature.[18]

The above observations may seem like technical "academic" theses rather than a matter of positions taken up by ordinary religious practitioners, but we think that ordinary, non-theologically trained believers in God would be utterly bewildered if asked to entertain the possibility that God had a beginning or might cease to exist or was created by the Big Bang. This would be akin to asking whether $1 + 1 = 2$ is only true on Tuesdays or whether the concept of justice likes lettuce, evident nonsense. We are not claiming here that it is obvious such religious believers are right in thinking of God as necessarily existing; ours is the more modest claim that (from the standpoint of Abrahamic theism) the idea that God can or should be explained by something external to God does not make sense.[19] Geradus Vendler Leeuw writes, "The religious significance of things ... is that on which no wider or deeper meaning can follow. It is the meaning of the whole."[20]

Actually, this understanding of God and the cosmos is what motivates some philosophers to claim that our cosmos, its existing at all and continuing to exist, is better explained on theism rather than naturalism. Given naturalism, the existence of the cosmos is a brute, not further explainable fact. Bertrand Russell, J. L. Mackie, and others have been explicit on this point: The cosmos just is, without further explanation. Mackie went so far as to propose that our contingent cosmos might have come into existence without any cause whatsoever:

There is a priori no good reason why a sheer origination of things not determined by anything should be unacceptable, whereas the existence of god with the power to create something out of nothing is acceptable.[21]

---

[17] God's being self-existing is not the same as claiming that God is self-creating (*causa sui*). The former implies that God's reality is self-sufficient (requiring no external cause), whereas the second makes a different claim that God might create God, which seems to be incoherent (this appears to involve God having to exist before God exists).

[18] One needs to keep in mind here that in philosophy an explanation of something (an event, an idea, the meaning of a term, a rule, or whatever) is a matter of making it understandable or intelligible. Such explanations can involve causation, but they can be noncausal (we explain $1 + 1 = 2$, for example, without claiming that $1 + 1$ somehow caused there to be 2).

[19] Going back to Chapter 2, we recall Gareth Moore's suggestion that God might be like the equator would be deemed absurd from the perfect-being theological point of view. The existence of the equator depends on mapmakers, whereas the reality of God does not depend on God-makers.

[20] Gerardus Vander Leeuw, *Religion in Essence and Manifestation: A Study in Phenomenology*, trans. J. E. Turner (London: George Allen & Unwin, 1938), p. 680.

[21] J. L. Mackie, *The Miracle of Theism* (Oxford: Oxford University Press, 1983), p. 94.

The Gates Are Closed

Mackie's proposal prompted this reply by William Craig:

Does Mackie sincerely believe that things can pop into existence uncaused, out of nothing? Does anyone in his right mind believe that, say, a raging tiger could suddenly come into existence uncaused out of nothing, in this room right now? The same applies to the universe, if prior to the universe there was absolutely nothing – no God, no space, no time – how could the universe possibly have come to exist?[22]

If theism is true, then there is a noncontingent source and an account of the cosmos that does not require any further accounting. An argument like this can be developed quite independently of theism by simply raising a question about why our contingent cosmos exists or why there is not a different one. Arguably a successful answer to this question will lead to recognizing a necessarily existing being, leaving open whether or not such a being is God.[23] Perhaps the necessarily existing being does not have all the divine attributes. So, the question about the existence of the contingent cosmos may be advanced without having any in-advance assumption about God at all. At the conclusion of that argument, however, philosophers can appeal to additional arguments that enhance theism, such as the teleological argument or the argument from the emergence of consciousness.[24] One reason to resist Crane's atheism is that "the world around us" may need an explanation in terms of that which transcends it. From a religious point of view, the existence of the cosmos, like the existence of the epic *Ramayana* or a beautiful calligraphic Quranic manuscript, begs for us to look beyond it to understand its origin and nature.[25]

Even if we have some reason to recognize the transcendent to explain the cosmos, what about the further point that we cannot experience the transcendent? We propose that it is unreasonable to rule out *in principle* or *by*

---

[22] W. L. Craig, "The Kalam Cosmological Argument" in *Philosophy of Religion: An Anthology*, edited by L. Pojman (Boston: Wadsworth Publishing, 1998), p. 2. John Cottingham aptly points out that recent claims that our universe might have emerged from fluctuating quantum energy would not count as our universe coming into being from nothing. "Fluctuating energy may be 'nothing' in the sense that it contains no atoms or molecules, but it is not *nothing at all*. Quantum theory, for all its impressive success, does not remotely undermine the unshakeable logical maxim '*ex nihilo, nihil fit*'; from nothing, nothing comes." "Transcending Science" in *New Models of Religious Understanding*, edited by Fiona Ellis (Oxford: Oxford University Press, 2018), pp. 26–27.

[23] For a careful account of this point, see *Necessary Existence*, by Alexander Pruss and Joshua Rasmussen (Oxford: Oxford University Press, 2018). For recent defenses of the cosmological argument, see Timothy O'Connor's *Theism and Ultimate Explanation: The Necessary Shape of Contingency* (Oxford: Wiley-Blackwell, 2012) and Michael Aleida's *Cosmological Arguments* (Cambridge: Cambridge University Press, 2018).

[24] See *Contemporary Philosophical Theology*, by Charles Taliaferro and Chad Meister (London: Routledge, 2016), chapter 4.

[25] The claim here concerns what many religious practitioners believe about how the cosmos without a divine sustaining cause would seem enigmatic; we do not thereby attribute to such practitioners a William Paley watchmaker argument. On Paley, see Taliaferro's *Evidence and Faith*, chapter 6. We address the possibility of there being a novel without a novelist in chapter 7.

definition experiences such as those cited in Chapter 2 and at the outset of this chapter. We believe that it is very difficult to limit experience to the five senses or to what can be empirically confirmed or explained only by the natural sciences. Under common circumstances we can experience almost limitless emotions, thoughts, ideas, works of art, and imaginary objects (which we can describe poetically). And we can perceive values like the power of love to overcome hate or recognize the ugly yet seductive nature of vanity.[26] We can experientially respond to the danger of fascism or an impending economic recession, lament the lives lost in remote wars, and so on. We may well restrict terms like *witness* to experiences that are more direct or immediate than others (compare an eyewitness to a crime with someone who observed it weeks later via a video recorder). But we suggest that terms like *experience* – even when it comes to cases of when a person professes to experience the divine – are harder to rule out on definitional terms. On this point, we are impressed by Kai-man Kwan's proposal that we should treat reported experiences of all sorts holistically and with a trust that is critical (weighing the reasonability of the claim with what we otherwise reasonably believe about reality). There are, of course, some limits on experience. Assuming there is no Loch Ness Monster, experiencing it will be limited to looking at an out-of-focus photograph and some dodgy sonar readings. Some limits to experience will depend on conceptual, linguistic, and ethical factors: without mathematical expertise, it would be difficult to experience the elegance of a sophisticated mathematical proof. Enjoying someone's fluency in Nahuatal, the language of the Aztec people, would be difficult without proper linguistic proficiency. A white nationalist who abhors Asian immigrants would be unlikely to empathize with the profound suffering of a Hmong child as described in Anne Fadiman's *The Spirit Catches You and You Fall Down*, an account of failures in communication and empathy by hospital personnel. Granted those limitations, we propose that in ordinary, overwhelmingly evident circumstances our experience goes far beyond the austere confines of the empirical sciences. We readily recognize in our experience good and bad, beautiful and ugly reasons, desires, and ideas as explanatory that would not be captured, described, or explained in the sciences. If we only allowed for the authority of physics, chemistry, and biology, we would not be able to account for our writing this book or you reading it because of our shared interest in religion and aesthetics.[27]

Howard Wettstein shares Crane's view that religion is not principally about beliefs. Wettstein is a practicing, observant Jew who engages in prayer and

---

[26] See "Are You Experienced?" by Charles Taliaferro in *Jimi Hendrix and Philosophy*, edited by Theodore Ammon (Chicago: Open Court, 2017), chapter 9.
[27] We follow Thomas Nagel when he claims: "the universe revealed by chemistry and physics, however beautiful and awe-inspiring, is meaningless." *Secular Philosophy and the Religious Temperament*, p. 8. See also Nagel's *Mind and Cosmos* (Oxford: Oxford University Press, 2013).

The Gates Are Closed

worship but "without metaphysics."[28] As a philosopher, however, he does have a metaphysics: naturalism, which recognizes the natural world without anything supernatural.[29] He seeks to identify religious practice with emotions like awe, rather than focusing on beliefs. He claims his position is supported by the leading twentieth-century Jewish philosophical theologian Abraham Joshua Heschel, whom he cites:

> Awe rather than faith is the earliest attitude of the religious Jew ... In Judaism, yirat hashem, the awe of God, or yirat shamayim, the awe of heaven, is almost equivalent to the word "religion." In Biblical language the religious man is not called "believer," as he is for example in Islam [Mu'min] but yare hashem [one who stands in awe of God].[30]

A key demarcating the practicing Jew from someone who is secular, is not so much the affirmation or denial of the truth about some philosophy of God, but whether religious themes, values, and teachings play a fundamental role in one's life.[31] The case for or against religious life is not principally about evidence, but about what is effectively central to a person:

> Coming to or leaving religious life has more in common with falling in or out of love. Alternatively, it is a bit like finding a work of literature powerful. One does or one does not. In thinking about love, or about literature, we are not tempted to bring to bear concepts like intellectual justification, proof, and the like. My sense is that these concepts are probably not particularly germane to religious change or indeed to religious commitments or rejection.[32]

Wettstein compares religious practitioners to mathematicians who may be not merely proficient in math, but also experts who yet may be agnostic or have no belief of any kind about the reality of numbers.[33]

What emerges is an interesting dichotomy between Wettstein's life as a philosopher and as a religious practitioner. As a religious practitioner, Wettstein uses realist language:

> In prayer (when it goes well), I have the sense of the presence of the divine, of making contact. But ask me about the party on the other end and one of two things will happen: either I will beg to be excused for not having too much to say, or else we will have a very long talk about how difficult a matter it is that is in question.[34]

The practice of prayer appears to involve making contact with the divine (ostensibly this is not just experiencing oneself or something one knows with certainty to be fictional). To enter such a practice, he needs to "suspend disbelief" as a philosopher. He is aware of the tradition and testimony we

---

[28] Howard Wettstein, *The Significance of Religious Experience* (Oxford: Oxford University Press, 2012), chapter 13. "Metaphysics" is sometimes used as a technical term, but here the term simply refers to what is the case. So, to have a metaphysics is to have a view about what there is. In this use, the terms "metaphysics" and "ontology" mean the same.
[29] Ibid., 48, 51–53.   [30] Ibid., p. 29.   [31] Ibid., p. 89.   [32] Ibid., p. 23.
[33] Ibid., pp. 26, 66, 212–213.   [34] Ibid., p. 211.

have appealed to in Chapter 2 in which persons report feeling in the presence of God, but he laments the serious disanalogy between such apparent experiences of God and ordinary perception. "Ordinary, everyday perception by contrast, is reliably repeatable. One can return to a room and typically see exactly what one expects to see."[35]

We agree that mere belief in the divine, without attended emotions, practices, action, is an empty religious life. Also, it would be puzzling to claim to be an observant Jew and yet not have Jewish teaching and practice play a foundational role in one's life. Moreover, if Judaism did have a foundational role in one's life (one acted as if there is a God of justice and love, one seeks to love one's neighbor as oneself), then it might well be that such a person, even if she did not believe the relevant metaphysic, is more deeply devout than someone who believes the metaphysic but is unmoved by it in terms of feeling and action. But we find Wettstein's examples puzzling: Can one be in awe of God without believing (or hoping or trusting or assuming) that there is a God? We think this is implausible. And it seems similarly implausible to think that falling in or out of love can dispense with beliefs. Indeed, it would be unusual, if not conceptually absurd, to claim to love another person without having (and desiring) all sorts of (justified, true) beliefs about the person. We can adore fictional subjects like Jane Austen's Mr. Darcy, but we love them as fictional subjects who have no awareness of us and certainly cannot return love. The example of mathematicians who can be experts without having beliefs about what numbers are does not seem a fitting analogy, given that mathematicians do not pray to numbers or believe that numbers created and lovingly sustain the cosmos.[36]

Wettstein's reported religious experience actually supports the notion that we can experience the transcendent. Recall that Wettstein writes that, in prayer, "I have the sense of the presence of the divine, of making contact." This is especially significant, in our view, as Wettstein is having this apparent contact with the divine despite the fact that, *as a philosopher*, he believes there is no divine reality with whom to be in contact. We further suggest that Wettstein's criterion for reliable perception seems one dimensional: Sure, our perception of seeing furniture in rooms mostly involves "exactly what one expects to see," but shouldn't we be open to a more dynamic understanding of experiencing the divine than experiencing furniture?[37] Jerome Gellman comments on Wettstein's comparing the experience of furniture and the experience of God:

---

[35] Ibid., p. 138.
[36] This is an important objection to Wettstein's use of mathematicians as an analogy with religious believers, as argued by Laura Ekstrom in "Religion on the Cheap" in *Oxford Studies in Philosophy of Religion*, edited by J. Kvanvig (Oxford: Oxford University Press, 2015), pp. 87–113.
[37] Actually, experiencing furniture and its properties or meaning may turn out not to be altogether inert. You see a chair in a room, leave, and then return a day later; the chair may have changed from being your property to being the property of your ex-spouse who just divorced you.

The Gates Are Closed

Wettstein is thinking of God as a stationary, inert object that should be accessible at all times, if accessible at all. This is surprising, since Wettstein likes to stress the multifarious images of God in the religious life which strongly suggest a fluid, dynamic God.[38]

Wettstein's own practice of praying might go some of the way to identifying a practice: *Often (though not always), deep, sincere prayer leads practitioners to have an experience of what they take to be the presence of the divine, making contact with a transcendent, divine being.*[39]

Wettstein's claim that his philosophy of religious experience has some support from the work of Abraham Heschel may be due to the stress Heschel places on the role of being in awe of God. But for Heschel, awe is an element of encountering *the reality of God* as experienced in prayer and prophecy. He says, "To the prophet, God is always apprehended, experienced, and conceived of as a Subject, never as an object."[40] While Heschel contends that "no image must be fashioned, no concept formed" of God, he nonetheless affirms God's passionate presence in the world. God "is moved and affected by what happens in the world, and reacts accordingly. ... This notion that God can be intimately affected ... basically defines the prophet's consciousness of God."[41] Heschel's spirituality is a vigorous affirmation of God as a passionate presence.

Like Crane and Wettstein, Roger Scruton is skeptical about claims to experience a transcendent God. We shall present his position and critically assess it without speculating on the ways in which Scruton may be inspired by other philosophers.[42] Scruton advances a major bifurcation between causes and reasons. For Scruton, to ask for the cause of an event is very different from asking for the reason for an event. According to him, if we are concerned with the causation of anything, from the cosmos as a whole to explaining cancer, we must appeal to science:

[E]verything in the natural world, human thoughts and action included, happens in accordance with scientific laws so that the same laws govern events in the atom and events in the galaxy, even in the ocean and events in the mind.[43]

---

[38] Jerome Gellman's review of Wettstein's *The Significance of Religious Experience* in the *Notre Dame Philosophical Reviews*, March 22, 2013.

[39] Wettstein's further description of the phenomenology of such prayerful contact suggests (to us) realism rather than mythology: Wettstein describes prayer as an "experience of intimacy, of sharing one's longing, pains, joys and the rest" (p. 172). Such experiences at least appear to be a sense of intimacy with the divine, a sharing of one's longings with God. Interestingly, Wettstein writes that he has "great confidence in the power of religious practice and the virtues of the religious life" (p. 27), even though, from his naturalist point of view, such practices involve engaging "wholeheartedly with mythology" (p. 172). In our view, there seems to be a profound tension between the ostensible realism of his experience and his theoretical commitment to naturalism.

[40] Abraham Heschel, *The Prophets* (New York: Harper, 1962), p. 485.   [41] Ibid., pp. 274, 224.

[42] Evidently, Scruton is indebted to Kant's view of causation and to Ludwig Wittgenstein's private language argument and suspicion about self-reference.

[43] Scruton, *The Face of God*, p. 4.

Scruton thereby seems to hold that the causes of our thinking (neurological explanations of your reading this sentence) must involve the same laws that govern the rest of the cosmos, mental or nonmental. From a scientific point of view, Scruton affirms that there is no cause of the cosmos itself. "There is no final explanation of why the world exists; it just does. Indeed, there is something incoherent about the question 'why?' asked of the existence of the world."[44] But, Scruton claims, that does not mean there is no *reason* why the world exists. Evidently, reasons come into play in the context of meaning and practice, as opposed to science. Scruton writes about how prayer can enable us to find *the reason why the world depends on God*:

The relation of dependence that binds the world to God gives the reason why things are as they are. But this reason is not a cause. In referring to the ultimate reason of things we are dealing with another kind of answer to the question 'why?' and another meaning of *therefore*. And this is what gives sense to the life of prayer.[45]

Scruton suggests that prayer and other practices might give us reason to believe in something quite different from what can be disclosed in science:

The communion is the real presence of God among us, and it is from such acts of participation that we come to see who God is and how he relates to us. It is through communion that we come face to face with God.[46]

Perhaps one advantage to Scruton's position is that there is no direct conflict between science and religion, as they are concerned with different domains. One of the reasons Scruton offers for God playing no causal role in the world is his view that God is beyond space and time. Given that God is not spatiotemporal, God cannot be the object or explanation of the ostensible experience of God. "If God is a transcendent being who lies outside the space-time continuum, there is a deep, perhaps even a necessary truth that God has no causal role to play in the beliefs that target him – or in any other event in space and time."[47] Scruton believes that any account of religious experience can make no appeal to God or the transcendent. "The best explanation of our belief in the transcendental can make no reference to the transcendental."[48] Despite excluding God from the world of causation, Scruton affirms a realist view of God's omnipresence:

He [God] is in and around us, and our prayers shape our personal relationship with him. We address him, as we address those we love, not with the 'why?' of explanation, but with the 'why?' of reason and the 'why?' of meaning.[49]

Perhaps akin to Wettstein's combination of naturalism and religion, Scruton appears to adopt naturalism when it comes to science but, unlike Wettstein, theistic realism when it comes to reason and meaning:

---

[44] Ibid., p. 4.   [45] Ibid., p. 13.   [46] Ibid., p. 20.
[47] Roger Scruton, *The Soul of the World* (Princeton: Princeton University Press, 2014), p. 9.
[48] *The Face of God*, p. 18.   [49] Ibid., p. 13.

If the usual claims of faith are true, God is transcendental. He is not part of nature and not a possible object of scientific enquiry. No scientific explanation of religious belief could possibly refer to him. It follows that, if there is an explanation, it will be 'naturalistic': it will explain religious belief in terms of forces and functions that make no reference to God.[50]

Scruton has an interesting concept for what constitutes a person. He is reluctant to think of a person as an object, preferring instead to think of the self as a perspective: "The self is not a thing but a perspective." Scruton comes close to denying the self is part of the real world and denies that he can observe himself, partly because he seems to favor observation largely in the context of science while denying the existence of observation due to introspection or self-awareness:

The subject is in principle unobservable to science, not because it exists in another realm but because it is not part of the empirical world. It lies on the edge of things, like a horizon, and could never be grasped 'from the other side', the side of subjectivity itself. Is it a real part of the real world? The question begins to look as though it has been wrongly phrased. I refer to myself, but this does not mean that there is a self that I refer to. I act for the sake of my friend, but there is no such thing as a sake for which I am acting. Sakes are not objects in the world of objects. Neither are selves.[51]

He refers to knowing what he is thinking "without observation."[52]

Scruton's position on religion and science is vexing. We believe he gives the natural sciences too much of a domain – namely "everything in the natural world" including thoughts and action. We agree that the same laws of nature that are used to account for inanimate processes (law of gravity) obtain for accounting for the mental life of persons and animals, but we propose that processes involving thoughts, desires, ideas, reason, and so on essentially involve more than the laws used to explain nonthinking processes. If we are asked what is the smallest perfect number (a number equal to the sum of its divisors, including one, but not including itself), we would respond "6" because we reason that $6 = 1 + 2 + 3$, and there is no smaller number that is perfect. We submit that this intentional thinking is the cause, in part, of why we say what we do. On a vastly, radically different scale, if God's causal power is the reason why the cosmos exists, we suggest that God's causal power is *the cause of why the cosmos exists*. The reasons why the *Ramayana* was composed and translated (and the reason why there is a copy on our desk) must be part of the causes of why copies of the epic are where they are around the world.

We are baffled by Scruton's claim that explaining why (causally why) people claim to experience God can make no appeal to God or the transcendent. It seems as though Scruton thinks a necessary condition for being recognized as a cause is that the cause must be explainable scientifically, which seems to involve

[50] Ibid., p. 31. [51] Ibid., pp. 32–33. [52] Ibid., chapters 2 and 3.

empirical descriptions. But empirical descriptions have their limits. As Patrick McNamara points out in *The Neuroscience of Religious Experience*:

> We can't see subjective experiences, and thus it is a bit harder (although not impossible) to measure them. We are one step removed from the object of study because we have to measure reports about experience instead of experiences themselves.[53]

When we do get reports of experiencing God from people who do not believe there is a transcendent God, how might one explain that without employing the concept of a transcendent God (and perhaps their reasoning that such a being would be incoherent)? And if someone believes in a transcendent God due to arguments or experiences, how might that be explained without at least being open to the reality or unreality of this transcendent God having a causal role in the world?[54] Given the plausible view that mathematical properties (numbers and their relations) are not spatial (and perhaps timeless), it seems that the transcendent has to be invoked whenever anyone engages in mathematical reasoning.[55]

Scruton's view of persons is, at the least, very counterintuitive. First, it is odd to think of a person as being the same thing as a perspective. It makes sense to think of persons having perspectives, but not so if we imagine there can be a perspective without a person having that perspective. Scruton entertains the possibility that persons ("the subject") are not part of the real world. He asks whether the subject is "a real part of the real world?"[56] We think the most evident fact we are capable of knowing *is* the reality of ourselves and our subjective states, much more evident than our knowledge of events and things that are independent of mind and experience. As Richard Fumerton observes:

> This much is certain. We are directly and immediately aware of paradigmatically mental properties such as visual appearance and pain. Through that awareness we gain non-inferential knowledge that such properties are exemplified. This knowledge is the best sort of knowledge imaginable. There is no surer place to start one's ontological commitments. The awareness that allows foundational knowledge of these properties also allows one to think directly about these properties. When one thinks of searing pain, for example, one is (typically) not thinking of it as that state, whatever it is, that results

---

[53] Patrick McNamara, *The Neuroscience of Religious Experience* (Cambridge: Cambridge University Press, 2009), p. 10.

[54] The work of Fiona Ellis is especially important at this juncture. She has mapped out an interesting position called "expansive naturalism." She argues for the unsatisfactory nature of narrow, eliminative naturalists, noting that a liberal naturalism that recognizes consciousness, normativity, and other values is far more convincing. She then contends that once one's naturalism has so expanded, it is not so implausible to embrace theism; see her book *God, Value, and Nature* (Oxford: Oxford University Press, 2014). Examples of liberal naturalists include David Macarthur and Mario De Caro, though time will tell whether they might expand their naturalism a little in the direction of theism in the future.

[55] See "Abstract Objects: Bringing Causation back into Platonism," by Charles Taliaferro, *Revista Portuguesa de Filosofia* 71 (4), 2015, pp. 769–780.

[56] *The Face of God*, p. 32.

from damage to tissue and produces pain-healing behavior. One is not (merely) thinking about the property that typically results from laying one's hand on a red-hot burner. Rather, one is thinking of the searing pain as the property it is.[57]

What is the source of Scruton's skepticism about the self? When he writes "I refer to myself, but this does not mean that there is a self I refer to," we ask: Then, what could it mean to refer to oneself unless there is a self?[58] It is absurd to deny that in our self-awareness we are aware of ourselves as subjects, as individuals who endure over time and have perspectives. The analogy that a self could be like "a sake" is highly surprising: Of course, if you do something for the sake of your friend (comfort her when she experiences a loss), there are two selves (you and your friend) and there is also compassion (an emotion) and experience. Each of these factors needs to be accommodated in any reasonable account of the transaction. What about Scruton's point that just because we use the term *sake* meaningfully and truly does not mean there is such a thing as a sake? Grammatically and conceptually, the term *sake* does not refer to a thing; it refers instead to the purpose of something ("let's be good for goodness sake"). There are no such *things* as sakes. Perhaps a better analogy would be this: just because you can meaningfully and truly refer to the average plumber ("The average plumber has 2.5 children"), it does not follow that they are things, the average plumbers and their 2.5 children. Still, we submit that our self-awareness is very different from referring to some abstract mathematical "object."

Scruton employs a Wittgensteinian rationale (not unlike Gareth Moore) to try to dismiss what we know directly about our mental states. Scruton claims:

There is a difference between knowing what pain is and knowing what pain is like. But to know what it is like is not to know some additional inner fact about it: it is to recall the memory of "how it felt." We are dealing with familiarity rather than information. "What it's like" is not proxy for a description, but a refusal to describe.[59]

We believe this radically distorts our experience of pain. When we say that we are feeling pain, we are indeed describing, at a fundamental level, how we are feeling. In fact, if we are not describing how we are feeling when we report feeling pain, then there is nothing (in our view) that would count as a description of anything. This is a paradigmatic case of a description.

By way of an appreciative view of Scruton's work, we suggest that his artful depiction of religious life in the world of meaning and reason provides some evidence that the experiences have a bearing on our understanding of causation in the real world. Consider the following passage in which Scruton first derides

---

[57] *Knowledge, Thought, and the Case for Dualism*, pp. 218–219.
[58] On the primacy of first-person awareness, see Lynne Baker's *Naturalism and the First-Person Perspective* (Oxford: Oxford University Press, 2013). On the observability of the self, see Roderick Chisholm's *Person and Object* (London: George Allen and Unwin, 1976).
[59] *The Face of God*, p. 32.

the case for experiencing the transcendent, but then endorses a religiously significant picture of the world:

> The philosophical question is not whether we can connect the experience of the "numinous" case by case with some transcendent origin – for that is impossible – but whether we can present a picture of the world that enables us to interpret the religious experience in that way. If we can get this far, then we have made way for the only thing that can sustain the truth of what we feel, which is trust in a personal God who reveals himself.[60]

We suggest that if the latter has some experiential support, its support is relevant to the first philosophical question of whether such experiences in toto (taken together rather than focusing on only a single case) may support the notion that the numinous, divine reality is indeed experienced. Our reasoning here is similar to our view that Scruton's own experience – in this case, of death – supports a more substantial view of the self than he embraces. Scruton writes:

> In death we confront the body voided of the soul, an object without a subject, limp, ungoverned and inert. The awe that we feel in the face of death is a response to the unfathomable spectacle of human flesh without the self.[61]

We interpret this experience as partly grounded on the awareness that people are not just perspectives, but substantial individuals who may perish while their bodies survive (as corpses).

In our view, Crane, Wettstein, and Scruton have not offered compelling evidence against the plausibility that persons can have some experience of the God of Abrahamic faiths or the experience of the divine through the Bhagavad Gita.

A PHENOMENOLOGY OF FACE-TO-FACE DISCLOSURE

The Bhagavad Gita, the Hebrew Bible, the Christian Bible, and the Qur'an contain multiple pictures of divine revelation. Among the many is the notion of encountering the divine in a face-to-face disclosure: Krishna and Arjuna, Moses at Mount Sinai, Jesus of Nazareth and his contemporaries, the Angel Gabriel and Mohammad. Reports of such encounters reveal a world (or worlds) thoroughly suffused with *embodied conscious awareness*, involving *the availability and openness on behalf of persons to the transcendent*. We believe the pathway to appreciating such possible (or prospective) encounters involves seeing how some aesthetic experiences can be cognitive apertures; taking seriously the protean primacy of consciousness; and attending to ethical and religious attunement.

Aesthetic, cognitive apertures: As we have seen, Scruton seems to recognize the potential, revelatory nature of religious experience. He goes so far as to affirm that such experience mediates the divine: "The experience of the sacred is

---

[60] *The Face of God*, p. 165.   [61] Ibid., p. 161.

therefore a revelation, a direct encounter with the divine."[62] And yet he is reluctant to entertain that this involves the divine causally interacting with persons (in the real world). His reluctance has left some of his critics wondering whether Scruton leaves us with a merely aesthetic appreciation for religion. Brian Hebblethwaite questions whether Scruton is similar to the character Sebastian Flyte in Evelyn Waugh's novel *Brideshead Revisited*.[63] He cites this dialogue between Sebastian and his friend Charles Ryder. Charles asks Sebastian about his Roman Catholic faith:

> "But, my dear Sebastian, you can't seriously *believe* it all."
> "Can't I?"
> "I mean about Christmas and the star and the three kings and the ox and the ass."
> "Oh yes, I believe that. It's a lovely idea."
> "But you can't *believe* things because they are a lovely idea."
> "But I *do*. That's how I believe."[64]

Hebblethwaite makes this comparison with reluctance, but his worry is not out of place if Scruton embraces the primacy of naturalism.

Contrast Scruton's naturalism with Simone Weil's experience of beauty in the world. In her view, beauty provides evidence of God coming among us. For her, this meant the incarnation:

In everything that gives us the pure authentic feeling of beauty there really is the presence of God. There is as it were an incarnation of God in the world and it is indicated by beauty. The beautiful is the experiential proof that the incarnation is possible.[65]

Weil offers an intimate picture of God in causal interaction with the world: "The Beauty of the world is Christ's tender smile for us coming through matter. He is really present in the universal beauty."[66]

For Weil, the experience of beauty is not so much a reactive attitude to the world, but an aperture – an opening, portal, or conduit – through which she (we) may experience the transcendent. To defend the coherence and importance of this understanding of aesthetic experience, it is not essential to argue that the religious perceptual claims are as reliable as our claims to see other persons and the world. An experience of the divine can be a bona fide experience of the divine even if the subject(s) do not know that the experience is veridical. We contended earlier that Wettstein's own experience of making contact with the

---

[62] Scruton, *An Intelligent Person's Guide to Philosophy* (London: Duckworth, 1996), p. 96.
[63] Brian Hebblethwaite, "Metaphysical and Doctrinal Implications" in *The Religious Philosophy of Roger Scruton*, edited by James Bryson (London: Bloomsbury, 2016), chapter 6.
[64] Evelyn Waugh, *Brideshead Revisited: The Sacred and Profane Memories of Captain Charles Ryder* (Boston: Little, Brown and Company, 1979), pp. 86–87.
[65] Simone Weil, *Gravity and Grace*, translated by E. Crawford and Mario von der Ruhr (London: Routledge and Kegan Paul, 1952), p. 137.
[66] Simone Weil, *Waiting on God*, translated by E. Crawford and Mario von der Ruhr (London: Fontana, 1959), p. 120.

divine may be genuine even in the case when he, as a philosopher, is skeptical about the existence of God. The term *revelation* is not always a success term insofar as the person experiencing a revelation must be certain that it is a revelation. What philosophers call "success terms" are those that require that the speaker is successful in making a claim, as in "I know the Pope is in Rome today"; the statement would not be true if the Pope was not in Rome. But "I think the Pope is in Rome today" may be true even if the Pope is not in Rome. In terms of revelation claims, we suggest that you actually might experience a revelation and yet not know that it is a revelation. After all, in a religious or secular context, a person may authentically reveal their commitment to justice through marches, manifestos, sacrificial acts protecting the vulnerable, and so on, even if very few, if any, people recognize such a revelation or disclosure of the person's character.[67]

The primacy of consciousness: In addition to recognizing how aesthetic, religious experiences can be understood as apertures for encountering the divine, we propose that the significance of religious experience can be amplified when we take seriously the protean primacy of consciousness. As we argued in Chapter 2, the vantage point of the natural sciences rests on the prior trust in our first-person experiences. The threat from the sciences to eliminate consciousness from one's worldview is akin to the short story "The Shadow" by Hans Christian Anderson. In that tale, a man's shadow takes on an independent life and, in the end, has him killed. The story is disturbing because we know that shadows are not objects in themselves, but only a deprivation of light. Analogously, the sciences only have meaning and reliability insofar as they rest on conscious, self-aware subjects. Making us aware of this dependency is one of the tasks of philosophy, as Thomas Nagel has observed:

Philosophy in general is the most systematic form of self-consciousness. It consists in bringing to consciousness for analysis and evaluation everything that in ordinary life is invisible because it underlies and pervades what we are consciously doing.[68]

Nagel's invocation of the invisible underscores our response to Scruton. While Scruton treats persons and their mental states as not observable or visible to the natural sciences, that is a reason to recognize the limits of the natural sciences and, in our view, bring to explicit self-awareness the consciousness we have of ourselves as persons.

Both Hindu and Buddhist traditions have stressed the reality and importance of consciousness. In Hinduism, *brahmavidya*, or "supreme science," is aimed at the investigation of human conscious experience in its search for an underlying,

---

[67] As it happens, we suggest that a person may be justified in believing an experience is genuinely revelatory of the divine even if she is not justified in believing she is justified in believing/trusting in the revelation. For support, see William Alston's "Level Confusions in Epistemology" in *Midwest Studies in Philosophy*, vol. 5, edited by P. A. French, T. E. Uehling, and H. Wettstein (Minneapolis: University of Minnesota Press, 1980), pp. 135–150.

[68] *Secular Philosophy and the Religious Temperament*, p. 9.

absolute reality. In an illuminating essay called "Buddhism and Science," B. Alan Wallace takes note of how Western science in the modern era has focused on nature as independent of consciousness. In early modern science, it was not thought that such a science could threaten our confidence in the reality of our conscious, subjective states. Newton, for example, never dreamed that his laws of motion could explain why two persons might fall in love and their bodies move toward each other out of desire. Wallace makes the case that, historically, Buddhist thinking was more anchored in the recognition of the reality of subjective experience than in Western thought:

> While [Western] science has overwhelmingly focused on the objective, quantifiable, physical universe in order to gain power over the natural world ... Buddhism is primarily focused on understanding subjective, qualitative states of consciousness as a means to liberate the mind from its affective tendencies (klesha) and obscurations (avarana). ... The rigorous, experiential examination of the mind has been central to Buddhism from the start.[69]

Wallace goes on (properly, in our view) to contend that the first-person inquiry into the nature of consciousness should not be ruled out as nonscientific:

> While such [Buddhist] introspective inquiry may seem more philosophical than scientific, consider the definition of the scientific method as "principles and procedures for the systematic pursuit of knowledge involving the recognition and formulation of a problem, the collection of data through observation and experiment, and the formulation and testing of hypotheses." ... There is nothing in that definition that insists on a third-person observation or quantitative analysis, especially for phenomena that are irreducibly first-person in nature.[70]

The importance of our being aware of our embodied conscious life comes to the fore when considering a common philosophical case for skepticism. Classical arguments designed to lead us to doubt our perception are often based on thought experiments in which we are not embodied as we think we are, but subject to deception. (Could we be brains in a vat, deceived by a powerful demon or scientist?)[71] While philosophical thought experiments can help extend our thinking beyond our mental habits and help keep our imaginations dynamic, a universe shaped by severe skepticism of our normal, healthy perception – that we are embodied with consciousness – has to end in tears.

Religious and ethical attunement: In addition to being open to experiential apertures and the protean primacy of consciousness, an appreciation for

---

[69] B. Alan Wallace, "Buddhism and Science" in *The Oxford Handbook of Religion and Science*, edited by Philip Clayton and Zachary Simpson (Oxford: Oxford University Press, 2006), 25.
[70] Ibid., p. 32.
[71] Descartes' classic proposal that we might be deceived by an evil demon can now be updated by Nick Bostrom's proposal, the simulation hypothesis, according to which what we think is real is a simulation powered by a post-human civilization.

religious experience may be enhanced by taking religious and ethical attunement seriously. In the West, the importance of the virtues in philosophical inquiry goes back to Plato. According to Plato, one needs virtue to inquire into the nature of virtue:

> It is barely possible for knowledge to be engendered of an object naturally good, in a man naturally good; but if his nature is defective, as is that of most men, for the acquisition of knowledge and the so-called virtues, and if the qualities he has have been corrupted, then not even Lynceus could make such a man see. In short, neither quickness of learning nor a good memory can make a man see when his nature is not akin to the object, for this knowledge never takes root in an alien nature; so that no man who is both naturally inclined and akin to justice and all the other forms of excellence, even though he may be quick at learning and remembering this and that and other things ... will ever attain the truth that is attainable about virtue.[72]

This seems sensible; a person with the vices of vanity, jealousy, envy, illicit anger, and so on will be more hampered in reflecting on justice than someone who has the virtues of fair-mindedness, intellectual courage, and humility. The importance of virtuous inquiry is also recognized in Hindu teaching. The Mundaka Upanishad offers this portrait of the teacher–student relationship:

> To that student who approaches in the proper manner, whose mind is calm and who is endowed with self-control, the wise teacher should fully impart the knowledge of Brahman, through which one knows the true and imperishable Person.[73]

Here are similar passages from the Upanishad on how inquiry requires virtue and the avoidance of vice:

> One who has not abstained from evil conduct, whose senses are not controlled and whose mind is not concentrated and calm cannot gain the Self through knowledge.
> By truth this self can be grasped – by austerity, by right knowledge, and by a perpetually chaste life. It lies within the body, brilliant and full of light, which ascetics perceive, when their faults are wiped out.[74]

In the context of religious experience, we propose that some of the virtues that are important are akin to the virtues in interpersonal relations.

In the twentieth century, there have been some important works, mostly by those in the personalist, phenomenological tradition, focused on the nature of personal interrelationships, sometimes used to shed light on religious experience. The Jewish philosophical theologian Martin Buber explored this path. He differentiated the impersonal relations (which he called I-it relationships) with a personal one (I-thou). For Buber, the I-thou

---

[72] *Plato's Epistles*, translated by G. R. Morrow (Indianapolis: Bobbs-Merrill, 1962), pp. 240–241.
[73] Cited by Anantanand Rambachan, *The Advaita Worldview: God, World, and Humanity* (Albany: State University of New York, 2006), p. 19.
[74] Cited by Rambachan, p. 19.

relationship recognizes the sanctity of other persons and sheds light on our ultimate relationship with God. Another important contributor to the phenomenology of the face-to-face encounter is Emmanuel Levinas.[75]

Gabriel Marcel similarly wrote of the profound ways in which persons can be radically available to one another:

> It will perhaps be made clearer if I say the person who is at my disposal is the one who is capable of being with me with the whole of himself when I am in need; while the one who is not at my disposal seems merely to offer me a temporary loan raised on his resources. For the one I am a presence; for the other I am an object.[76]

While Marcel's focus here is on human-to-human exchanges, his concept of presence amplifies the symmetrical, reciprocal personal relations we have highlighted in religious experience.

Marcel is a philosopher who may be taken as having some sympathy with Crane and Scruton insofar as he believes that the transcendent resists full comprehension:

> There is an order where the subject finds himself in the presence of something entirely beyond his grasp. I would add that if the word "transcendent" has any meaning it is here – it designates the absolute, unbridgeable chasm yawning between the subject and being, insofar as being evades every attempt to pin it down.[77]

But Marcel does not equate the transcendent with "transcending experience." Marcel writes, "There must exist a possibility of having an experience of the transcendent as such, and unless that possibility exists the word can have no meaning."[78]

In Chapter 4, we engage in an aesthetic inquiry into the meaning of five religious traditions and secular alternatives. Religious experiences such as the one prompted by reading the Bhagavad Gita, which we cited at the beginning of this chapter, can utterly change one's sense of the meaning of life. John Cottingham's account of the meaning of Christian religious awareness of the divine applies to the enhanced sense of the meaning of life we see in the Bhagavad Gita:

---

[75] See Levinas' *Ethics and Infinity*, translated by R. A. Cohen (Pittsburgh: Duquesne University Press, 1985), pp. 95, 98, 119. Merleau-Ponty also developed a related, important phenomenology of perceptual experience that likened our encounter with the world to a face-to-face relation. See his *The Visible and the Invisible*, translated by C. Lefort (Evanston: Northwestern University Press, 1968). We highly recommend Glen Mazis' *Merleau-Ponty and the Face of the World: Science, Ethics, Imagination, and Poetic Ontology* (New York: SUNY Press, 2016).

[76] G. Marcel, *Philosophy of Existentialism*, translated by M. Harai (New York: Citadel, 1995), p. 40.

[77] Marcel, *Tragic Wisdom and Beyond*, translated by S. Jolin and P. McCormick, edited by J. Wild (Evanston: Northwestern University Press, 1973), p. 193.

[78] Marcel, *The Mystery of Being*, volume 1, *Reflection and Mystery*, translated by G. S. Fraser (London: The Harvill Press, 1951), p. 46.

The sense that our acts are eternally subject to divine evaluation ... seems deeply to enhance their significance [as] a source of joy to a being of supreme wisdom and love. This amplifies and as it were confirms the meaningfulness that they already had on earth, and protects them against the erosion of time and contingency, shielding them against the backdrop of impermanence against which nothing in the long run matters.[79]

---

[79] John Cottingham, "Meaningfulness, Eternity and Theism" in *God and Meaning*, edited by Joshua Seachris and Stewart Goetz (New York: Bloomsbury, 2016), p. 135.

4

The Perception of Gates

> Like art and religion, philosophical systems have as their content a certain conception of life and the world. They do not originate in conceptual thought but deep in the life of the individuals who have erected these systems.
>
> Wilhelm Dilthey[1]

In the midst of a fierce storm with brilliant light and flashing fire, four bronze figures emerge with the faces of a man, lion, bull, and eagle. There is a profusion of extended wings, along with lightning, wheels, a scroll, and a prophet, who is commissioned to exhort Israel to repentance, warning about the forthcoming fall of Jerusalem.

The thunderous, cascading opening passages of the sixth-century BCE Book of Ezekiel in the Hebrew Bible led some twentieth-century commentators to speculate whether it was actually a description of an alien spaceship landing. What seems more reasonable to assume is that interpreting the sacred texts of great religious traditions requires acquaintance with the meaning and history of the people and cultures in which these texts took shape.

In this passage, Ezekiel, a captive exile in Babylon, has a vision that corresponds to the iconography of the Babylonian zodiac. The image of a divine chariot traversing the skies (heavens) was widely employed in the ancient world to acknowledge the dependency of those on Earth on the forces moving above them. Ezekiel understands the vision to be a message of hope for the Jews in exile. They have not been abandoned by Yahweh; they are remembered.

In this chapter we offer an aesthetic investigation into the meaning of life and the meaning *in* life, in the context of the Abrahamic faiths, Hinduism,

---

[1] Dilthey cited by Meyer Schapiro, *Worldview in Painting—Art and Society* (New York: George Braziller, 1999), p. 19.

Buddhism, and their secular, naturalist alternatives. We begin by proposing a framework for this investigation.

A MATTER OF WORLDS

One may use the term *the world* to refer to *everything that is the case*.[2] In this sense, we are all in the same world. There is nothing wrong with this usage, but it does not immediately lend itself to appreciating how many of us live in profoundly different contexts and cultures. Due to ethnicity, economics, personal experience, and philosophies, some communities or groups live in virtually different worlds. When it comes to religions, these may themselves be thought of in terms of diverse worlds. In *Coming to Our Senses*, Morris Berman observes:

> "Sacred" and "secular" are not just convenient intellectual categories; they are lived experiences. ... To live in a world in which a person's touch was believed to be able to (could?) cure a specific disease is a very different psychic experience in which such things are regarded as impossible (and, perhaps as a result, do not occur).[3]

We propose that Judaism, Christianity, Islam, Hinduism, Buddhism, as well as other religions, and their secular alternatives may be thought of as different worlds where one may enter, leave, visit, be born into, and die. Using the term *world* here is broader than when using terms like *the art world* or *the world of sports*, which designate areas of life in virtue of special interests or practices. Rather, the great world religions involve claims that speak to all of life or everything that is the case.[4] In the *Bhagavad Gita*, Krishna declares, "There is nothing that exists separate from me."[5] There is reason to believe that some religions, such as Judaism, evolved over time to make claims of maximal scope. Some passages in the Hebrew Bible (Psalms 82 and 95; Micah 4:5) suggest there may be gods other than the God of Israel, but monotheism is explicitly secured in Judaism by the late prophets ("I am God, and there is no other." Isaiah 45:22).[6]

The worlds of the five world religions overlap at many points. And in some settings, people may live in more than one world: perhaps practicing Hinduism

---

[2] This is reflected in the first line of Wittgenstein's *Tractatus Logico-Philosophicus*.
[3] Morris Berman, *Coming to Our Senses* (New York: Simon and Schuster, 1989), p. 121.
[4] In technical philosophical terms, our use of the term *world* matches some uses of the term *possible world*. See Plantinga's account of possible worlds as maximal states of affairs, *The Nature of Necessity* (Oxford: Clarendon, 1974). The use of the word *world* in our sense is observed by C. S. Lewis in his *Studies in Words* (Cambridge: Cambridge University Press, 1967), pp. 258–260.
[5] *Bhagavad Gita* 7.7.
[6] See "Kaufman and Recent Scholarship: Toward a Richer Discourse of Monotheism," by Benjamin Sommer, in *Yehezkel Kaufman and the Reinvention of Jewish Biblical Scholarship*, edited by Job Jindo, Benjamin Sommer, and Thomas Staubli (Fribourg: Academic Press, 2017), pp. 204–239.

in meditation, Buddhism in social relations, and entering a secular world when doing business. The metaphor of picturing religions as worlds complements the metaphor of the practice of philosophy as a form of movement or travel, for example, the journey from a cave to the light. In Ancient Greece, the term *philosophizing* was used to describe traveling, as when Solon was said to leave Athens to philosophize, or travel.[7] Hannah Arendt recommended that when we entertain different worldviews, we think of ourselves as visitors, not in the sense of being mere tourists, but, as visitors, we imaginatively enter into different worlds while retaining our own identities. Arendt commended seeing the world from various perspectives without uncritically abandoning one's point of view and adopting another's. "Visiting" does not mean, she says, "passively accepting another's thoughts or merely exchanging prejudices."[8] C. S. Lewis makes a related point about reading works of literature:

> In reading great literature I become a thousand men and yet remain myself. Like the night sky in the Greek poem, I see with a myriad of eyes, but it is still I who see. Here, as in worship, in love, in moral action, in knowing, I transcend myself and am never more myself when I do.[9]

Conceiving of religions and their secular alternatives as worlds is akin to the way some philosophers think of works of art. Some philosophers of art refer to the world of Flannery O'Connor, the world of Virginia Woolf, the world of J. R. R. Tolkien, and so on. These worlds have their own imaginarium (the boundary and nature of the imagined world). We rightly do not expect O'Connor's escaped convict in "A Good Man Is Hard to Find" to burst into Woolf's dinner party in *To the Lighthouse*. And we are correct in thinking that Tolkien's elves and hobbits live in Middle Earth as opposed to the American Deep South of O'Connor or a summer home on the Isle of Skye with Woolf.[10] In the course of engaging Wettstein's work in Chapter 3, we proposed that the nature and significance of religious beliefs are profoundly different from our approach to literature – religious believers do not think of God or Allah or Brahman as fictional beings or beings limited by geography. But the ways in which we engage with works of art can model how we assess religious worlds and their secular alternatives. We shall explore these, employing the principle of charity (sometimes called a principle of rationality or humanity), investigating the internal coherence of worlds and their support (or conflict) with what we know in general, and drawing on the test of time.[11]

---

[7] Herodotus, *History*, 1, 30.
[8] H. Arendt, *Lectures on Kant's Political Philosophy* (Brighton: Harvester Press, 1982), p. 43.
[9] C. S. Lewis, *An Experiment in Criticism* (Cambridge: Cambridge University Press, 1961), pp. 140–141.
[10] See Taliaferro's *Aesthetics: A Beginner's Guide*.
[11] Our objection to Wettstein's assimilation of religious belief to the ways in which (fictional) literature can move us was that it does not take seriously the evident realism that defines religious devotion (awe) and practice. We note here an addendum that our assessment of fiction, even

There are, of course, many different ways of entering, leaving, and abiding in the five religious worlds and secular alternatives. One may do so through study, first-hand experience, meditation, living among those who are practicing a religion or living a secular life, taking vows, making declarations (for example, the shahada "There is no God but Allah, and Muhammad is his prophet"), or undertaking a rite of entry such as circumcision or baptism. Given the phenomenological perspective of this book, we stress the importance of experience in these explorations. Morris Berman asks a provocative question:

> Who knows more about medieval sainthood – the historian who compiles data on age and nationality, or the one who goes to a monastery, and sits in a cell for several months in complete silence?[12]

We think doing both, as well as studying sacred texts (and more), would be better than either alone.[13] We especially commend the way that the arts can assist in our "travels" or "visits" to different religious and philosophical worlds.

Being in a world religion will admit of degrees. For example, one would not be partaking of communion in the world of Christianity without some shared understanding of the rite. In his *Natural History of Religion*, David Hume tells a story involving a new convert to Christianity named Benedict:

> Having been well instructed and catechized, he at last agreed to receive the sacraments of baptism and the Lord's supper. The priest, however, to make everything sure and solid, still continued his instructions: and began the next day with the usual question, "How many Gods are there?" "None at all," replies Benedict; for that was his new name. "How! None at all!" cries the priest. "To be sure," said the honest proselyte. "You have told me all along that there is but one God: And yesterday I ate him."[14]

The tale of Benedict's participation in the Lord's supper (also referred to as communion, the Eucharist, mass) is humorous because Benedict is treating communion as a case of ordinary eating and drinking as opposed to receiving a sacrament in which one communes with the presence of the imperishable Jesus Christ through receiving the consecrated bread and wine. A predicament like Benedict's in the world of Christianity would occur if someone thought the world of Hinduism was centered on worshiping an elephant-headed god who

---

outrageous fairy tales, commonly has realist elements. So, while it would be absurd to measure the success of Tolkien's *The Lord of the Rings* in terms of the evidence for or against the existence of wizards and Ents, it would be on the mark to assess the portrayal of virtue and vice, courage and cowardice, friendship and enmity, and the view that the natural world is wondrous. This would involve assessing a fairy tale in light of what we believe to be true and valuable about reality.

[12] Morris Berman, *Coming to Our Senses*, p. 115.
[13] For an illuminating treatment of studying sacred texts, see *Religious Reading: The Place of Reading in the Practice of Religion*, by Paul Griffiths (Oxford: Oxford University Press, 1998).
[14] David Hume, *Natural History of Religion*, chapter 12, the 1889 ed. [1757], online.

brings good luck to travelers. Yes, many Hindus venerate Ganesha, but such popular devotion, as well as devotion to a whole panoply of gods, needs to be understood in light of overriding ideas about Brahman and the many ways a single divine reality may be manifested in abundant modes and figures.

We have highlighted an amusing case of when someone might not have fully passed through a gate into a world religion, but it also needs to be readily acknowledged that some of the ways of entering into different worlds, religious or secular, are lamentable when they involve compulsion (including, literally, kidnapping), violence or the threat of violence, subjugation, exploitive material or social incentives, manipulation, lies, or damaging misinterpretations. Religion as practiced by individuals, communities, and institutions is not invulnerable to horrible abuses, as history and the present day show us.

In this chapter we consider the aesthetics and meaning of life from the standpoint of secular naturalism. We then explore the aesthetics and meaning of life in five religions, focusing largely on how they differ from a secular alternative. A key difference is that the religious worlds all embrace a broader vision of the sacred. That is, both secular and religious worlds can involve the sacred by recognizing what is deeply valuable, irrevocably precious, and worthy of profound reverence, but religious worlds connect this meaningful terrain in light of a transcendent reality (God, Allah, Brahman, Nirvana). This does not make the religious worlds better or more worthy of our allegiance; there is simply an important, overall difference. We go on to investigate how religious worlds overlap and develop new terrain. We propose that, ideally, a serious search for the meaning of life should take into account both secular and religious worldviews, and we reflect on the task of evaluating different worldviews.

SECULAR NATURALISM

Secular naturalism is the most widely held position in Western philosophy today. As noted in Chapter 1, naturalism comes in two forms: strict, scientific naturalism and liberal or broad naturalism. Strict naturalists only recognize as real what is or will be recognized by the natural sciences (physics, chemistry, biology).[15] In Chapter 2 we advanced a version of the knowledge argument to conclude that there is more to being human than can be captured by the natural sciences. It is possible to have an exhaustive knowledge of another person's body, all neurological processes, and so on, and yet have no knowledge at all of the person's mental states. If a person's mental states are the very same thing as her bodily states, then to know one is to know the other. We are confronted with

---

[15] There is some tension among strict naturalists on this point insofar as some place substantial confidence in the current state of the natural sciences, whereas others appeal to what the natural sciences will describe and explain under ideal conditions, perhaps when the natural sciences are complete (if ever). Strict naturalism would fit what, in Chapter 1, was referred to as *scientism*.

the evident reality of consciousness and its being ostensibly distinct from our brain and bodily processes. As Colin McGinn points out:

> The property of consciousness itself (or specific conscious states) is not an observable or perceptible property of the brain. You can stare into a living conscious brain, your own or someone else's, and see there is a wide variety of instantiated properties – its shape, colour, texture, etc. – but you will not thereby see what the subject is experiencing, the conscious state itself.[16]

Based on the evident reality of conscious states, we believe that forms of naturalism that deny the reality of conscious states are unacceptable. Our thesis is that the world of strict naturalism cannot (or does not) account for values and evident experiences. We cannot enter the world of strict naturalism without abandoning what we know is true: We are consciously existing, self-aware persons. This realization is at the heart of aesthetic personalism.

Liberal naturalists go beyond the natural sciences and recognize the reality of consciousness, the mental, and more, including ethical and aesthetic values; though the liberals remain naturalists insofar as they deny the existence of God, the soul, an afterlife, miracles, and what might be called "supernaturalism" (though for reasons noted in Chapter 1 we find the term *supernatural* problematic).

We believe that liberal naturalism is monumentally more plausible than strict naturalism, although neither form accounts for the existence and endurance of the cosmos the way theism can. In what follows in this book, we use the term *naturalism* to designate liberal naturalism. What is it like to live in the world of naturalism?

Naturalists may be described as optimists or pessimists. One may be a pessimist when one believes that human evolution is far from progressive or good. Denying any afterlife means that all humans and other animals perish at death. The deaths of billions of people in poverty, childhood, and so on are irreversibly tragic; given naturalism, there is no life after life in which there might be redemption or overcoming of sorrow. The most pessimistic naturalists are antinatalists, who argue that the probability of giving birth to fulfilled persons is so low that people should not procreate.[17]

More optimistic naturalists believe that evolution is progressive. On this view, at least many human lives are improving over time; we are living longer and, some hold, evolving ethically such that we are (gradually) coming to an expanding understanding of justice.

Charles Darwin may have occupied a position in between optimism and pessimism. On the one hand, he wrote about how, while it might have been the case that persons evolved to favor all sorts of horrors, we in general will favor justice over time (though such progress may be frustratingly slow, as

---

[16] Colin McGinn, *The Problem of Consciousness* (Oxford: Basil Blackwell, 1990), pp. 10–11.
[17] David Benatar is a leading antinatalist today.

Secular Naturalism

Darwin lamented the toleration of the practice of slavery, which he found abhorrent). This optimistic note has to be qualified by two points: Darwin predicted that in the future the stronger races will exterminate the weaker ones, and Darwin was himself troubled by the idea, which he thought confirmed scientifically, that all life will perish one day.[18]

The current scientific prediction is that all life in our solar system will perish in five billion years when our sun will turn into what is called a red giant and its outer layer will consume our planet. In his famous 1903 essay, "A Free Man's Worship," Bertrand Russell offers this portrait of our beginning and our end:

> That man is the product of causes which had no prevision of the end they were achieving; that his origin, his growth, his hopes and fears, his loves and his beliefs, are but the outcome of accidental collocations of atoms; that no fire, no heroism, no intensity of thought and feeling, can preserve an individual life beyond the grave; that all the labors of the ages, all the devotion, all the inspiration, all the noonday brightness of human genius, are destined to extinction in the vast death of the solar system, and that the whole temple of man's achievement must inevitably be buried beneath the debris of a universe in ruins – all these things, if not quite beyond dispute, are yet so nearly certain, that no philosophy which rejects them can hope to stand. Only within the scaffolding of these truths, only on the firm foundation of unyielding despair, can the soul's habitation be safely built.[19]

The stark aesthetic realism of this portrait is often praised for its stripping away any pretense of some ultimate consolation.

Russell's depiction of the naturalist position in terms of "unyielding despair" is noteworthy for not resorting to philosophical antidotes to such despair. In an argument that was forged in Ancient Greece, some philosophers reasoned that we should no more fear our nonexistence after death than we find our past nonexistence vexing prior to our birth. Evidently, Russell thought our future nonexistence is a profoundly different matter: The perishing of all people and the annihilation of all we create casts a shadow over our lives, whereas the fact that human life had a beginning does not.[20]

There is another philosophical antidote to despair that deserves mention. Imagine all life ceases to be in five billion years and, eventually, there is not the slightest trace of there ever having been life in our galaxy. It would still nonetheless be forever true that life did emerge and endure for billions of years in what was once called the Milky Way. It would still be forever true that we existed, we had ancestors and descendants, we human beings included monsters like Hitler and courageous sages like Dorothy Day and Gandhi; in fact, it would be forever true that all events in our history occurred as they did, replete with all

---

[18] See the account of Darwin in our *The Image in Mind*, chapters 3 and 5.
[19] Russell, "A Free Man's Worship," 1903, widely reprinted and available online.
[20] Samuel Scheffler has argued that many of the projects we value presuppose there will be a future with people able to benefit from our work. See his *Death and the Afterlife* (Oxford: Oxford University Press, 2016). See also the entry "The Afterlife," by William Hasker and Charles Taliaferro, in the free, online *Stanford Encyclopedia of Philosophy*.

their beauty as well as ugliness.[21] We are not invested here in undermining a vision that offers consolation in dire cosmic conditions. Yet we worry that even if there are everlasting truths, such a vision would reinforce Russell's "unyielding despair." On the hypothesis that all persons (all life) will be annihilated, no one will know these truths or find meaning, weep over loss, or take delight in any great events. The truths themselves would be lifeless abstractions with no meaning to persons or other conscious beings. The everlasting truth that there were once loving persons is not by itself a joy-filled vision.

Some naturalists seek to replace a concern for finding a purpose *of* life with seeking meaning *in* life. Consider the proposals by Simon Blackburn and Ronald Dworkin. Blackburn develops the following account of meaning in life:

Another option for meaning ... is to look only within life itself. This is the immanent option. It is content with the everyday. There is sufficient meaning for human beings in the human world – the world of familiar, and even humdrum doings and experiences. In the immanent option, the smile of the baby, the grace of the dancer, the sound of the voices, the movement of a love give meaning to life. For some, it is activity and achievement: gaining the summit of the mountain, crossing the finish line first, finding the cure, or writing the poem. These things last only a short time, but that does not deny them meaning. A smile does not need to go on forever in order to mean what it does. There is nothing beyond or apart from the process of life. Furthermore, there is no goal to which all these processes tend, but we can find something precious, value and meaning, in the processes themselves.[22]

Dworkin advocates a similar position:

When you do something small well – play a tune or a part or a hand, throw a curve or a compliment, make a chair or a sonnet or love – your satisfaction is complete in itself. There are achievements within life. Why can't life be an achievement complete in itself, with its own value in the art in living it displays?[23]

How might one assess the world of secular naturalism? At this stage, we suggest that if there is good reason to think naturalism is true, then we have little choice but to commit ourselves to what Blackburn calls immanent meaning and forego wishing things were different. The aesthetics of a naturalist world may be just what we find in our everyday experience: Life is suffused with precious values and occasions for creativity and justice (what may rightly be described as the sacred), notwithstanding the eventual overriding Russellian vision of unyielding despair.

---

[21] This claim is neutral about the truth of determinism and the status of free will. The claim is simply that whatever and however human history unfolds, it will be forever true that history occurred. For a consoling appeal to an atemporal point of view, see *Arguing for Atheism*, by Robin Le Poideven (London: Routledge, 1996).

[22] Simon Blackburn, "Religion and Respect" in *Philosophers without God: Meditation on Atheism*, edited by Louise Antony (Oxford: Oxford University Press, 2007), p. 190.

[23] Ronald Dworkin, *Religion without God* (Cambridge: Harvard University Press, 2013), p. 158.

Five Religious Worlds

The valued events and persons (in the Blackburn–Dworkin list) are indeed valuable and recognized as valuable in the great world religions. Both secular naturalists and religious practitioners can recognize the sacred beauty that surrounds us. The impermanence of such goods has, however, been lamented by both religious and secular philosophers and artists.[24] Many have experiences where the true value of material and shared comforts calls out to something beyond one's subjective instances of judgment. Christian Wiman, a contemporary American poet and essayist, recalls, while recovering from cancer treatments, this need for grounding experience in something bigger than oneself:

Nine years later in New York, reeling from treatments, turning as ever to poetry for both refuge and release, I opened [Susan] Howe's book of elliptical sympathies and extreme grief and found her trying to salvage meaning from some ancient source:

"Nietzsche says that for Heraclitus all contradictions run into harmony, even if they are invisible to the human eye. Lyric is transparent – as hard to see as black or glare ice. The paved roadway underneath is our search for aesthetic truth. Poetry, false in the tricks of its music, draws harmony from necessity and random play. In this aggressive age of science, sound-colored secrets, unperceivable in themselves, can act as proof against our fears of emptiness."

I read this passage over and over. (It is itself darkly transparent.) It still seems to me a fresh and useful description of what poetry ("sound colored secrets") can do and why we read and need it ("proof against our fear of emptiness"). It is also [a] beautiful – and, I think, accurate – description of what an experience of God can be and do in our lives. Instead of the paved roadway being our search for aesthetic truth, though – of what value would that be, finally? can there even be aesthetic truth without some other, more ultimate truth as precedent – I would say that the road is our search for *spiritual* truth. This is why a poet's technical decisions are moral decisions, why matters of form and sound have existential meaning and consequences.[25]

FIVE RELIGIOUS WORLDS

We are highly selective in our account of the five religions as worlds. Each maintains that something is not right (not just or not wise or good or fitting) in life. The religions differ slightly in their view of the source of this predicament: Some claim that the problem is sin (a violation of the will and nature of God/Allah/Brahman), or ignorance, or it may be that terrible suffering is built into the very structure of reality. But with each of these religions' claims we are not left utterly hopeless. We begin with an overview of what these religions have in common and then consider some of their differences.

---

[24] For example, Schopenhauer's "Vanity of Existence." The impermanence of ourselves and the world is a core teaching of Buddhism. It also underlies ascetic traditions in Hinduism and the Abrahamic faiths.
[25] Christian Wiman, *He Held Radical Light: The Art of Faith, the Faith of Art* (New York: Farrar, Straus and Giroux, 2018), pp. 25–26.

All five traditions are united in sharing significant values: the golden rule; the good of mercy and compassion; the ill of greed; and the emptiness of the pursuit of mere worldly glory through self-aggrandizement at the expense of others, by usurping just powers, and by subjugating the vulnerable.[26] We see this later point in the Hebrew Bible/Christian Old Testament in many places, such as the testimony of Solomon (Book of Ecclesiastes) on the emptiness of pursuing only earthly pleasures. And in Islam there are abundant divinely revealed precepts calling for almsgiving (zakat), justice, mercy, and condemnation of those who oppress widows and children. In the Upanishads we see that the call to wisdom involves unmasking the hollowness of mere worldly goods. Yama (or Death) reveals to the boy Nachiketa the emptiness of only sensual pleasures. The founder of Buddhism, Siddhartha Gautama, who came to be known as the Buddha or Enlightened One, set out on the path of seeking enlightenment because he wanted to discover the root of suffering. On this point, the five religious worlds differ from ancient cultures that applaud worldly glory (in Greek *kleos*). Glory in the world of Homer was often a matter of what was won on the battlefield in a victory over one's foes. It consisted in winning fear and awe among one's contemporaries and for future generations. In the Abrahamic faiths and theistic Hinduism, glory (worship, awesome fear, and reverence) is due to the divine, rather than to be given to rapacious human rulers. In most forms of Buddhism, the quest for glory is challenged by a critique of the concrete individual self as illusory (anatta).

In the Abrahamic faiths and theistic Hinduism that envision God as all-knowing, as well as in forms of Buddhism that attribute omniscience to the Buddha, there is no person anywhere – no matter how hidden in prison, oppressed by a government, ostracized by their culture, persecuted because of sexual orientation – who is hidden or invisible to God or the Buddha. There is evidence that this powerful affirmation of the way in which nothing is hidden from an all-good God accounts, in part, for the spread of Christianity and Islam. What Thomas Cahill writes about Christianity can also be said of the spread of Islam, and about what many in the Greco-Roman world found appealing about Judaism:

Christianity's claim that all were equal before God and all equally precious to him ran through class-conscious, minority-despising, weakness-ridiculing Greco-Roman society like a charged current. It is no wonder, really, that the primitive church seemed almost a fairyland harbor to women, who had always been kept in the shadows, and to

---

[26] This is not to deny the presence of many of these values in the world of naturalism. For an accessible defense of relevant objective values and natural law, see C. S. Lewis' *Abolition of Man* (New York: MacMillan, 1947).

slaves, who had never before been awarded a soupçon of social dignity or political importance.[27]

An omniscient point of view of God can be consoling to those suffering from isolation and censure, and worrisome to tyrants and other victimizers.

At the outset of Chapter 1, we cited some theologians, such as McCabe and Lash, who think of God as so different from "everything" that God is not "anything." We suggest that the idea of God being so wholly other than the created order is better thought of as a way of correcting the treatment of the divine as familiar and falling into anthropomorphism (seeing God as a kind of superhuman). There is a place for this correction to anthropomorphism, while seeking to avoid anthropophobia, or excessive fear of seeing something in human terms. This warning about making the divine after one's own image goes back to the pre-Socratic philosopher Xenophanes who speculated:

But if cattle and horses or lions had hands, or were able to draw with their hands and do the work that men can do, horses would draw the forms of the gods like horses, and cattle like cattle, and they would make their bodies such as they each had themselves.[28]

Actually, we have some sympathy with those Xenophanes is scolding. So long as the cattle et al. realize that the divine is more than what they are picturing, perhaps no harm is done.[29]

In his recent book, *God, Soul and the Meaning of Life*, Thaddeus Metz writes:

The more God were like us, the more reason there would be to think we could obtain meaning from ourselves, absent God. On the other hand, the more God were utterly unlike us and radically other, perhaps for being atemporal or absolutely simple, the less clear it would be whether we could truly understand His nature or how we could obtain meaning by relating to Him.[30]

The literature in which God is sensed to be *intimately present, loving, supremely good, and compassionate* implies that God is sufficiently like us so

---

[27] Thomas Cahill, *Mysteries of the Middle Ages and the Beginning of the Modern World* (New York: Random House, 2006), p. 44.
[28] Xenophanes, *The Presocratic Philosophers*, edited and translated by G. S. Kirk and J. E. Raven (Cambridge: Cambridge University Press, 1957), p. 168.
[29] But one case of contemporary anthropomorphism may be singled out as quite unfortunate. In *The God Delusion*, Richard Dawkins identifies "The God Hypothesis" as "There exists a superhuman, supernatural intelligence who deliberately designed and created the universe and everything in it, including us" (London: Bantam, 2006), p. 52. There are three problems. We know of no one in the Abrahamic traditions who would describe God as "superhuman." In Chapter 2 we offered reasons for thinking of God as "supernatural" as inappropriate. The hypothesis is also wildly off base insofar as there is no reference to values; the concept of God in the Abrahamic faiths and theistic Hinduism is believed to be good, even maximally good and worthy of worship.
[30] Thaddeus Metz, *God, Soul and the Meaning of Life* (Cambridge: Cambridge University Press, 2019), p. 23.

that these terms make sense. And yet God is sufficiently unlike us so that being in relationship with this transcendent being is decisively astounding and profoundly transformative. Metz is introducing an idea of scale or proportion. This presents a picture of truth as being fitted and tensed to our intelligence and experience. There is an example of this kind of scale in the Christian understanding of the impact of the death of Christ in the Gospel of Matthew, when an earthquake occurs at the time of Christ's death.[31]

If Christ is both God and human, then the death of Christ, in one's imagination, might lead to more destruction than an earthquake splitting rocks. But there is something fitting in this narrative with the Trinitarian understanding of God in Christianity. Christ is both God and human, not as a blending of the two, but both present in Christ. In the narrative of redemption, Christ's holiness is marked in death as shaking the firmament, but not destroying it. The other event recorded in Matthew, coinciding with the earthquake, is the tearing of the veil of the temple. This inner veil separated the Jews from the holy of holies, the unclean from the ark of the covenant. The splitting of the veil of the temple in two, from top to bottom, signifies for Matthew the new covenant with God. Now God and his people can be together, face-to-face.

Let us take note of some variations between religious worlds about the meaning of life, beginning with Hinduism and then Buddhism. Hinduism has a face-to-face revelation of the divine with avatars and Buddhism includes an encounter with the all-seeing Compassionate Buddha.

There are many forms of Hinduism, including forms that are theistic, polytheistic, pantheist, panentheistic, and even atheistic. We highlight only two: Advanta Vedanta and Vishishtadvaita (qualified nondualism). Both are based on an appeal to Hindu sacred texts, the Vedas and the Upanishads.

According to Advanta Vedanta, our deepest, truest self is identical with Brahman. All individuals, and indeed all apparently distinct objects, are understood to be analogous to disrupted droplets of water in an eternal and boundless ocean. In reality, all is one, all is nondistinct, and all is Brahman. The Advanta Vedanta school does distinguish nirguna Brahman (Brahman without attributes) from saguna Brahman (Brahman with attributes), but the latter is the illusory Brahman and is merely an aid for the unenlightened. Shankara (circa 788–820 CE) is the central philosopher who defended this view. "Brahman is," Shankara claims, "the Reality, the one Existence. Because of the ignorance of our human minds, the universe seems to be composed of diverse forms; but it is Brahman alone."[32] Ramanuja (1017–1137) adopted a qualified nondualism, according to which Brahman exists and the world exists, and Brahman and the world are not identical.

---

[31] Matthew 27:51.
[32] Shankara, *Vivekachudamani Crest-Jewel of Discrimination*, translated by Swami Prabhavananda, (Los Angeles: Vedanta Press, 1947), p. 70.

While these schools of Hinduism differ – and there is much debate on whether deliverance, or moksha, of individuals involves absorption into Brahman or whether the individual ceases to be or a variation in which the individual remains an individual but united with Brahman – the final end is described in the Upanishads as persons merging into bliss and wisdom. "Brahman is understanding, bliss."[33] Becoming united with Brahman is: "An ocean, one, the seer becomes, without duality ... this his highest bliss."[34] "When all desires which shelter in the heart detach themselves, then does a mortal man become immortal: to Brahman he wins through."[35] The meaning of life in this world seems supreme (the term *Brahman* is sometimes translated as "the Supreme"). Such a blissful, perhaps boundless end is in stark contrast with the world of naturalism.

Most Buddhist traditions, like Hindu traditions, accept some form of reincarnation, which is often based on a nonmaterialist view of the soul or individual. Both Buddhism and Hinduism uphold belief in karma (from *kri* "to do"), a belief that our actions have consequences morally. To believe in karma is, in part, to believe that we live in a moral universe, a world in which justice ultimately triumphs; the vicious will experience the effects of their ill; the good will experience goodness. Buddhism is sometimes thought of as teaching that the ultimate end of the individual is annihilation (*Nirvana*, or *Nibbana*, comes from the term for "blowing out"). But this needs to be set in the context of the tradition that the Buddha himself was not annihilated when he attained enlightenment. On the contrary, he lived and taught for another forty-five years. Buddhist scripture, in fact, records that hundreds of living men and women have attained Nirvana. While Buddhism is rightly seen as being opposed to the view that selves are concrete individual substances, it is not obvious that Buddhism teaches the ultimate extinction of the individual rather than the extinction of illusion, hatred, and selfish craving. One reason for thinking that Nirvana is the annihilation of hatred and egocentric greed rather than absolute extinction of the individual is that Nirvana is often described as "happiness supreme."[36] This implies there is someone who is experiencing "happiness supreme."

There are, in fact, different understandings of Ultimate Reality within the various streams and schools of Buddhist thought. In one major Buddhist school, referred to as Madhyamika (school of the Middle Way) and developed by Nagarjuna (circa 150–250 CE), Ultimate Reality is understood to be *sunyata*, which is translated as "Emptiness" or "The Void." It may seem at first glance that Emptiness and Ultimate Reality are contradictory concepts. How can something fundamentally real be empty or void? But Buddhists of the

---

[33] Brihadaranyaka Upanishad in *Hindu Scriptures*, translated by R. C. Zaehner (London: Dent, 1960), 3.9, p. 60.
[34] Ibid., p. 68.   [35] Ibid., p. 71.
[36] Udana, II, I (The Minor Anthologies of the Pali Canon), p. 3.

Madhyamika school (and of most schools, in fact) understand "being real" as "being independent of other things." Fundamental reality, in typical Buddhist metaphysics, is emptiness; there is no "thing" insofar as a thing has independent existence. All apparent substantial entities, whether galaxies, mountains, trees, or people, are abstractions of events or processes which are dependent on other events or processes. While such "things," including our very selves, appear to be substantial entities, in fact they are not. They seem to be enduring substances, but this is because we abstract from different experiences that occur and then reify substantial entities, including a substantial self, from all of this. Yet they are only processes; in reality, all is in flux. One Buddhist text, in which the following verse is ascribed to the Buddha himself, puts it this way:

> Impermanent are all component things,
> They arise and cease, that is their nature:
> They come into being and pass away,
> Release from them is bliss supreme.[37]

In another writing attributed to the Buddha:

The five aggregates, monks, are *anicca*, impermanent; whatever is impermanent, that is *dukkha*, unsatisfactory; whatever is dukkha, that is without *attaa*, self. What is without self, that is not mine, that I am not, that is not my self. Thus should it be seen by perfect wisdom (*sammappa~n~naaya*) as it really is. Who sees by perfect wisdom, as it really is, his mind, not grasping, is detached from taints; he is liberated.[38]

Nagarjuna offers this exposition: "When the notion of an Atman, Self, or Soul ceases, the notion of 'mine' also ceases and one becomes free from the idea of I and mine."[39]

In a close study of the end state, K. N. Jayatilleke argues that Nirvana in Theravada Buddhism involves neither extinction nor identification with divinity nor, he argues, was Buddha unconcerned about Nirvana:

Nirvana is ... the Transcendent Reality, whose real nature we cannot grasp with our normal minds because of self-imposed limitations. It is a state of freedom, power, perfection, knowledge and perfect happiness of a transcendent sort.[40]

The Abrahamic traditions – Judaism, Christianity, and Islam – all share a theistic affirmation of God as the creator and sustainer of the cosmos, who becomes known in human history through prophecy and other forms of revelation. Christianity affirms that Jesus of Nazareth is God and man in the incarnation; whereas this is denied in Judaism and in Islam. (The Qur'an

---

[37] Mahaa-Suttana (*Diigha Nikaaya*, 2013), p. 16. Available online.
[38] Samyutta Nikaya, "The Three Basic Facts of Experience" (2013), 22.45. Available online.
[39] Nagarjuna, *Mulamadhyamakaarika (The Fundamental Wisdom of the Middle Way)*, translated by E. J. Garfield (Oxford: Oxford University Press, 1995), 22.45.
[40] K. N. Jayatilleke from his book *The Message of the Buddha*, cited from *The Philosophy of Religion Reader*, edited by Chad Meister (London: Routledge, 2008), chapter 16, p. 185.

acknowledges Jesus as a prophet, his miraculous birth, the important role of Mary his mother, Jesus' teaching, and Jesus not being killed but raised up by God. See Qur'an 3:45–48; 4:157–158; 5:75; 5:116–117; 43:61–65.) Judaism is strictly monotheistic, which has historically been the basis for rejecting the Christian idea that God is Triune. Islam is explicit in rejecting the Trinity. Christianity and Islam have traditionally upheld the idea that individuals do not perish at death but come to be in the presence of God (heaven) or remote from God (hell). There is reason to think that Judaism did not include a belief in an individual afterlife in its early history. But this belief developed later, as seen in Job 19:26–27: "After my skin has been destroyed, yet in my flesh I will see God; I myself will see him with my own eyes – and not another's. How my heart yearns within me." It also appears in Isaiah 16:19: "But your dead will live." (See also Daniel 2:1–3 and 12:2; Ezekiel 37:1–14.) One of the sources for the emergence of a belief in life after death was that a God of love and power would not allow death to have the last word for God's people.

Let's ask: Why would belief in an all-powerful, loving God lead anyone to think life after death is desirable or plausible? Let's return to the meaning in life advanced by Blackburn and Dworkin. Some of Blackburn's examples of meaning are well chosen to make these points: a smile of a baby lasting forever would be bizarre on two fronts – a person remaining a baby forever sounds like a science-fiction horror story, and we all cringe at fake smiles. Someone dancing forever would have to become tedious. Someone summiting a mountain is an inspiration, but someone summiting, descending, and then summiting again reminds us of the myth of Sisyphus and his endless rolling of a stone up a hill, seeing the stone roll back down, and then hauling the stone up again (a classic case of pointlessness). Dworkin's cases too serve his purpose. Offhand, it would be churlish to play a tune, partake in some project, offer a compliment, build a chair, or make love and then insist that such events or feats or sexual unions are of no value unless endlessly repeated. But what is missing in these accounts is imagination: What if we were not hampered by the limits of our current biology (in which our organs are doomed to failure at certain points), and we could engage in increasingly enriching values in relationship with a maximally excellent being (God/Allah/Brahman) and boundless different creatures?[41] In some forms of Hinduism, for example, the preparation for one's death involves a meditative readiness to shed one's dying body.[42] Philip Kitcher suggests that to entertain such a possibility of life after life stems from "regret at being human," but that would only be the case if "being human" meant those who perish at biological death, whereas it appears that the majority of the world

---

[41] See "Why We Need Immortality," by Charles Taliaferro, *Modern Theology* 6:4, 1990, pp. 367–377.

[42] Significant Hindu meditations involve being detached from one's bodily sensations and even, at the point of death, taking leave of one's body. See, for example, Eknath Easwaran's *The End of Sorrow*, volume 2 of his *The Bhagavad Gita for Daily Living*.

population who use terms for human beings do not believe that all persons perish at death.[43] From their point of view, it is Kitcher's view of what it is to be human that is regrettable: They believe humans are not by their very nature annihilated at death.

In terms of the value of a possible afterlife, some philosophical theologians embrace the idea that goodness is diverse or multiform (*bonum est multiplex*).[44] Imagine you love your child (following Hume, we will call him Benedict), who grows up to be a graceful dancer, who relishes exchanges with others by voice and all other means of communication, who will have a lover who makes chairs, and so on. Further imagine you think it is a real possibility that death will not annihilate Benedict but might be a gateway that transforms him into being active in a world of endless challenges and opportunities for pursuing with others the good, the true, and the beautiful. If you truly love Benedict, wouldn't you hope the latter is the case? This need not be a matter of self-love; imagine it is certain that you will perish, but it is not certain that Benedict will. We suspect that, given the ending of annihilation versus what is believed to be abundant life, the significance of the imagined ending may well reflect the values and loves you have in this life. David Velleman offers the following view of how endings can shape the meaning of narratives:

> The emotion that resolves a narrative cadence tends to subsume the emotions that preceded it: the triumph felt at a happy ending is the triumph of ambitions realized and anxieties allayed; the grief felt at a tragic ending is the grief of hopes dashed or loves denied. Hence the conclusory emotion in a narrative cadence embodies not just how the audience feels about the ending; it embodies how the audience feels, at the ending, about the whole story. Having passed through emotional ups and downs of the story, as one event succeeded another, the audience comes to rest in a stable attitude about the series of events in its entirety.[45]

Belief in an afterlife is not necessarily to believe in some future postmortem good. After all, in the Homeric literature, life after death seems like a listless, shadowy affair compared with this life. The *Iliad* contains testimony from a dead person who said it would be better to be a live dog than a dead lion.[46] And as we shall note in a closing section of this chapter, many religions, including those discussed in this book, have promoted a vision of an afterlife of endless

---

[43] Kitcher, *Life after Faith: The Case for Secular Humanism* (New Haven, CT: Yale University Press, 2014), p. 100.
[44] Some who believe that human persons survive death believe that they may thereby cease to be human, as when persons reincarnate in nonhuman animal bodies or are recreated by God in a glorified or transformed body.
[45] David Velleman, "Narrative Explanation," *The Philosophical Review*, 112:1, 2003, p. 19
[46] For a famous recent case for the undesirability of an afterlife, see "The Makropulos Case: Reflections of the Tedium of Immortality" in Bernard Williams' *Problems of the Self* (Cambridge: Cambridge University Press, 1973) pp. 82–100. For a reply, see John Fischer's "Why immortality is not so bad" in the *International Journal for Philosophical Studies* 2(2), 2008, pp. 257–270.

Five Religious Worlds

torment. But matters differ in the Benedict thought experiment in the context of an ecstatic understanding of reality and beauty of shared love between God and creatures such as what we find in the *Divine Names*, attributed to Dionysius the Areopagite:

In God, the eros desire is outgoing, ecstatic. Because of it lovers no longer belong to themselves but to those whom they love. God also goes out of himself ... when he captivates all creatures by the spell of his love and his desire. ... In a word, we might say that Beauty-and-Goodness is the object of the eros desire and is the eros desire itself.[47]

For the Abrahamic faiths, the ultimate end of life involves happiness. In the sixth-century classic *The Consolation of Philosophy* by Boethius, the figure Lady Philosophy[48] reminds him that:

The whole concern of men, which the effort of a multitude of pursuits keeps busy, moves by different roads, yet strives to arrive at one and the same end, that of happiness. ... In all of these things it is obviously happiness alone that is desired; for whatever a man seeks above all else, that he reckons the highest good. But we have defined the highest good as happiness; wherefore each man judges that state to be happy which he desires above all others. ... And you also, earthly creatures that you are, have some image, though hazy, in your dreams of your beginning; you see, though with a far from clear imagination yet with some idea, that true end of your happiness. Your natural inclinations draw you towards that end, to the true good.[49]

Anselm of Canterbury (1038–1109) offers a similar outlook:

It ought not to be doubted that the nature of rational beings [was] created by God ... in order that, through rejoicing in him, it might be blessedly happy. ... Man, being rational by nature, was created ... to the end that, through rejoicing in God, he might be blessedly happy. ... God ... [made man] for the purpose of eternal happiness.[50]

The personal nature of the world of Christianity is revealed in much of the art it has inspired. Consider this personalization of divine attributes in William Langland's *Piers the Ploughman*:

I drew back in the darkness and went to the depths of the earth. And there, in accordance with Scripture [Psalm 85:10], I dreamt that I saw a maiden come walking from the West, and looking towards hell. Mercy was her name, and she seemed a very gentle lady, courteous and kind in all she said. And then I saw her sister come walking quietly out of the East, and gazing intently westwards. She was very fair, and her name was Truth, for

---

[47] *Divine Names* in *The Roots of Christian Mysticism*, edited by Oliver Clément, p. 22.
[48] There has been speculation that J. R. R. Tolkien's Lady Galadriel, the Royal Elf, in *The Lord of the Rings* is inspired by the figure of Lady Philosophy.
[49] Boethius, *The Consolation of Philosophy*, translated by D. R. Slavitt. (Cambridge: Harvard University Press, 1973), pp. 233, 235, 241.
[50] St. Anselm, *Anselm of Canterbury: The Major Works*, edited by Brian Davies and G. R. Evans (Oxford: Oxford University Press, 1988) pp. 315–316.

she possessed a heavenly power that made her fearless. ... "I give way," said Truth, "You are in the right, Mercy. Let us make our peace together, and seal it with a kiss."[51]

Judaism and Islam are more reticent to use what they would consider such anthropomorphic imagery of the divine (though Judaism includes imaging wisdom as a person, often female). We engage Judaism and Islam on happiness and blessedness in Chapter 5.

In all, the five religious worlds we have considered offer a profoundly different aesthetic alternative to Russell's vision of unyielding despair. While they offer an alternative to the annihilation of all persons, they do not differ from Russell in thinking there will be an end of the Earth and the cosmos. In Judaism and Christianity, there is prophecy of a new creation (Isaiah 65:17; 2 Peter 3:12–13). In Islam there will be an end of the Earth as we know it and then resurrection (Qur'an 101). In Hinduism, there is some traditional teaching that our cosmos will be destroyed and then there will be a cosmic regeneration.[52] In Buddhism, there is no consensus in terms of cosmology, but the transitory, the impermanence of the cosmos, is a cardinal teaching.

THE SEARCH FOR THE MEANING OF LIFE SHOULD INCLUDE THE EXPLORATION OF BOTH RELIGIOUS AND SECULAR WORLDS

While in this book we defend the importance of subjective, first-person, aesthetic points of view, we propose that the meaning of what we say, what we do, and how we live is not a matter of only subjective assessment. It is possible that there is a massive difference between our assessment of ourselves as humble altruists committed to justice, and our virtuous character, when in fact we turn out to be utterly vain, selfish, and disposed only to look as though we are committed to justice. Who and what we are will involve our subjective, conscious experiences and choices, but what we actually do and our true identity will stretch beyond our own experience and choices. We can examine this idea under the light of different worlds.

Imagine naturalism is true. If that is right, then those of us who worship, venerate, or pray to God are actually directing our lives in light of an illusion, on our projection or image of God. It may be that we will never know that atheism is true. It could be that those in such God-centered traditions will reap benefits for themselves and others (perhaps there will be greater justice), but it will still be at the cost of believing something false. If the human species survives and

---

[51] William Langland, *Piers the Ploughman*, translated by J. F. Goodridge (Harmondsworth: Penguin Books, 1974), pp. 220–229.
[52] For Hindu and Buddhist approaches to eschatology, see "Hindu Eschatology," by David Knipe (pp. 170–190) and "Buddhist Eschatology," by Jan Nattier (pp. 151–169) in *The Oxford Handbook of Eschatology*, edited by Jerry Walls (Oxford: Oxford University Press, 2008).

comes to know the truth of naturalism, the history of such religious belief will be written as the history of an illusion (as Sigmund Freud proposed).

On the contrary, imagine the Abrahamic faiths and theistic Hinduism turn out to be an accurate vision of reality. Setting aside traditional concepts of heaven and hell, it would mean that even in this life those who lived without any regard to the divine were missing out on a profound aspect of reality. One would be living a life that is missing the divine cadence revealed by Krishna as like a thousand suns, the Hebrew vision of God as holy, and the Christian vision of Christ as the essence of life.

Imagine you are a follower of Ayn Rand, committed to what she called the virtue of selfishness. You are single-mindedly focused on power and achievement. And yet, imagine further that the Buddhist no-self theory of the self (anatta) proves to be the case. What you have spent your whole life seeking turns out to be an illusion. The truth of most forms of Hinduism would also undermine Rand's valorization of selfishness. The Hindu philosopher Eknath Easwaran draws on William Law to describe what he sees as the illusory satisfactions of living a life in which (to use Rand's term) selfishness is considered a virtue: "A life devoted to the interests and enjoyments of this world, spent and wasted in the slavery of earthly desires, may be truly called a dream, as having all the shortness, vanity, and delusion of a dream: only with this great difference, of when the dream is over nothing is lost but fictions and fancies; but when the dream of life is ended only by death, all that eternity is lost, for which we were brought into being [a divine life]."[53]

It may be instructive to clarify our position in relation to a possible objection. In "The Meaningfulness of Lives," Todd May objects:

Basing life's meaningfulness on the existence of a deity not only leaves all atheists out of the picture but also leaves different believers out of one another's picture. What seems called for is an approach to thinking about meaning that can draw us together, one that exists alongside or instead of religious views.[54]

First, we are not claiming life is meaningful only if there is a God (or if a life is lived faithfully in the presence of God, *Coram Deo*). Second, there is much in common among religions, which also affirm the immanent goods identified by Blackburn and Dworkin. Therefore, our proposal about the meaning of life is not principally about leaving lots of people out. But we do propose that the truth or falsehood of theism or Buddhism or naturalism or other worldviews does impact the meaning of our lives. The truth of any of these worldviews that value compassion *means* that those who live without compassion and instead have contempt for those they deem inferior are not living a beautiful life. Contrary to what they think, they may be creating a hell for other people.

---

[53] Law cited by Easwaran in *The End of Sorrow*, p. 42.
[54] Todd May, "The Meaningfulness of Lives," in *Modern Ethics in 77 Arguments*, edited by P. Catapano and S. Critchley (New York: Liveright Publishing Company, 2017), p. 4.

We adopt a realist view of worlds in that we think the truth of these worlds has important implications for the way things are. John Searle has noted how some recent thinkers have a visceral (aesthetic) disgust for realism:

> I have to confess ... that I think there is a much deeper reason for the persistent appeal of all forms of anti-realism [or relativism] and this has become obvious in the twentieth century: it satisfies a basic urge to power. It just seems too disgusting, somehow, that we should be at the mercy of the "real world."[55]

Disgusting or not, we propose that not all views of reality (especially when they are incompatible) can be true. There may be two consoling responses, though: Perhaps the real world turns out to be a site of great flourishing, a place for joy (in the end) and not endless disgust. Second, incompatible worlds may not be equally true, but they might have an equivalent level of evidence in their favor, and so it is not possible for there to be any triumphal claims to know with certainty that one world is true and others false.

We suggest that if we truly value our lives, we have reason to consider the meaning of our lives in light of religious worldviews and their secular alternatives.

So, how might we assess worlds or worldviews?

ASSESSING WORLDS

Assessing religious and secular worlds may involve some of the same principles involved in assessing works of art. We highlight how worlds may be evaluated internally and externally, engaging in comparative criticism (comparing worlds in terms of clarity, scope, and power to shed light on our experience); using a principle of charity; and examining the worlds' development over time. The latter employs what philosophers of art have referred to as the test of time. In the arts, the test of time measures the extent to which works of art are appreciated over time. Those works of art valued over generations have a greater presumption of value than those that are considered but not valued. This evaluation has to be understood in the context of knowing that many aspects of a culture determine value, including the value of monetary investment in art. Also, many works of art do not become widely appreciated due to the invisibility of the maker. So, while we can use the test of time to think about how a work stays alive in the imaginations of generations who value it as art, we know this list of enduring works is limited by the forces that sustain access to the work. In assessing worlds or worldviews, a test of time pertains to their resilience in terms of criticism, new findings in the sciences and humanities, and moral development.[56]

---

[55] John Searle, *Mind, Language and Society: Philosophy in the Real World* (New York: Basic Books, 1998), p. 17.
[56] Alasdair MacIntyre has done much to promote this method, taking note of how Christian tradition was not destroyed but has been refined over the centuries by such events as the

Worlds may be assessed internally. By internally, we mean evaluating a world in its own terms. Is the world internally consistent? Two examples of potential inconsistency will suffice to make the point: In theistic traditions it is widely held that God is good or maximally excellent, omnipotent, and omniscient. It is further believed that enormous evil exists. These traditions also hold a firm view of virtues and vices, justice and injustice. This is all part of what is traditionally known as the problem of evil. Can these beliefs about good and evil be coherently believed, or do they involve a contradiction?[57] Buddhism also faces a challenge: Can one believe in reincarnation and, at the same time, believe that there is no self? In reincarnation, it appears that there must be something – a soul or subject or mind – that endures over time in different bodies. But if you think there is no such thing, how can there be reincarnation?[58]

Worlds may be assessed externally. How does a religious or secular world accord with what we know (or have some reason to believe with evidence) independent of the worldview? Is there a conflict between a worldview and what we know from the sciences, not just the natural sciences but also anthropology, sociology, and psychology? Is the religious or secular world compatible with what we know experientially of our self-awareness as conscious agents, responsible for ourselves and others? Especially relevant for this book, does the world enhance or complement or inhibit our independent experience of beauty and ugliness? Anthony O'Hear proposes that our sense of beauty provides some sign, or indication, that reality includes a transcendent being:

Where ... do we get a sense that, despite the problems of alienation thrown up by science and morality, we are nevertheless at home in the world? Where else, except from a sense, at times strong, at times fleeting, that despite all the horrors and dilemmas and problems, the world and human life are beautiful, and that this sense is not mere projection on our part? ... It is above all in aesthetic experience that we gain the fullest and most vividly lived sense that though we are creatures of Darwinian origin, our nature transcends our origin in tantalizing ways.[59]

Comparative evaluations: There can also be objections to a religious world from the standpoint of a different world. For example, naturalists often affirm the primacy of the physical world. From the standpoint of a confident

---

rediscovery of the work of Aristotle, the rise of modern science, and so on. For philosophy of art, see *The Test of Time: An Essay in Philosophical Aesthetics*, by A. Savile (Oxford: Clarendon Press, 1982).

[57] For a survey of theistic responses to the problem of evil, see *Contemporary Philosophical Theology*, by Charles Taliaferro and Chad Meister (London: Routledge, 2016), chapters 6 and 7.

[58] We believe this objection can be met by treating the teaching of annihilation as not involving the complete annihilation of the self. Death involves the dissolution of the psychophysical unity that makes up the self, but not the perishing of every aspect of the self (or mind or soul).

[59] Anthony O'Hear, *Beyond Evolution: Human Nature and the Limits of Evolutionary Explanations* (Oxford: Clarendon, 1997), p. 202.

affirmation of the physical world, the very idea of a nonphysical God may seem absurd. Consider this charge by Anthony Kenny:

If we reflect on the actual way in which we attribute mental predicates such as know, believe, think, design, control to human beings, we realize the immense difficulty there is ... applying them to a putative being which is immaterial, ubiquitous and eternal. It is not just that we do not, and cannot, know what goes on in God's mind, it is that we cannot really ascribe a mind to God at all. The language that we use to describe the contents of human minds operates within a web of links with bodily behavior and social institutions. When we try to apply this language to an entity outside the natural world whose scope of operation is the entire universe, this web comes to pieces, and we no longer know what we are saying.[60]

Given a naturalist starting point, this may be a forceful argument and challenge. But, as we have proposed in Chapters 1 and 2, there is good reason to think that we have a much clearer idea about the mind (subjectivity, consciousness, experience) than we do of mind-independent bodies. Kenny writes with confidence about our grasp of bodily behavior and social institutions, but it may be countered that any such confidence must rest on a prior certainty in individual self-awareness and consciousness. We propose that you would not have any idea which body or which society is yours unless you have some antecedent awareness of yourself as a self. That does not mean that the idea of God as an immaterial reality is coherent, but it means that we have some reason to temper our ruling out as nonsense an idea of God based on our view of a mind-independent world, because we lack a clear view of such a world. While we began Chapter 2 with critically challenging Bertrand Russell's depiction of the Jews' "invisible Yahweh," we appreciate Russell's view that contemporary science has revealed to us a world that is far stranger than common sense would suggest. He observed that "Matter has become as ghostly as anything in a spiritualist séance."[61]

Principle of charity: In personal relations, especially in communication, philosophers refer to the principle of charity (sometimes called a principle of humanity or rationality), according to which we should not (without good evidence) distrust another's speech and action in the worst way possible. Rather, other things being equal, we should try to interpret each other positively. This is operative in both personal relations and in assessing works of art. Even the most celebrated work of art cannot survive a hostile critic. H. G. Wells disparages Henry James with a withering analogy:

It [any novel by James] is like a church lit but without a congregation to distract you, with every light and line focused on the high altar. And on the altar, very reverently placed, intensely there, is a dead kitten, an egg-shell, a bit of string.[62]

---

[60] Anthony Kenny, *What I Believe* (London: Continuum, 2006), pp. 52–53.
[61] Bertrand Russell, *An Outline of Philosophy* (London: Routledge, 1927), p. 78.
[62] H. G. Wells, *Boon* (New York: George H. Doran, 1915), 4.3.

Or think of Virginia Woolf's assessment of T. S. Eliot when he became a Christian: "Tom Eliot, who may be called dead to us all from this day forward. He has become an Anglo-Catholic, believes in God and immortality, and goes to church. I was really shocked. A corpse would seem to me more credible than he is. I mean, there's something obscene in a living person sitting by the fire and believing in God."[63]

In terms of assessing religious and secular worlds, hostile reviews can resort to what some call toxic speech. We suggest that the assessment of worlds should be in light of what appears to be the better expression of the worlds rather than what appears to be the worst. Consider the following three cases.

In assessing Hinduism one can focus on Hindu militants who are champions of Hindutva, or "Hinduness," who see India as ideally a Hindu state. This political Hinduism supports a combination of nationalism and an exclusionary religious identity in opposition to Muslim, Christian, and secular populations. Or, instead, one can give central attention to Mahatma Gandhi, Ramakrishna, and Vivekananda, who promoted a multireligious society of Hindus, Muslims, Christians, and others living in peace. A principle of charity would draw us closer to the latter group as representatives of Hinduism than to the first. The Vedas and the capacious, loving portrait of the divine in the Bhagavad Gita give decisive weight to seeing the Hindutva party as not being a paradigm case of Hinduism.

A principle of charity is sorely needed in western conceptions of Islam. Sadly, some critics focus on the so-called Sword Verse: "Fight and slay the pagans wherever ye find them, and seize them, beleaguer them, and lie in wait for them in every stratagem" (Qur'an 9:5). But what needs to be appreciated is the context. This sura addresses the question of how to respond to an enemy when that enemy has violated a treaty. The chapter further teaches that there should be a pause of several months to permit repentance and reconciliation before responding. And it adds that if the offending party does repent then "open the way for them." This passage has nothing to do with attacking innocent individuals or with advocating war against those who desire to coexist in peace and harmony. Sword verses need to be set beside verses such as this: "There is no compulsion in religion" (2:256). On pagans who reject the Prophet's message: "yet pardon them, and say 'Peace!' Soon they will learn" (43:89). "Those who believed, and the Jews and Christians, and whoever has believed in God and the Last Day and performed good works, they shall have their reward with their Lord" (2:62).

Consider a third case. In *God Is Not One: The Eight Rival Religions That Run the World – and Why Their Differences Matter*, Stephen Prothero offers the following portrait of Christianity, which we find problematic:

---

[63] From Virginia Woolf's letter to her sister Vanessa in 1928. See *The Letters of Virginia Woolf*, edited by Nigel Nicholson and Joanne Trautman (New York: Harcourt Brace Jovanovich, 1977), pp. 457–458.

When I was a professor at Georgia State University in Atlanta, I required my students to read Nazi theology. I wanted them to understand how some Christians bent the words of the Bible into weapons aimed at Jews and how those weapons found their mark at Auschwitz and Dachau. My Christian students responded to these disturbing readings with one disturbing voice: the Nazis were not real Christians they informed me, since real Christians would never kill Jews in crematories. I found this response terrifying, and I still do, since failing to grasp how Nazism was fueled by ancient Christian hatred of Jews as "Christ killers" allows Christians to absolve themselves of any responsibility for reckoning with how their religion contributed to these horrors.[64]

We agree that self-identified Christians and their institutions have fostered anti-Semitism and participated in varying degrees in the Holocaust. Martin Luther's teachings and views regarding Jews (especially *On the Jews and Their Lies*, 1543), the Jewish ghettos, the expulsion of Jews from Spain and England, and persecution throughout Europe are all examples of this. But we side with the students in claiming that the major Nazi theologians were not Christian. Joseph Goebbels, Martin Bormann, and Heinrich Himmler were overtly hostile to Christianity. Alfred Rosenberg taught that Jesus was an Aryan and not Jewish. He outlawed the publication and dissemination of the Bible; altars in churches had to display a copy of Hitler's *Mein Kampf*. According to Joseph Goebbels, the Reich Minister of Propaganda: "The Fuhrer is deeply religious, though completely anti-Christian. He views Christianity as a symptom of decay. Rightly so. It is a branch of the Jewish race. This can be seen in the similarity of their religious rites. Both [Judaism and Christianity] have no point of contact to the animal element, and thus, in the end they will be destroyed."[65] The very heart of Nazism was profoundly hostile to Christianity.

While we agree that many Christians fueled Nazism, not all Christians did so, and many fought Nazism.[66] A principle of charity applies when comparing the five traditions we address in this book.

Might it be the case that given their differences, the evidence for one religion would be evidence against the credibility of the others?

Evidence that any of the world religions recognizes the basic goodness of immanent goods (such as those identified by Blackburn and Dworkin) should be some evidence of its authentic goodness. Any evidence that above these

---

[64] Stephen Prothero, *God Is Not One: The Eight Rival Religions That Run the World – and Why Their Differences Matter* (New York: HarperOne, 2010), p. 10.

[65] *The Goebbels Diaries 1939–1941*, edited and translated by Fred Taylor (London: Hamish Hamilton, 1982), December 29, 1939. One major obstacle for Nazis to be regarded as Christian is that, except for a few heretics like Marcion in the second century, Christianity is virtually inconceivable without the Old Testament, which is thoroughly Jewish.

[66] In our view, to think of Kittel and other Nazi "theologians" as Christian is not credible. Compare them with Dietrich Bonhoeffer, the theologian, anti-Nazi dissident, and founding member of the Confessing Church (founded to counter a pro-Nazi Protestant Reich church). As we are writing this book in the tradition of personalism, it is worthy of note that one of the greatest personalists in the twentieth century, the German Catholic philosopher Dietrich von Hildebrand (referenced in Chapter 1), was a formidable, public opponent of Hitler.

immanent goods, there is some transcendent good, should count, in our view, in considering the merits of such worlds. And there are some significant overlaps. For example, while it seems as though Hindu thought about individuals becoming one or being united with the divine seems antithetical to Abrahamic thought, this is not obvious. Many Christian mystics and students of mysticism speak about the highest state attainable as one that involves "that pure surrender of selfhood, or 'self-naughting,' which the trials of the dark night tended to produce."[67] Irenaeus speaks of "those who see God are in God, and receive His splendor."[68] W. R. Inge writes, "The last stage of the journey, in which the soul presses towards the mark and gains the prize of it[s] high calling is the unitive or contemplative life, in which man beholds God face to face, and is joined to Him."[69] Similar claims can be found in Meister Eckhart and the author of the *Theologica Germanica*. R. C. Zaehner, himself a Christian, observes, "Christianity agrees with Hinduism in that it insists that the immortal self can only be found if the empirical self, the 'I' dies."[70] Some of the common chords of the five religious traditions have led prominent philosophers of religion to stress the unity or complementariness of religions (John Hick, Ninian Smart, Huston Smith, Dianne Ecke).[71]

Test of time: As noted earlier, philosophers of art have proposed that one sign that a work of art is valuable is if it has been appreciated as valuable over time. One may also evaluate a religious tradition for how it addresses problems over time. So, what about cases of when sacred texts like the Hebrew–Christian Bible seem to countenance genocide (Deuteronomy 2:3–34; 3:3–6; 7:21; 7:16; Joshua 6:21)? What about Biblical condemnation of homosexuality (Leviticus 20:13; Romans 1:26–27)? What about Biblical passages condoning slavery? The New Testament has been used to require obedience to unjust rulers (Romans 13) What about the teaching in Abrahamic traditions of hell? Could an all-good, all-just God condemn people to eternal torment?

One sign of resilience or virtue is when religious change is brought about by reasons that are inherent in the tradition itself. That seems to be the case in the Abrahamic traditions on slavery. Tragically, slavery has been virtually coextensive with human history. Its practice has been considered normal and natural (by Aristotle among others). It is not surprising that the Bible has multiple passages tolerating or even managing slavery, because slavery was evident in Egypt, Babylon, throughout Greece, in the Roman Empire, and in every Middle Eastern society. But the Abrahamic teaching that all persons are made in the image of God took hold in leading multiple abolition movements.

---

[67] Evelyn Underhill, *Mysticism*, pp. 497–498.
[68] Irenaeus, *Against Heresies*, edited by A. Roberts and J. Donaldson (Grand Rapids: Eerdmans, 1956), Book IV, Ch. 20, para. 5.
[69] W. R. Inge, *Christian Mysticism* (London: Charles Scribner's Sons, 1899), pp. 52–53.
[70] R. C. Zaehner, *Evolution in Religion* (Oxford: Clarendon Press, 1971), p. 97.
[71] As representative, see Diana Eck's *Encountering God* (Boston: Beacon Press, 1993).

Christian figures like William Wilberforce, Charles Spurgeon, John Wesley, Harriet Beecher Stowe, Sojourner Truth, Harriet Tubman, and others powerfully fought slavery on religious grounds.

Keith Ward makes note of how many of the world religions endorse principles or teachings that "self-correct" what appears to us now as moral failures:

> Each tradition has developed sophisticated ways of overriding those texts with other and usually later interpretations that stress what is quite clearly more basic – the command of God to have compassion and mercy.[72]

Interpreting sacred texts and past history through the lens of what religious practitioners today believe is love and justice has created what may be called *a hermeneutic of love*. It is on this basis why many interpret the conquest narratives in the Hebrew Bible/Christian Old Testament as either hyperbolic or as parables. A similar hermeneutic is in play when a case is made for the permissibility of same-sex unions in some Christian traditions (recognized by some Christian churches in the United States, for example), notwithstanding a handful of Biblical passages to the contrary. See, for example, Gareth Moore's *Christianity and Homosexuality*.[73]

Any overview of the aesthetics of the five religious worlds has to take into account the remarkably vivid portraits of hell. There have been vivid speculations about how persons might be eternally burned. How might it be the case that a body could be continuously burned forever? Marcus Minucius Felix offered this proposal: "That clever fire burns the limbs and restores them, wears them away and yet sustains them, just as fiery thunderbolts strike bodies but do not consume them."[74] At least one twentieth-century philosopher, David Lewis, cites the teaching on hell as his primary rationale for atheism.[75] There have been some philosophical defenses of traditional views of hell.[76] But there is also a long tradition of universalism, according to which all persons will eventually be saved through a face-to-face encounter with the God of overwhelming love.[77] There are multiple representatives of this far-reaching view of divine love. Isaac of Nineveh writes:

---

[72] Keith Ward, *Is Religion Dangerous?* (Grand Rapids: Eerdmans, 2006), p. 36.
[73] Cited in Chapter 2.
[74] Cited in *Rethinking Hell*, edited by C. M. Date et al. (Cambridge: Lutherworth Press, 2013), p. 13.
[75] David Lewis, "Divine Evil" in *Philosophers without Gods*, edited by Louise Antony (Oxford: Oxford University Press, 2007). For a good historical overview of views of hell, see Allen Bernstein's *The Formation of Hell: Death and Retribution in the Ancient and Early Christian Worlds* (Ithaca, NY: Cornell University Press, 1993).
[76] For an overview and critical evaluation, see *The Logic of Damnation*, by Jerry Walls (Notre Dame: University of Notre Dame Press, 1992).
[77] See Lindsey Hall's *Swinburne Hell and Hick's Universalism* (Aldershot, UK: Ashgate, 2003).

Assessing Worlds

As a handful of sand in the boundless ocean, so are the sins of the flesh in comparison with God's providence and mercy. As a copious spring could not be stopped up with a handful of dust, so the Creator's compassion cannot be conquered by the wickedness of creatures.[78]

We propose, then, that assessing the aesthetics of the five religious worlds and secular alternatives needs to take a long view, surveying strengths and weaknesses over time.

As we turn to the topic of beauty in the Chapter 5, it is fitting to conclude with A. E. Taylor's view of the long history of religion and aesthetics and the mixture of authentic and inauthentic claims. Taylor contends that the history of human responses to a sacred, transcendent reality – which he refers to as the numinous – involves a mix of spurious and what he takes to be authentic encounters. He compares this with the history of human conceptions of beauty. Notwithstanding there being sham religious and aesthetic aberrations, Taylor makes a forceful case for authenticity in religion and aesthetics:

> It is *conceivable* that the majority of objects men supposed to be beautiful are not beautiful; that most of the acts human societies have thought morally noble have only been thought so because our current moral notions are perverted by false sentimentalism, that most of the statements which have been acclaimed as profound truths are only plausible errors; it is *certain* that spurious beauty, sham virtue, flashy half-truths do often impose on mankind. But just as the fact that bad pictures and bad music are often admired, and spurious heroism often belauded, is no proof that there is no true beauty or moral heroism, so the aberrations of silly, lewd, or cruel worships are no proof that there are not events, things, persons, really endued with the numinous quality. If there are, then we may expect the task of distinguishing the true numinous from the counterfeit, or the more fully from the imperfectly numinous, to prove at least as difficult as that of discriminating true beauty from false. The education of mankind in recognition of the numinous should, by all analogy, be as slow and hard a business as their training in the discernment of beauty, and we might anticipate that, in both cases, the training would only advance pari passu with, and in close dependence on, the general mental development of man.[79]

---

[78] Isaac of Nineveh, "Ascetic Treatises" in *The Roots of Christian Mysticism*, p. 306. Similar statements about God's overwhelming compassion can be found in work by Gregory of Nyssa, John Cassian, John Climacus, Julian of Norwich, and others.
[79] A. E. Taylor, *The Faith of a Moralist*, Series II (London: Macmillan and Co. 1951), pp. 186–187.

5

The Beautiful Gate

Where there is no vision, the people perish.

Proverbs 29:18

Religious traditions hold the sacred to be beautiful and desecration to be ugly. Is this a glib, pious claim, masking a sentimental attachment to outdated categories? Or, is beauty still a guiding force in understanding what is valuable? Should our sense that an event or a person's act is ugly guide our judgment?

Hans Urs von Balthasar, a twentieth-century theologian, developed a theology of beauty. He submitted that without an allegiance to beauty, along with her "sisters" truth and goodness, our lives would be fallow and loveless. Life would also be without religious devotion:

> We no longer dare to believe in beauty, and we make of it a mere appearance in order the more easily to dispose of it. Our situation today shows that beauty demands for itself at least as much courage and decision as do truth and goodness, and she will not allow herself to be separated and banned from her two sisters without taking them along with herself in an act of mysterious vengeance. We can be sure that whoever sneers at her name as if she were the ornament of a bourgeois past – whether he admits it or not – can no longer pray and soon will no longer be able to love.[1]

Balthasar is working within a Platonic Christian tradition that understands beauty as a foundational category, sometimes called a transcendental. In this tradition, beauty leads to the rightful order of the soul (*ordo amoris*). But even without this theological context, one can readily understand the protean power of beauty. Roger Scruton observes:

---

[1] Hans Urs von Balthasar, *The Glory of the Lord: A Theological Aesthetics*. Volume I: Seeing the Form (San Francisco: Ignatius Press, 1982), p. 18. See also Guy Sircello's *Love and Beauty* (Princeton: Princeton University Press, 1989), chapter 1, "Reviving Love."

Introducing Beauty

Beauty can be consoling, disturbing, sacred, profane; it can be exhilarating, appealing, inspiring, chilling. It can affect us in an unlimited variety of ways. Yet it is never viewed with indifference: beauty demands to be noticed; it speaks to us directly like the voice of an intimate friend. If there are people who are indifferent to beauty, then it is surely because they do not perceive it.[2]

One of the most influential Western philosophical works on beauty involves a series of speeches on love given at a drinking party in ancient Greece. Written in the fourth century BCE by Plato, the *Symposium* (from the Greek *symposion* for "drinking party") depicts a banquet held in the home of a tragedian playwright. While there are seven main male characters in attendance, there is an eighth contributor: Socrates, the narrator, tells us what he learned from a wise woman, Diotima, on love and beauty. According to Diotima, we start a journey to the beautiful itself by first loving particular beautiful bodies and then ascend on a ladder to greater beauties until we come to a wonderful and supreme, absolute beauty, the source of boundless creativity and delight.

One section of this chapter focuses on Diotima's vision of ascent to beauty, and its religious and philosophical significance. Another section addresses the challenge of relativity about beauty: Is beauty merely in the eye of the beholder? The third section engages beauty from the position of a God's-eye point of view. While the idea of an ideal aesthetic observer can be and has been used for exploitive purposes, it can also be emancipatory. It is emancipatory when one apprehends there are no aspects of anyone's life (however ignored or shamed socially) unknown by a God of love.[3] We propose that our lack of visibility to each other is related to our lack of allegiance to such a comprehensive view from everywhere.

Before addressing Diotima's discourse on beauty, we begin with some general observations about beauty.

INTRODUCING BEAUTY

Virtually all cultures recognize beauty. Beauty is most often thought of as that which pleases aesthetically (our attention is riveted by light streaming through trees). Or it is the object of delight (a melody befriends us). Beauty seems to pervade ordinary and extraordinary life, encompassing domestic interactions (the guest–host relationship) to dramatic heroism. It is almost always seen as something good. In ancient Greece the concept of the good and the beautiful were treated as joined. The Greek term for *beauty* (*kallos*) was not distinguished

---

[2] Roger Scruton, *Beauty* (Oxford: Oxford University Press, 2009), p. ix.
[3] Our valuing a God's-eye point of view is not the same as valuing the exposure of our interior lives to everyone, especially to an encroaching, powerful government or corporation. On the difference between our being known to God (or being the object of a God's-eye point of view) and being known by sinister forces, see Taliaferro's "Does God violate your right to privacy?" in *Theology*, May 1989, pp. 190–196.

from the *good* (*agathon*). A truly beautiful person was a good person or a person with excellence (*arête*).

There has also been a long-standing recognition across cultures that outward or external beauty (a beautiful face) differs from inward or spiritual or soulful beauty (the beauty of a person's character, intentions, emotions). Much mythology, folklore, sacred scripture, and philosophy bears out the turmoil that stems from being deceived into thinking that someone who is externally beautiful is also inwardly beautiful and, conversely, mistakenly thinking someone must be ugly inwardly on the grounds of some perceived defect or ugly appearance. In the *Symposium* the distinction between outward and inward beauty is on display in the most handsome and alluring lover, Alcibiades. Here is an account of his physical beauty from the first- and second-century Greek biographer and essayist Plutarch in *Lives*:

> As regards the beauty of Alcibiades, it is perhaps unnecessary to say aught, except that it flowered out with each successive season of his bodily growth, and made him, alike in boyhood, youth and manhood, lovely and pleasant... Even the lisp that he had became his speech, they say, and made his talk persuasive and full of charm.[4]

And yet with all this external, sensuous magnetism, Alcibiades was notoriously unreliable and self-indulgent. True to form, at the dinner party he is intoxicated and, rather than offering a discourse on the love of beauty, he only complains that Socrates has resisted Alcibiades' attempt at seducing him (both men and women found Alcibiades almost irresistible).

The link between beauty and goodness finds support well outside ancient Greece. In Judaism, God's overwhelming greatness and high beauty is praised:

> Whoever looks at him is instantly torn;
> whoever glimpses His beauty immediately melts away.
> Those who serve Him ... their hearts reel
> and their hearts grow dim at the splendour
> and the radiance of their King's beauty.[5]

In the *hadith* Muhammad proclaims: "God is beautiful and loves beauty."[6] In Hinduism, the divine is represented as Satyan (truth), Shivam (goodness), and Sundaram (beauty). Beauty, or Sundaram, coincides with the highest good and so something thoroughly beautiful must also be good. African aesthetics also offers support for aligning beauty and goodness. In Yoruba discourse, for example, *ewa* (the term most frequently translated as "beauty") is directly linked with goodness. The Yoruba people make a distinction between

---

[4] Plutarch, *Lives*, translated by Bernadotte Perrin (London: William Heinemann, 1916), vol. 4, p. 5.
[5] These verses are found in The Greater Hekhalot in *The Penguin Book of Hebrew Verse*, edited by T. Karmi (Harmondsworth, UK: Penguin Books, 1981), p. 196.
[6] *Beauty in Arabic Culture*, by Doris Behrens Abonseif (Princeton: Marcus Weiner Publishers, 1999), pp. 17, 19.

outward ewa and inward ewa. Outward ewa concerns physical appearance and behavior, whereas inner ewa is thought of as moral beauty. Stephen David Ross describes the joining of beauty and goodness in many cultures:

> In the earliest cultures known, before written history, and in China, Egypt, the Islamic world, and sub-Saharan Africa, beauty was and still is a term of great esteem linking human beings and nature with artistic practices and works. Human beings – men and women – their bodies, characters, behaviors, and virtues are described as beautiful, together with artifacts, performances, and skills, and with natural creatures and things: animals, trees, and rock formations. In such cultures, beauty, goodness, and truth are customarily related. Ancient Greece and China were no exceptions. In the Confucian tradition, Kongzi (sixth to fifth century BCE) emphasized social beauty, realized in art and other human activities. Two centuries later, Daoism united art and beauty with natural regularity and purpose, and with human freedom.[7]

In this chapter we assume that the reality of beauty and its goodness is supported across cultures.

DIOTIMA'S LADDER

Returning to Diotima, there is some reason to believe Diotima was the name of an actual person, for in his dialogues Plato rarely used names that did not refer to actual people.[8]

According to Diotima, we should first appreciate particular beautiful things such as a specific beautiful body. We are then naturally led to love greater, more general beauties. Socrates reports Diotima's instructions:

> A lover who goes about this matter correctly must begin in his youth to devote himself to beautiful bodies. First, if [Love] leads aright, he should love one body and beget beautiful ideas there, then he should realize that the beauty of any one body is brother to the beauty of any other and that if he is to pursue beauty of form he'd be very foolish not to think that the beauty of all bodies is one and the same. When he grasps this, he must become a lover of all beautiful bodies, and he must think that this wild gaping after just one body is a small thing and despise it.[9]

We are to begin, then, in the embodied world, and this leads us gradually to ever higher beauties. It is as though the experience of a specific individual beauty

---

[7] Stephen David Ross, "Beauty" in *The Encyclopedia of Aesthetics* (Oxford: Oxford University Press, 1998), p. 237.

[8] While we follow A. E. Taylor in thinking of Diotima as an actual person of that name, it has been recently speculated that Diotima was the fictitious name for Aspasia of Miletus, the brilliant partner of Pericles. See *Socrates in Love: The Making of a Philosopher*, by Armand D'Angour (London: Bloomsbury, 2019). In the *Symposium*, Socrates reports that Diotima "is the one who taught me the art of love" (201c). Socrates tells Diotima that he is "your student, filled with admiration" (206b).

[9] *Symposium* 210a,b. This element of despising lower goods was rejected by Christian Platonists, especially in medieval and early modern philosophy (e.g., Cambridge Platonism).

opens us up to an irresistible love of greater beauty. For those who think there is no necessity of going from the particular to the general, one might at least concede that there is some reason to do so. After all, in loving one person, isn't it natural or at least reasonable to love or appreciate and be grateful to the people and events that helped the person grow into your beloved? Climbing Diotima's ladder involves growing out of one beauty and traveling upward to a greater beauty. Climbing the ladder also gives rise to the idea of expansion. When you love someone or something and you take pleasure in the cherished one, you experience an expansion of your identity. To take a trivial example, if you take great pleasure in a sports team, you might well choose to use the possessive pronoun: Manchester United becomes *your team*. Many of the ancient philosophers held that it is the very nature of pleasure to expand the soul, and they conversely held that the nature of pain or suffering contracts the soul.[10] Perhaps when one comes to love higher beauties, there is a sense in which these higher beauties become yours through the experience of delighting in them. Diotima continues:

After this he must think that the beauty of people's souls is more valuable than the beauty of their bodies, so that if someone is decent in his soul, even though he is scarcely blooming in his body, our lover must be content to love and care for him and seek to give birth to such ideas as will make young men better. The result is that our lover will be forced to gaze at the beauty of activities and laws and to see that all this is akin to itself, with the result that he will think that the beauty of bodies is a thing of no importance.[11]

The ongoing ascent then involves an emancipating, ever-expanding philosophical, beautiful awareness of the nature of reality. Diotima continues:

After customs he must move on to various kinds of knowledge. The result is that he will see the beauty of knowledge and be looking not at beauty in a single example ... but the lover is turned to the great sea of beauty, and, gazing upon this, he gives birth to many gloriously beautiful ideas and theories, in unstinting love of wisdom.[12]

At the summit, the love naturally overflows with fecundity in which he or she gives birth to awesome creative productivity. The highest point of the beautiful involves a final transcendence of all images and the fulfillment of what Diotima describes as true virtue:

[Beauty] always is and neither comes to be nor passes away ... [Beauty] is not beautiful this way and ugly that way ... This is what it is to go aright ... into the mystery of Love: one goes always upwards for the sake of the Beauty ... If someone were to see the

---

[10] Richard Sorabji notes that in much ancient Greek philosophy "distress is the judgment that there is bad at hand and that it is appropriate to feel a shrinking. Pleasure is the judgement that there is good at hand and that it is appropriate to feel an expansion." *Emotion and Peace of Mind: From Stoic Agitation to Christian Temptation* (Oxford: Oxford University Press, 2000), pp. 29–30. See also pp. 37, 48.
[11] *Symposium* 210c.   [12] Ibid., 210d.

Beautiful itself, absolute, pure, universal ... only then will it be possible for him ... to give birth to true virtue.[13]

This ascension to the beautiful, and thus to true virtue, as a process and consummation of true love, stands in dramatic contrast to the Homeric desire for worldly fame and domination on a battlefield.

Before assessing Diotima's vision, consider Plato's view of desire. While Plato (perhaps inspired by Diotima) spoke of beauty itself, he also thought of beauty as the proper object of love. That which is beautiful is that which calls for or deserves our loving delight. Love, for Plato and many of the ancient Greeks, involves desire, or Eros, which may or may not involve what we would call the erotic. In the following myth or parable, love is pictured as the offspring of Poros, the personification of plenty, and Penia, the personification of poverty:

As the son of Poros and Penia, his lot in life is set to be like theirs in the first place, he is always poor, and he's far from being delicate and beautiful ... he is tough and shriveled and shoeless and homeless, always lying on the dirt without a bed, sleeping at people's doorsteps and in roadsides under the sky, having his mother's nature, always living with Need. But on his father's side he is a schemer after the beautiful and the good; he is brave, impetuous, and intense, an awesome hunter, always weaving snares, resourceful in his pursuit of intelligence, a lover of wisdom through all his life, a genius with enchantments, potions, and clever pleadings.[14]

Love or Eros, then, is full of energy and stealth, and even inclined to philosophy (the love of wisdom), while also feeling need and a keen lack of satiation or fulfillment. In a sense, a person who desires is always seeking what the person lacks. From a Platonic point of view, if you are strong now, it makes no sense for you to desire strength. It is because we lack beauty that we seek it. And in so doing, we take the first step in the direction of beauty. It is a deeply Platonic thesis defended to our day, that if something is good, it is good to love it.[15] If you love beauty, your love is itself beautiful. If, for example, justice is both good and beautiful, then loving justice is both good and beautiful. Someone may claim to love justice and do nothing to promote justice; but with power and authenticity, a lover of justice would naturally honor justice in her or his life and actions. Platonists through the centuries have endorsed similar notions with respect to all the virtues: to love wisdom is itself wise. As Plato suggests at the beginning of his masterpiece the *Republic*, the love of the good and the beautiful is an inherently youthful enterprise. It is not for those who are content with the loss of desire in old age, but for those at any age who are filled with a restless desire for the good.

With some qualifications (noted below) we believe the Diotima–Platonic notion of desire is plausible, but we think a shared loving desire and

---

[13] Ibid., 211b–212b. [14] Ibid., 203d.
[15] See Roderick Chisholm, *Brentano and Intrinsic Value* (Cambridge: Cambridge University Press, 1986).

satisfaction can be coextensive. A lover and a beloved need not always be striving for what they lack.[16]

Our claim is not that Diotima and Plato are clearly right about beauty and goodness, but we suggest that a Platonist has a defensive strategy against some possible objections. If you have reason to believe something is genuinely beautiful and yet morally base, you have a reason to challenge Plato. But keep in mind that a proper counterexample must be a case when the very same thing in the same respect would have to be beautiful and ethically wrong (e.g., a beautiful serial killer would not, for example, be a convincing counterexample).

The Platonic heritage strongly reemerged in the late twentieth century. One of the leading figures in this Platonic revival was Iris Murdoch. In *The Sovereignty of Good*, Murdoch writes movingly about the curative, emancipatory character of beauty:

Beauty is the convenient and traditional name of something which art and nature share, and which gives a fairly clear sense to the idea of quality of experience amid changes of consciousness. I am looking out of my window in an anxious and resentful state of mind, oblivious of my surroundings, brooding perhaps on some damage done to my prestige. Then suddenly I observe a hovering kestrel. In a moment everything is altered. The brooding self with its hurt vanity has disappeared. There is nothing now but kestrel.[17]

Notice how Murdoch finds in the love of beauty a cure for the self-preoccupied seeking of reputation and personal glory. This recalls the historical contrast in the West between the love of beauty and the violent passion for glory and fame.[18] Murdoch reflects on beauty and desire:

Good is the magnetic centre towards which love naturally moves. False love moves to false good. False love embraces false death. When true good is loved, even impurely or by accident, the quality of the love is automatically refined, and when the soul is turned towards Good the highest part of the soul is enlivened. Love is the tension between the imperfect soul and the magnetic perfection which is conceived of as lying beyond it. (In the *Symposium* Plato pictures Love as being poor and needy.) And when we try perfectly to love what is imperfect, our love goes to its object via the Good to be thus purified and made unselfish and just. The mother loving the retarded child or loving the tiresome elderly relation. Love is the general name of the quality of attachment and it is capable of infinite degradation and is the source of our greatest errors; but when it is even partially refined it is the energy and passion of the soul in its search for Good, the force that joins us to Good and joins us to the world through Good. Its existence is the unmistakable sign that we are spiritual creatures, attracted by excellence and made for the Good. It is a reflection of the warmth and light of the sun.[19]

---

[16] Such experiences may border on cases of when there is an ostensible transcendence of time, as hinted at in T. S. Eliot's *Four Quartets* and his reference to the still point of the turning world. See Taliaferro's *The Golden Cord*.
[17] Iris Murdoch, *The Sovereignty of the Good* (London: Routledge, 2007), p. 82.
[18] See Taliaferro's *Aesthetics: A Beginner's Guide*, chapter 1.
[19] *The Sovereignty of the Good*, p. 100.

Other philosophers who have been instrumental in a renaissance of an aesthetics of beauty include Mary Mothersill, Guy Sircello, and Elaine Scarry.[20] Murdoch and each of these philosophers recognize beauty as a response to what is valued. Things, persons, events are not beautiful because they give us delight; they give us delight because they are beautiful.[21]

The notion that beauty instills in us desire is supported by Alexander Nehamas:

Beautiful things don't stand aloof, but direct our attention and our desire to everything else we must learn or acquire in order to understand and possess, and they quicken the sense of life, giving it new shape and direction.[22]

Some Christians have made use of a kind of ascent from the beauty of this world to the next. Abbot Sugar of St. Denis in the twelfth century describes the way in which an aesthetically rich, beautiful church can lead one to ascend toward Heaven:

Thus, when – out of my delight in the beauty of the house of God – the loveliness of the many-colored gems has called me away from external cares, and worthy meditation has induced me to reflect, transferring that which is material to that which is immaterial, on the diversity of the sacred virtues: then it seems to me that I see myself dwelling, as it were, in some strange region of the universe which neither exists entirely in the slime of the earth nor entirely in the purity of Heaven; and that, by the grace of God, I can be transported from this inferior to that higher world in an anagogical manner.[23]

Roger Scruton takes note of the intentional role of Gothic churches in offering a glimpse of the Heavenly City:

It is clear from Abbot Sugar's account of the building of St. Denis ... that the architecture [s] of the Gothic churches were motivated by a perceived relationship between the finished church and the Heavenly City of Christian speculation. ... Each great church can be considered as a concatenation of smaller structures, of aedicules, fitted together as arches, chapels, windows and spires, and so can be seen as an assembled city, rather than as a single entry minutely subdivided.[24]

---

[20] See Mary Mothersill's *Beauty Restored* (Oxford: Clarendon Press, 1984) and Guy Sircello's *A New Theory of Beauty* (Princeton: Princeton University Press, 1975) and *Love and Beauty* (Princeton: Princeton University Press, 1989). We address the work of Elaine Scarry below.
[21] See Hans Urs von Balthasar's *The Glory of the Lord: A Theological Aesthetics*, Volume VII: *Theology: The New Covenant*, translated by Brian McNeil (San Francisco: Ignatius Press, 1989), p. 22. It is worth noting that some delights can themselves be beautiful and enhance beauty. The desire that another person lives a beautiful life may itself be beautiful, and a shared awareness of this desire might enhance a beautiful friendship.
[22] Alexander Nehamas, *Only a Promise of Happiness: The Place of Beauty in a World of Art* (Princeton: Princeton University Press, 2007), pp. 80–81.
[23] Cited by Umberto Eco in *Art and Beauty in the Middle Ages* (New Haven: Yale University Press, 1959), p. 14.
[24] Roger Scruton, *The Aesthetics of Architecture: God in Imagination* (Princeton: Princeton University Press, 1979), pp. 74–75.

The Talmud includes a vision of a ladder of ascent in which persons can ascend to Jacob, whose beauty reflects the beauty of Adam.[25]

Some challenge the idea that the ascent takes us to a comprehensive good. Nehamas suggests beauty can only create smaller communities:

> Aesthetic judgment, I believe, never commands universal agreement, and neither a beautiful object nor a work of art ever engages a catholic community. Beauty creates smaller societies, no less important or serious because they are partial, and, from the point of view of its members, each one is orthodox – orthodox, however, without thinking of all others as heresies… What is involved is less a matter of *understanding* and more a matter of hope, of *establishing* a community that centers around it – a community, to be sure, whose boundaries are constantly shifting and whose edges are never stable.[26]

Later in this chapter, we use an ideal aesthetic observer theory to counter the notion that there is no way to reach a consensus about beauty. But we note here that the scope of that which is beautiful may be so wide that it can indeed lead to many, incommensurate communities. This is widely acknowledged in religious traditions that recognize the good of married life as well as the good of the monastic tradition of celibate monks and nuns. Arguably, both forms of life have value but cannot be measured on a single scale. In contrast to Nehamas' skepticism about beauty being a basis for a stable life, consider Elaine Scarry's philosophy of beauty.

Scarry argues for a much larger role for beauty, understanding its role in our lives to ignite in us nothing less than the desire for truth. Beauty is not static, but comes into our field of awareness and departs without our ability to control its arrival or its leaving. In her critique of Kant's early theory of aesthetics, we agree about the belittling and diminution of beauty in the academy. In Kant's aesthetics, beauty came to stand in contrast with the sublime, and beauty was given a gender: female. Flowers, in Kant's list, are beautiful. The (male) sublime became a category that not surprisingly includes power, mountains, tall trees, night, nobleness, and righteousness. Kant created a lens to look at the world expressed through his values of power, truth, and goodness. We do experience the aesthetic realm in all kinds of variety. Depending on our age, our experiences, our particular pasts, we are motivated to pay attention to different things over time. For Scarry, beauty not only demands our attention (arriving without invitation), but it also exerts a pressure on us to share the beauty. Scarry realigns beauty with truth by giving it the status of being in service to benefit all, and, most intriguingly, beauty creates a desire in us to distribute beauty.

While Scarry is moving a Platonic understanding of beauty forward in our time, the image of climbing the ladder and abandoning "lower" beauties is

---

[25] See Chalm Reines' "Beauty in the Talmud," *Judaism*, vol. 14 (1973), pp. 100–107; see p. 102.
[26] Alexander Nehamas, *Only a Promise of Happiness: The Place of Beauty in a World of Art*, p. 77.

countered by Scarry's story of realizing the beauty of a palm tree. She had earlier thought palm trees to be ugly, in fact, worthy of being hated. In this encounter, Scarry doesn't reevaluate or abandon her love of sycamores and birch trees. Instead, she feels the correction inside her about the beauty of the palm tree to lead her to ask questions about what other beauty she has missed. Where else has she been wrong? *This question* is how beauty ignites the desire in us for truth.[27]

Rather than ascending a ladder and abandoning lower beauties as we ascend, we may find the image of a fountain more instructive – its seemingly endless source of flowing water is an image that can help us understand beauty as irreducible, generous, and in motion.

For those who worry about the lack of consensus on what is beautiful, Jacques Maritain reminds us that beauty is not to be confused with perfection. He writes:

> Anything perfect is totally terminated and without any lack and leaves nothing to be desired – and therefore lacks the longing and "irrational melancholy" of which Baudelaire spoke – it is lacking a lack. A totally perfect finite thing is untrue to the transcendental nature of beauty. And nothing is more precious than a certain sacred weakness, and that kind of imperfection through which infinity wounds the finite.[28]

An articulate aesthetic of imperfect beauty is found in the Japanese aesthetic of wabi-sabi. It is derived from Buddhist teaching and the recognition of imperfection, transience, and suffering. While its lineage is long, its latest manifestation is found in Japan in raku and Hagi ware pottery. Wabi-sabi is also expressed in Bonsai designs that incorporate hollowness and deadwood highlighting the passage of time, the flower arrangements of Ikebana, and the Japanese tea ceremony. Some of the aesthetic characteristics valued in this worldview include simplicity, intimacy, and roughness. While different from Greek ideals of symmetry and proportion, it is a religious worldview that encompasses spiritual longing in its recognition of material impermanence.

THE ARRIVAL OF BEAUTY

In Hinduism *Rasa* refers to aesthetic emotions, as noted in Chapter 1. It translates in English as "tincture, essence, flavor." Aesthetic experience is being cast as the tasting of a flavor. This perception of taste breaks through the walls of the one (the person) asleep to the soul, which is predisposed to have sympathy. The idea of beauty "breaking through" occurs in the West as well, in the fairy tale of Sleeping Beauty who is awakened by the prince arriving at the

---

[27] *On Beauty and Being Just*, by Elaine Scarry (Princeton University Press, Princeton and Oxford, 1999).
[28] Jacques Maritain, *Creative Intuition in Art and Poetry* (New York: Bollingen Foundation, 1953), pp. 195, 142, 144, 167.

right time and greeting her. Mentioned earlier, Iris Murdoch called it an "unselfing" when describing a moment she was taken out of herself by the sight of a kestrel soaring. Margaret Miles went further in describing the perception of beauty as an activity and a skill. She uses the example of seeing a bluebird and experiencing a burst of sharp happiness (the aesthetic of the description here is being pierced, broken into, quick, and unanticipated). Then, upon reflection, she realizes that the experience of seeing the bluebird is itself happiness.[29]

Edgar Allen Poe, known for his excursions into cavelike conditions of the human psyche, saw through the darkness he was exploring:

> It is the instinct for beauty which makes us consider the world and its pageants as a glimpse of a correspondence with Heaven. ... It is at once by poetry and *through* poetry, music and *through* music that the soul divines what splendors shine behind the tomb.[30]

What is meant by *through*? Is it the idea that our experiences of poetry and music deliver us somewhere? Or that beauty reveals a lack in ourselves that we are awakened to? In *The Sleeping Beauty*, literary scholar and Episcopal priest Ralph Harper offers a nuanced treatment of contemporary feelings of homesickness and nostalgia, our longing for justice and a foundation for flourishing. Harper writes in the Platonic tradition, according to which we each have some primordial, perhaps even inchoate sense of goodness. His use of the term "nostalgia" is not at all in the vicinity of the sentimental.

> Homesickness or nostalgia is an involuntary conscience, a moral conscience, it is positive rather than prohibitory. It reminds a person, by way of giving him the experience, of the good he has known and lost. Nostalgia is neither illusion nor repetition; it is a return to something we have never had. And yet the very force of it is just that in it the lost is recognized, is familiar. Through nostalgia we know not only what we hold most dear, but the quality of experiencing that we deny ourselves habitually.[31]

BEAUTY IN THE EYE OF THE BEHOLDER?

In ancient Greece, there were skeptics about beauty and goodness. Protagoras was famous for his notion that man is the measure of all things. Sophists claimed that they could make a good argument look weak and vice versa. Plato's Socrates in the dialogues confronts them, arguing for a realist view of beauty and goodness as well as truth. There were modest disagreements about proportion, symmetry, and the like, but a general Platonic stance had authority in the medieval world. Consider Plotinus:

---

[29] Margaret Miles, *Reading for Life* (New York: Continuum, 1997).
[30] Edgar Allen Poe, cited in Maritain's *Creative Intuition in Art and Poetry*. The citation is Baudelaire's translation of a passage in Poe's *The Poetic Principle*.
[31] Ralph Harper, *The Sleeping Beauty* (Cambridge: Cowley Press, 1985), pp. 20–21.

Beauty in the Eye of the Beholder? 101

We hold that all the loveliness of this world comes by communion in Ideal-Form. All shapelessness whose kind admits of pattern and form, as long as it remains outside of Reason and Idea, is ugly from that very isolation from the Divine-Thought. And this is the Absolute Ugly: an ugly thing is something that has not been entirely mastered by pattern, that is by Reason, the Matter not yielding at all points and in all respects to Ideal-Form. But where the Ideal-Form has entered, it has grouped and coordinated what from a diversity of parts was to become a unity: it has rallied confusion into co-operation: it has made the sum one harmonious coherence: for the Idea is a unity and what it moulds must come into unity as far as multiplicity may.[32]

But in the modern era, we come to David Hume:

Beauty is no quality in things themselves: It exists merely in the mind which contemplates them; and each mind perceives a different beauty. One person may even perceive deformity, where another is sensible of beauty; and every individual ought to acquiesce in his own sentiment, without pretending to regulate those of others.[33]

And there has been some skepticism about the meaningfulness of our aesthetic experience. Consider A. J. Ayer:

Such aesthetic words as "beautiful" and "hideous" are employed ... not to make statements of fact, but simply to express certain feelings and evoke a certain response. It follows ... that there is no sense attributing objective validity to aesthetic judgments, and no possibility of arguing about questions of value in aesthetics.[34]

What should we make of these challenges? Let's start with Hume.

Hume did not hold that beauty, aesthetics, and judging art are completely relative to just any beholder. Beauty may be in the eye of the beholder, but it is important that *the beholder actually sees and experiences the art or object*. Sometimes misinformation, faulty sensory organs, prejudice, egotism (you like the painting only because you painted it and despise another painting because someone else painted it), or lack of emotional maturity can obscure and utterly undermine aesthetic judgment. Some proper attunement is essential in order to observe works of art, just as it is needed in our personal interaction with others. Dan Zahavi has provided a close study on how autism can impair the ability to interpret the emotions of others.[35] In Chapter 7 we will address the kinds of affective states that can enhance or obscure our interpretations of works of art in ways that are analogous to our interpretations of each other.

Hume himself thought that there would (or, perhaps, should) arise some convergence on recognizing what we judge to be beautiful and excellent in art:

---

[32] Plotinus, 22, I.6.
[33] David Hume, *Of the Standard of Taste and Other Essays*, edited by J. Lenz (New York: Bobbs-Merrill, 1965), p. 136.
[34] A. J. Ayer, *Language, Truth and Logic* (New York: Dover, 1952), p. 113.
[35] See *Subjectivity and Selfhood: Investigating the First-Person Perspective*, by Dan Zahavi (Cambridge: Massachusetts Institute of Technology Press, 2005), p. 201.

Whoever would assert an equality of genius between Ogilby and Milton, or Bunyan and Addison, would be thought to defend no less an extravagance than if he had maintained a mole-hill to be as high as Teneriffe or a pond as extensive as the ocean. Though there may be found persons who give preference to the former authors, no one pays attention to such a taste and we pronounce, without scruple, the sentiment of these pretended critics to be absurd and ridiculous.[36]

Some philosophers have extrapolated from Hume an ideal aesthetic observer theory, according to which an ideal observer of some state of affairs (this could be a work of art or a natural object) would be one who was impartial, knows all facts about the state of affairs, and affectively grasps all its emotive features.[37] From that vantage point, the state of affairs is beautiful if it gives rise to aesthetic delight in the ideal observer, whereas it is ugly if it gives rise to displeasure or disgust.[38] We do not claim that this ideal perspective is consciously (or unconsciously!) assumed when persons make aesthetic evaluations; we instead propose that the theory idealizes the conditions we presuppose in sound aesthetic evaluations. There would be something absurd if we form the judgment that some artwork is beautiful while claiming it would be deemed ugly from a more accurate, impartial, and more robustly affective point of view.

The very idea of there being a vantage point greater than our own current point of view is an achievement that takes time. Zahavi describes how we come to recognize ourselves through our mirror image:

---

[36] David Hume, "Of the Standard of Taste," pp. 230–231.

[37] Charles Taliaferro, "The Ideal Aesthetic Observer" in the *British Journal of Aesthetics* 30 (1), 1990, pp. 1–13. See also Taliaferro's "The God's Eye Point of View" in *Faith and Philosophical Analysis*, edited by Harriet Harris and C. J. Insoke (Aldershot, Hampshire: Ashgate Publishing Ltd., 2013), chapter six; *Contemporary Philosophy of Religion* (Oxford: Blackwell, 1997), chapter five; "Relativizing the Ideal Observer Theory," *Philosophy and Phenomenological Research*, 49, 1988, pp. 123–138; and "The Environmental Ethics of an Ideal Observer," *Environmental Ethics* 10:3, 1988, pp. 233–250. On God being an ideal observer, see Linda Zagzebski's *Omnisubjectivity: A Defense of a Divine Attribute*.

[38] There is some controversy over Hume on values. Hume is famously associated with insisting one should not infer values from facts or reason from an "is" proposition (Jones is happy) to an "ought" proposition (Jones ought to be happy), but in his work on ethics and aesthetics he does identify what he proposes makes for proper foundations (in ethics this involves a high role for sympathetic imagination), and epistemically he seems very at home with advocating what we *ought* and *ought not* to believe. Subsequent Humeans like J. L. Mackie who find ethical oughts "queer" face the charge that their own commitments to normativity in epistemology look just as "queer." As should be apparent, we adopt phenomenological realism when it comes to values; that is, we think it evident in experience that we ought to love justice and find injustice both wrong and ugly. In our response to the Humean denial of objective values, we side with John Findlay: "It is easy to defeat Hume, that worst of phenomenological observers, phenomenologically: in experience fact and value come before us as married and not isolated, and in many cases they come before us as logically, necessarily married, not brought together by an arbitrary link of taste or decision". *The Transcendence of the Cave* (London: Routledge, 1967), p. 61.

The ability to recognize one's own mirror image is linked to an increasing ability to assume a detached perspective on oneself, and increasing ability to recognize the perspective of others on me. The mirror permits the child to see itself as it is seen by others.[39]

If this account is right, there need not be an actual ideal observer. Still, the notion of an ideal observer may be implicit in our practice of arguing about the beauty of states of affairs. If we disagree about whether, for example, Vincent van Gogh's painting *Starry Night* is beautiful, aren't we each going to seek out an impartial point of view and urge each other to look at Van Gogh's rendering of swirling clouds, stars, and the luminous night sky from that point of view?

The appeal to the vantage point of an ideal observer provides a response to the supposition that aesthetic judgments are without proper content because of our subjectivity. Of course, our aesthetic judgments are subjective in the sense that they will inevitably be fostered by individual subjects. But that does not undermine our seeking ever broader points of view in which we seek to see things from the perspective of others. By our critical detachment (Murdoch's unselfing) from the vain conviction that only our own point of view is correct, we can aspire to a more emancipatory way of experiencing each other, works of art, and the sacred.

From the standpoint of the ideal observer theory, the reason why, in Hume's cases, one person sees deformity while another sees beauty is due to the limited particularity of one or more parties. One person may judge J. K. Rowling's Harry Potter books as fraught with sacrilege, promoting witchcraft and wizardry prohibited by God. Another might judge the books to be creative, imaginative fairy tales about the triumph of goodness (wisdom, love, friendship) over evil (spite, envy, lust for power). Is this a case of irreconcilable conflict without any room for arguments? Not at all, as should be evident by the powerful case made in *From Homer to Harry Potter* for why Christians (even highly conservative ones) should love Rowling's work.[40]

Assessing the aesthetic merits of works of art is not at all a matter of what Ayer refers to as simply expressing feelings. Rather, we are concerned about whether literature/art reveal important truths (Anne Frank's *The Diary of a Young Girl* does offer a profound, intimate record of a young girl in hiding from the Nazis) or obscure the truth (*The Journals of Lewis and Clark* does not take seriously the injustice done by Europeans to Native Americans). If someone disdains W. E. B. Du Bois' *The Souls of Black Folk*, we want to know why. Is the reader a white supremacist? Or perhaps the critic believes the final essay on the sorrow songs is too consoling or optimistic? We think the book succeeds, illuminating "the problem of the color-line" and that fair-minded readers will appreciate Du Bois' eloquent blend of philosophy, sociology, and experience.[41]

---

[39] *Subjectivity and Selfhood*, p. 201.
[40] Matthew Dickerson and David O'Hara, *From Homer to Harry Potter* (Ada, MI: Brazo Press, 2006).
[41] See, especially, Taliaferro's "Relativizing the Ideal Observer Theory."

We propose that it is at this juncture – the ideal aesthetic observer theory and the religious understanding of a sacred view of all things – that the relationship between religion and aesthetics is most poignant. We believe that reflective aesthetic perception and assessment suggests the normative ideal of a God's-eye point of view. At the very least, it would be utterly bizarre to make an aesthetic evaluation (*The Soul of Black Folk* is brilliant) while at the same time claiming that if all the facts were known (about the book's composition, history, author, and so on) this evaluation would be completely undermined.

So, we do accept a mixed answer to the question: "Is beauty in the eye of the beholder?" Yes and no. Yes, beauty is a relational property. Beautiful persons, events, acts, things are beautiful if they ought to give rise to aesthetic delight and pleasure in an ideal observer (one who knows all the properties and relations involved, including all affective dimensions and is impartial). The ideal observer is not necessarily divine but could be a being of any kind that is capable of such a capacious, impartial, cognitive power. This is not a matter of caprice, but stability. The "eyes" that are best suited to discern beauty belong to those who are not mired in vice, but attuned to receptively perceive goodness. Eknath Easwaran offers this portrait of beauty and the eyes:

Beauty comes in the eyes from within. We have only to look at a mother looking at her child to see how gloriously beautiful her eyes become when she loves. Or look at a husband and wife who live together in love and harmony; what beauty comes into their eyes! Even when long lost friends meet at a class reunion, beauty leaps from within their eyes. All of us have beautiful eyes. But our eyes lose their beauty when we become angry, brood upon ourselves, nurse grievances, and become violent. The quiet mind, the heart full of love and forgiveness, lights up the eyes and reveals the beauty of the Lord through them.[42]

As we have focused more in earlier chapters on the ideal point of view of God in the Abrahamic faiths, we now highlight ideal observation in Hindu and Buddhist tradition.

As noted earlier, Hinduism has multiple philosophical strands. We have seen the contrast between Advanta Vedanta tradition and the more qualified theistic vision of Ramanuga. Both strands trace themselves back to the Upanishads. In the Maitri Upanishads, we read about Brahman:

Unthinkable, unformed, profound, concealed, faultless, compact, impenetrably deep, devoid of attributes and beyond the constituents of nature, pure, resplendent, the experience of nature's constituents, awe-inspiring, immutable, Yoga's Lord, omniscient, most generous, incommensurable, beginningless and endless, bountiful, unborn, wise, indescribable, all things emanating, the self of all, all things experiencing, Lord of all ... endless in power, ordainer... at peace, soundless, without fear or sorrow, contented bliss.[43]

We will not seek to synthesize what may seem paradoxical here (affirming that Brahman has no attributes but is omniscient, which is often classified as an attribute), but we note that some Christian philosophers make similarly

---

[42] Eknath Easwaran, *The End of Sorrow*, p. 332.   [43] Maitri Upanishad 7.1, 242.

Beauty in the Eye of the Beholder?

paradoxical claims (some affirm that God is omniscient, while also claiming that the simplicity of God entails that none of God's attributes are distinct). We note here, though, that the affirmation of there being an ideal, omniscient point of view has a place in Hinduism (Sanskrit for "all knowing" is *sarvajnah*). Indeed, in Hinduism God's omniscience is often tied to omnipresence. *Vishnu* means "all pervasive or the one who is everywhere."[44] Easwaran relates an amusing account of his appreciating the all-knowing, in this case all-hearing, divine point of view:

Nothing can take place without the power of the Lord. Sri Krishna used to say that the Divine Mother even hears the footfall of the ant. Ever since I read this I cannot look at an ant without imagining the Lord listening to the *thud, thud, thud* of its tiny feet.[45]

FIGURE 5.1 Juichimen Kannon, early eighteenth century CE, solid woodblock construction with traces of polychrome, 1959.72 Worchester Art Museum. Photo courtesy of Bridgeman Images.

---

[44] Eknath Easwaran, *Like a Thousand Suns: The Bhagavad Gita for Daily Living*, vol. 2, pp. 66, 221.
[45] Ibid., p. 152.

As for ideal observation in Buddhism, consider the Bodhisattva of Compassion known as Quanyin (Chinese) and Avalokiteshvara (Sanskrit). The bodhisattva is male in India and Tibet but is usually portrayed as female in China and Japan. The current Dalai Lama is believed to be the fourteenth incarnation of this bodhisattva. There are different forms of portrayal – two of the most common in Japan are the Senju Kannon (Thousand-armed Kannon) and the Juichimen Kannon (Eleven-headed Kannon). There are also many images of Kannon as a single figure without extra arms or heads.

Consider Juichimen Kannon (pictured on the previous page):

Atop the head of the main image, one can see ten heads facing all directions and one more head, often depicting Amida, the Buddha of Infinite Light and Life. A common explanation is that the ten heads facing a full 360 degrees symbolize that Kannon can perceive/hear what is going on in all possible directions – and by implication, undifferentiated compassion radiates in all directions to all who might call on Kannon. Another explanation is that each of the ten heads symbolizes one of the ten stages of enlightenment.

The twenty-fifth chapter of *The Lotus Sutra* (the most important and widely used Mahayana Buddhist text in Asia) is devoted to Kannon. Here the name of the bodhisattva is *Perceiver of the World's Sounds*, at least in Burton Watson's fine translation.[46] This name *Perceiver of the World's Sounds* is Kanzeon in Japanese, but it is usually shortened to Kannon. As the name implies, the Kannon is compassionate toward any suffering from any direction – and remember, suffering is the fundamental characteristic of this world of birth, life, death, rebirth (samsara). Here are the first two lines in Watson's translation of chapter 25 of *The Lotus Sutra*:

At that time the Bodhisattva Inexhaustible Intent immediately rose from his seat, bared his right shoulder, pressed his palms together and, facing the Buddha, spoke these words: "World Honored One, this Bodhisattva Perceiver of the World's Sounds – why is he called Perceiver of the World's Sounds?"

The Buddha said to Bodhisattva Inexhaustible Intent: "Good man, suppose there are immeasurable hundreds, thousands, ten thousands, millions of living beings who are undergoing various trials and suffering. If they hear of this Bodhisattva Perceiver of the Word's Sounds and single-mindedly call his name, then at once he will perceive the sound of their voices and they will gain deliverance from their trials.

This all-seeing perspective is in line with the ideal observer point of view. We believe that the notion of an ideal point of view is vital for our understanding that truth is not limited to human concepts, language, and experience. If truth were defined only by human concepts, language, and experience, then it appears that there would be no truths prior to the emergence of human concepts, language, and experience. This runs completely contrary to common sense and what most of us believe when we refer to what occurred before humans

---

[46] See *The Lotus Sutra* at http://nichiren.info/buddhism/lotussutra/.

came to be and what will be the case after our (highly probable) extinction. A concept of truth tethered to human limitations would also rule out the existence of truths inaccessible to human knowing. This anthropocentric view of truth may be both arrogant and dangerous. It can lead us to disregard aspects of life that may be of immense value, though they surpass human knowing.

We propose that a realist view of truth (there really are truths irrespective of whether they are graspable by human cognitive powers) goes hand in hand with the concept of a God's-eye point of view. Hilary Putnam declares: "The whole concept of realism lies in the claim that it makes sense to talk of a God's eye point of view."[47]

Such realism is part and parcel of the drive many of us have to make our lives – especially when oppressed – known to others. We can live in cultures with languages and institutions that outright ignore or deny outrageous grievances, harms, and suffering. The recourse to testimony, witness, bearing one's injuries in public is motivated largely by a passionate desire to expose and make known what elite and powerful persons and institutions seek to ignore and render invisible. One must be seen to be heard.

Consider three objections to a God's-eye point of view. The first returns us to considering the meaning of life, a second comes from Hilary Putnam, and the third stems from Pamela Sue Anderson's feminist critique of a God's-eye point of view.

The appeal to a God's-eye or ideal point of view implies that there is what may be called an objective meaning of life. This is what we advanced in Chapter 4. If naturalism is true, then theistic religious practices are not based on reality. There is no God to be worshiped or engaged through prayer and meditation. The meaning of the act of prayer is different if the God of Abrahamic faiths is real: You really can right now address the living Creator – the redeeming,

---

[47] Hilary Putnam, *Reason with a Human Face* (Cambridge: Harvard University Press, 1990), p. 23. A qualification is in order. While we believe that realism and a God's-eye point of view are coextensive, some philosophers accept realism while denying the coherence of a God's-eye point of view or omniscience. For example, some philosophers have argued that an omniscient being could not know future free acts of persons. It has been argued that it is true now that you will freely do some act tomorrow but no being can know what you will do. Some philosophers have argued against the possibility of omniscience on the grounds that while an omniscient being may know that Jones is in pain, God could not know that the proposition "I am in pain" is true when uttered by Jones. On this view, there could not be any being other than Jones who knows *that proposition* is true, and so there could not be a being that knows the truth of all propositions. See Patrick Grimm's "Some Neglected Problems of Omniscience," *American Philosophical Quarterly* 20, 1983, pp. 265–276. We do not believe these worries undermine the coherence of omniscience. For a reply to these objections, see *The Coherence of Theism* by Richard Swinburne (Oxford: Clarendon Press, 1993). Note that while some philosophers like Grimm deny that realism entails that omniscience is possible, it is far less controversial to claim that the actuality of omniscience (the affirmation that there is an omniscient being) entails realism. If there is an omniscient being, that being knows what is real and there is nothing about reality unknown to that being. The scope of omniscience would cover everything, including knowledge of all the points of view of all actual (and possible) persons.

omniscient, omnipresent God. If any (or all) of the religions addressed in our book are true, then those of us who are pursuing self-aggrandizement with rapacious greed at the expense of the vulnerable are committing sacrilege. The meaning of our lives will be different if none of these religious views of the sacred are true.

Consider this worry: E. D. Klemke thinks that life has no objective meaning. He probably means that life has no objective purpose: We were not created for the purpose of loving the creation and God, for example. Klemke thinks that what he calls *subjective meaning* should be our focus:

> It is true that life has no objective meaning. Let us face it once and for all. But from that it does not follow that life is not worthwhile, for it can still be subjectively meaningful. And, really, the latter is the only kind of meaning worth shouting about. An objective meaning – that is, one which is inherent within the universe or dependent on external agencies – would, frankly, leave me cold. It would not be mine. It would be an outer, neutral thing, rather than an inner, dynamic achievement. I, for one, am glad that the universe has no meaning, for thereby is man all the more glorious. I willingly accept the fact that external meaning is nonexistent … for this leaves me free to forge my own meaning.[48]

Given our understanding of "objective meaning," Klemke's position is incoherent. To put matters as clearly as we can, if there is subjective meaning – inner, dynamic achievements; freedom; and human glory – then this is an objective fact of the matter. Klemke is committed to holding that as a matter of objective meaning he is in actuality free (not constrained by God or gods or external agents, for example) to pursue projects he thinks are "worth shouting about."

Given the way we are using the term *meaning* as in *the meaning of life*, objective meaning is unavoidable. Whether we humans know it or not, there are objective truths about the world, what we say and do. The meaning of what we say or do is not entirely up to us. As noted in Chapter 4, we may think we are loving, fair-minded people when we could turn out to be depraved, exploitive, prejudicial disasters.

Klemke might make this reply: Who cares? Why should I be interested in a God's-eye point of view? It seems like a cold, neutral vantage point that has nothing to do with me.

Such a reply would be the equivalent of not caring about the truth of what you believe and the values you profess. Why bother to question whether you are actually a bigot, an exploiter of the people around you, a horror to many vulnerable, innocent people? Of course, a caveat is in order: Not all so-called

---

[48] E. D. Klemke, "Living without Appeal: An Affirmation of Life" in *The Meaning of Life: A Reader*, edited by E. D. Klemke and S. M. Cahn (Oxford: Oxford University Press, 1999), p. 172. For discussion on this passage, see T. J. Mawson's excellent book *God and the Meaning of Life* (London: Bloomsbury, 2016), pp. 2–4.

objective, impartial inquiry is truly objective and impartial. We address that problem when discussing Anderson's objection.

A second challenge comes from Hilary Putnam. He rejects the notion of a God's-eye point of view and substitutes instead an affirmation of multiple points of view:

> There is no God's eye point of view that we can know or usefully imagine: there are only various points of view of actual persons reflecting various interests and purposes that their descriptions and theories subserve.[49]

Putnam's "target" is a form of scientific realism that aims at a complete, fixed mind-independent view of reality. We very much agree with Putnam's important point that science itself is possible only if there are scientists who have their own interests, points of view, and purposes. A third-person, scientific worldview is not possible without there being first-person points of view, observations, reasoning, and so on. While we embrace that element in Putnam's position, we wholly endorse realism *and* the God's-eye point of view. We offer three points in response to Putnam.

First, we join Michael Loux, Peter van Inwagen, Roger Trigg, and many other philosophers who contend that realism is inescapable. Putnam's own account about points of view would make no sense unless he is truly affirming the reality of persons, purposes, and points of view. To put matters awkwardly, Putnam's alternative schema requires that persons and their points of view actually exist and not just exist from a particular point of view. Michael Loux maintains that some philosophers who contend that we cannot refer to reality, but only to conceptual schemes or points of view, forget that they are committed to believing in the reality of conceptual schemes or points of view.[50] Of course, some of our claims about reality will reflect our points of view; to go back to an example in Chapter 2, most of us would claim that the equator exists while realizing that the very idea of the equator is a reflection of cartography or mapmaking. But we would devolve into incoherence if we denied the reality of people who make and use maps.

Second, one reason to "usefully imagine" a God's-eye point of view is to foster epistemic humility. Namely, it underscores that we fallible human inquirers are not omniscient. We fail in terms of consistent impartiality; we often are subject to points of view that reflect narrow goals of self-interest. Referencing a greater point of view can remind us to stretch our own categories, perhaps even challenging the very human tendency to discount the value of other animals and forms of life.

Third, appealing to a God's-eye point of view is to appeal to a vantage point in which all persons, no matter how oppressed and marginalized, are seen, heard, and acknowledged. Of course this becomes no mere hypothetical

---

[49] Hilary Putnam, *Reason with a Human Face*, p. 50.
[50] Michael Loux, *Metaphysics* (London: Routledge, 1998), Introduction.

reference if there is truth in the Abrahamic faiths, Brahman, and the Compassionate Buddha. (As an aside, for someone to claim there cannot be a God's-eye point of view would be to claim that there cannot be a God or omniscience. Many atheist philosophers who claim there is no God do not go so far as to claim that it is impossible for there to be a God).[51]

It may be granted that an ideal observer account of beauty and aesthetics might clarify some of the values many of us have – values such as impartiality, use of imagination, and a commitment to knowing the facts as a basis for ethical evaluations. And yet the theory has received fierce criticism that it exalts a specifically gendered view of truth and values. Some philosophers like Pamela Sue Anderson propose that the ideal observer theory is a white, heterosexual ideal, or, more broadly, it tends to be used to reinforce male and females who are privileged:

> The rational subject who begins from the objective view-from-nowhere, understood in the sense of the God's eye view, may promote ideas of omnipotence and omniscience which have dangerous consequences for religious beliefs and values. Justifying questions of religious belief from a God's-eye view can simply reinforce the power of the biased beliefs of privileged men and women.[52]

In *Re-visioning Gender in Philosophy of Religion,* Anderson extends this point, contending that the ideal observer theory involves "the assumption that a philosopher can achieve the ideal observer position and be omniscient, omni-percipient [able to affectively appreciate the points of view of all parties] and impartial."[53] Even if it is not assumed that human philosophers can attain ideal observation, Anderson proposes that advocates of the theory have a desire for a God's-eye view and this desire readily leads a person to seek to gain the power to actively shape the world in accord with his or her assumption about ideal observation.

Note that in the first cited passage, Anderson's claim is that advocating the ideal observer theory *may* or *can* lead to ill effects. But almost any theory of

---

[51] For Hilary Putnam's views of religion, see his *Jewish Philosophy as a Guide to Life* (Bloomington: Indiana University Press, 2008). On God and truth: It is interesting to note that Nietzsche linked theism and realism. By his lights, if there is no God, there are no objective truths, just perspectives. *Tod Gottes = Tod Wahrheit.* We find Nietzsche's position incoherent on the grounds that he is committed to realism about perspectives (*viz.* the truth-claim that there are perspectives) and God (if atheism is true, then it is false to claim God exists; God's existence or nonexistence is not merely a matter of perspectives). A different line of reasoning is worthy of attention. Michael Dummett has recently appealed to theism in order to distinguish the way the world is (realism) from our varying perspectives: "The concept of the world as a whole is correlative to that of God as standing against the world. If that contrast is removed, no room remains for distinguishing the world as it is from the world as we experience it and find it to be." *Thought and Reality* (Oxford: Oxford University Press, 2006), p. 103.
[52] Pamela Sue Anderson, *A Feminist Philosophy of Religion* (Oxford: Blackwell, 1998), p. 34.
[53] Pamela Sue Anderson, *Re-visioning Gender in Philosophy of Religion* (London: Routledge, 2012), p. 46.

Beauty in the Eye of the Beholder?

values may or can lead to ill effects. Simply having a theory of justice of any kind can open up the possibility of having a bad theory of justice. The ideal observer theory (as defended in the literature) does not involve any claim whatsoever that human beings can become omniscient or should pursue or even desire omnipotence. It is more commonly defended as providing grounds for humility, acknowledging that while we should strive for impartiality, knowledge of the relevant facts, and affective sensitivity, we may fall woefully short of achieving ideal observation.[54] What we think is more dangerous would be accounts of ethics that deem impartiality a false ideal and so bias (prejudice, partiality) should not be challenged because bias is an inevitable part of the human condition.[55]

Anderson contrasts the appeal to an ideal point of view – which she describes as "detached ethical thought" and "seeing feminist ethics from a distance" – with the more embodied feminist point of view that stresses the relational project of achieving mutual recognition between persons.[56] Similar to our response to Klemke, we propose that advocating that we should treat ethics in a relational context would (naturally or ultimately) need a defense from an impartial point of view. It may be that cases arise when persons engaged in moral action cannot reflect impartially and it would be damaging to attempt to do so under certain circumstances. But even acknowledging this would imply that from an informed, impartial point of view it is not always good for agents to pursue impartiality.

We suggest that Anderson's objection about being detached may count against what some have described as an aesthetic point of view in which ethical judgment is suspended. But insofar as feminist ethics focuses on the true injuries of persons, the subordination of women to male forces, and the tendency to render invisible the needs and longings of women, then (by hypothesis) this would all be taken in by a God's-eye point of view. And if we apply the ideal observer theory to a theistic worldview or the eyes of the Compassionate Buddha, then it seems that the ideal observer theory would provide a philosophical foundation for fully recognizing the reality of such states or situations. It should be added that while Anderson describes the ideal observer theory as advancing "the objective view from nowhere," we see the theory as advancing the view from everywhere. This is akin to the classical theistic understanding of God's omniscience as a dimension of God's omnipresence (there is no place where God is not). This link between omniscience and omnipresence is not limited to Abrahamic traditions, but can

---

[54] Roderick Firth, "Ethical Absolutism and the Ideal Observer," *Philosophy and Phenomenological Report* 12 (3), 1951, pp. 317–345.

[55] It is interesting that those philosophers who defend what they call bias, do so from what they claim is an impartial point of view; see, for example, Louise Antony, "In Defense of Bias," Belgum lectures, St. Olaf College, March 2019.

[56] Pamela Sue Anderson, "What's Wrong with the God's Eye Point of View: A Constructive Feminist Critique of the Ideal Observer Theory" in *Faith and Philosophical Analysis*, Chapter 7.

be found in non-Christian and non-Islamic African religions. According to Abdulai Iddrisu, in African religions, "God is everywhere and can see and hear anything."[57] Whatever is done in plain sight or in secret, for the Dagombas, *Nati Tamlana nye ya*, meaning "the king of all kings has seen." God's omniscience is widely attested to in African religion. To the Akans of Ghana, God is "He Who knows and sees it all" and the Yoruba of Nigeria, "Only God is Wise," and the Dagombas "*Nawun ko nmi din sog'y*" meaning "Only God knows what is hidden. Nothing escapes God."

The objections we have considered from Klemke and Anderson speak to the vital concern at the intersection of religion and aesthetics. Let us return to Zahavi's reflection on the achievement of being able to see oneself as others see you. Merleau-Ponty observes how such an outlook engendered by seeing ourselves in a mirror can also occasion a sense of alienation from oneself:

> To recognize his image in the mirror is for him to learn that *there can be a view-point taken on him*. ... I am no longer what I felt myself, immediately, to be. ... I leave the reality of my lived *me* in order to refer myself constantly to the idea, fictitious, or imaginary *me*, of which the specular image is the first outline. In this sense, I am torn from myself, and the image in the mirror prepares me for another still more serious alienation, which will be the alienation by others.[58]

We acknowledge that the invocation of an ideal God's-eye point of view *can* be used to alienate one from oneself. But when the God's-eye point of view is understood to be the gaze of the compassionate Buddha, the loving awareness of Sri Krishna, the merciful all-knowing Allah, the eyes of the God of Jesus of Nazareth, and the God of Jeremiah and other Hebrew prophets, a person can experience a healing affirmation of one's integrity and health, a vision of a path for overcoming self-alienation and alienation from others.

---

[57] This passage and what follows are taken from Iddrisu's entry "African Religions" in *The Encyclopedia of Philosophy of Religion*, edited by Stewart Goetz and Charles Taliaferro (Oxford: Wiley-Blackwell, forthcoming).

[58] Merleau-Ponty, cited by Zahavi, *Self and Subjectivity*, p. 201.

6

Revealing and Concealing

> This intuition of the Real lying at the root of the visible world and sustaining its life is present in a modified form in the arts.
>
> Evelyn Underhill[1]

Art is generative by nature, revealing and concealing our intentions and identities. Form, by which we mean embodied content, has a unique relationship with each viewer, reader, or listener of call and response, and that is why the meaning of a work of art cannot be easily fixed or guaranteed. Art is a form of life.

The valence of a work of art is experienced over time. Even in works of art that fail to reach an impact many of us would consider profound, meaning can't be grasped in a glance or a moment of listening. Meaning in art often accrues by degrees as the world of the art's embodied content meets us in what we see, touch, hear, smell, and taste. And the world that art creates is formed through an act of poesis (from the Greek for *to make*), with intention, but not with a means to stabilize meaning(s) in its encounters with viewers over time, in some cases, millennia.[2] As a form of life, works of art may have not just histories but also biographies (extended narrative lives), and sometimes works of art die when they disappear from public view or consciousness.

---

[1] Evelyn Underhill, *Mysticism* (Nelson South, New Zealand: Renaissance Classics, 2012), p. 54.
[2] See *Poetry and the Fate of the Senses*, by Susan Stewart (Chicago: University of Chicago Press, 2002) for an extended essay on the role of the senses in lyric poetry. "What is the relation, then, of poetic making to other form-giving activities? Like all creative acts, poesis wrests form from nature without prior knowledge of ends or uses. Poesis thus exaggerates the possibilities of self-transformation available in all forms of art, for its intention cannot be fully known or totalized. The poet discovers his or her identity as a consequence of form-making – the role of the maker is not predetermined by either social convention or instrumental reason. The self is objectified, but not completed by the presentation of the form. And the form will always be more and less than a representation of its maker," p. 12.

We begin by considering a group of religiously significant artworks whose unintended ramifications conceal historical injustice. Following this, we look at an example of art whose concealment creates a possible intimacy in religious practice, being a positive example of how negation can function. We go on to reflect on seeing the sacred in Venetian art and conclude with considering how the sacred and profane can be layered in the work of a Dutch painter.

MENAGERIE PAINTINGS IN THE DUTCH GOLDEN AGE

There is a genre of painting in the seventeenth-century "Golden Age" of Dutch painting known as menagerie paintings. These works depict the natural world with rich attention to detail and a diverse abundance of animals and plants, both wild and domestic. The Rijksmuseum in Amsterdam has a collection of works by menagerie painter Melchior d'Hondecoeter, who specialized in painting birds and other animals. Our reflections on works of art touched on here are born mainly from time spent seeing the artworks in person over many years.

While D'Hondecoeter's work is exhibited and catalogued, this genre of paintings has generated little scholarship. This is puzzling because scholarship on the Golden Age of Dutch painting enjoys enormous attention in art history in the Netherlands, the United States, and the United Kingdom in particular. But menagerie paintings, and there are many of them, are considered unimportant and merely decorative.

The D'Hondecoeter painting we will consider is *The Menagerie*.

The animals are placed in the foreground as if on a stage and illuminated with intense light that creates deep shadows. The color is saturated and full of contrasting hues. The dense atmosphere, where they stand, sit, and perch, reflects the color one sees in the natural world when sunlight breaks through clouds and lights up portions of what is otherwise framed in darkness, like a storm on the horizon. Shaped by both Calvinist and Catholic thought in an era of intense scientific and geographic exploration, the menagerie paintings display a restored or redeemed landscape of idyllic calm.

Looking at what animals are depicted, one finds two squirrel monkeys from Central America, two white sulfur-crested cockatoos from Australia, a grey parrot from Africa, and a purple-naped lory from Indonesia (with a chain around its leg).

Installed originally at the Royal Palace (Het Loo, home of William III and Mary), the painting displays what in fact helped create the Golden Age in Holland, the expansive sea-trade empire in material goods like gold, spices, sugar, fruit, tea, and coffee, and in the slave trade. The Dutch had a controlling interest in shipping slaves to Spanish colonies in the seventeenth century, and they were the most expansive European power trafficking slaves in the history of Southeast Asia.

In a few instances, black Africans appear in Dutch paintings at this time, but usually in the guise of domestic help, not as portraiture and not as

Menagerie Paintings in the Dutch Golden Age

FIGURE 6.1 Melchior d'Hondecoeter, *The Menagerie*, oil on canvas, 135 cm × 116.5 cm, c.1690, Rijksmuseum, Amsterdam, Netherlands. Web Figure 1. Photo courtesy of Rijksmuseum.

enslaved. The persistence of justifying slavery and being instrumental in making it possible was based on the grounds that those being enslaved were nearer animals than humans, even contending that black Africans were close relations to nonhuman apes.[3]

Why, then, are black Africans and other traded slaves not depicted in the menagerie paintings in which the whole realm of nature is redeemed and restored? To portray the slaves in an aesthetically rich, redeemed nature, with the same kind of attention lavished on feather and fur, would have exposed what violence was being suppressed. To render is to give one's attention over to "other," and it can create tremendous intimacy. It is, if one is emotionally

---

[3] See *The Problem of Slavery in Western Culture*, by David Brian Davis (Oxford: Oxford University Press, 1988).

healthy, almost impossible to not develop empathy with what or who one is rendering.[4]

When we look at these paintings and realize who is not represented, content emerges, making visible a complex matrix of values and the widely shared history of exploitation and erasure.[5]

INTIMACY THROUGH CONCEALMENT

A different kind of concealment is found in the late black paintings of the mid twentieth-century American painter Ad Reinhardt. While insisting that his art did not have religious content, Reinhardt was keenly interested in Christian mysticism and contemplative practices of all world religions. He had a lifelong friendship with the Trappist monk Thomas Merton. Their friendship grew out of their time together as students at Columbia University in New York City in the 1940s.

Reinhardt's black paintings, made during the last seven years of his life, are not solid black surfaces. They include subtle geometric patterns or shapes that are discernible by close looking. Visually, they function the same way a Buddhist or Hindu mandala might. In this case, the painting directs the gaze of the viewer to a concentrated and still field, quiet and without reference to the material world.

In his book *New Seeds of Contemplation*, Merton writes:

But when the time comes to enter the darkness in which we are naked and helpless and alone; in which we see the insufficiency of our greatest strength and the hollowness of our strongest virtues; in which we have nothing of our own to rely on, and nothing in our nature to support us, and nothing in the world to guide us or give us light – then we find out whether or not we live by faith.

It is in this darkness, when there is nothing left in us that can please or comfort our own minds, when we seem to be useless and worthy of all contempt, when we seem to have failed, when we seem to be destroyed and devoured, it is then that the deep and secret selfishness that is too close for us to identify is stripped away from our souls. It is in this darkness that we find true liberty. It is in this abandonment that we are made strong. This is the night which empties us and makes us pure. Do not look for rest in any pleasure, because you were not created for pleasure: you were created for spiritual JOY. And if you do not know the difference between pleasure and spiritual joy you have not yet begun to live.[6]

---

[4] Perhaps it is because of this that there is the practice of *damnatio memoriae* or "condemnation of memory," in which a ruler or state seeks to erase all references and depictions of those whom they condemn.

[5] In preparing this manuscript, we learned that the Rijksmuseum is preparing *Slavery, an Exhibition*, which will be on display from September 2020 through January 17, 2021. The museum's website states: "This exhibition testifies to the fact that slavery is an integral part of our history, not a dark page that can simply be turned and forgotten about. And that history is more recent than many realize: going back just four or five generations you will find enslaved people and their enslavers."

[6] Thomas Merton, *New Seeds of Contemplation* (New York: New Directions Publishing House, 2007), pp. 258–259.

Intimacy through Concealment

FIGURE 6.2 Ad Reinhardt, *Abstract Painting no. 4,* 1961, oil on linen, Smithsonian American Art Museum, gift of S. C. Johnson & Son, Inc., 1969.47.71. Photo courtesy of Smithsonian American Art Museum.

Thomas Merton kept a small painting by Reinhardt in his cell for meditation. In creating works with such subtle and minute changes within the field of the image, Reinhardt created images of wordless contemplation, markers to pause and consider how value accrues for us in this silence.

Merton's reflections here are in the theological tradition of the way of negation (*via negativa*, or apophatic theology), in which the approach to God must paradoxically involve an experience of the divine through realizing what God is not. Merton used *via negativa* to discover his faith by stripping away false forms of life that created a barrier between himself and the life of God.

The writings of the philosopher and mystic theologian Nicholas of Cusa (1401–64) offer another way to think about how negation can play an important role in leading us, ultimately, to the positive way (*via positiva*, or cataphatic theology). In *On Learned Ignorance,* Cusa cautions us that the way of negation is more theologically reliable than the way of affirmation.

In theology negations are true and affirmations are inadequate and ... the negations that remove the more imperfect things from the most perfect are truer than other negations. It is truer, for example, to say that God is not stone than to say that God is not life or intelligence, and truer to say God is not drunkenness than to say that God is not virtue. It is the contrary with affirmations. Here it is truer to say that God is intelligence and life than to assert that God is earth, stone, or body.[7]

Cusa moves in his lifetime from *via negativa* spirituality to the encounter with God at the threshold of seeing and being seen by God. He developed the concept of the "wall of contradictions" beyond which God may be found. He employs the notion of "coincidence" to explore how the limits of reason bring us to contradictions (two irreconcilable things) that we must hold simultaneously. The humbling of our prideful reliance on discursive reasoning allows us to be open experientially to the presence of the all-seeing, all-loving God. Cusa says:

Consequently, when I am at the door of the coincidence of opposites, guarded by the angel stationed at the entrance of paradise, I begin to see you, O Lord. For you are there where speaking, seeing, hearing, tasting, touching, reasoning, knowing and understanding are the same and where seeing coincides with being seen, hearing with being heard, tasting with being tasted, touching with being touched, speaking with hearing, and creating with speaking. If I were to see just as I am visible, I would not be a creature, and if you, O God, did not see just as you are visible, you would not be God, the Almighty. You are visible by all creatures and you see all. In that you see all you are seen by all. For otherwise creatures cannot exist since they exist by your vision. If they did not see you who see, they would not receive being from you. The being of a creature is equally your seeing and your being seen.[8]

Cusa uses a work of art to conjure up the idea of God as all-seeing. A painting by Rogier van der Weyden, now lost, was of a figure whose eye seemed to follow viewers from whichever angle it was observed. Cusa offers an extraordinary meditative view on how God may be seen as having a face, but having a face that transcends all faces:

And how would one conceive of a face when one would transcend all faces, and all likenesses and figures of all faces, and all concepts that can be formed of a face, and all color, decoration, and beauty of all faces? Whoever, therefore, undertakes to see your face, so long as one conceives anything, is far removed from your face. For every concept of a face is less than your face, O Lord. And every beauty that can be conceived is less than the beauty of your face. Every face has beauty, but none is beauty itself. Your face, Lord, has beauty, and having is being. In this absolute beauty itself, which is the form that gives being to every form of beauty. O immeasurably

---

[7] *Nicholas of Cusa; Selected Spiritual Writings, On the Vision of God*, translated by Hugh Lawrence Bond, Classics of Western Spirituality Series (New York: Paulist Press, 1997) p. 127.
[8] *Nicholas of Cusa; Selected Spiritual Writings, On the Vision of God*, p. 253.

lovely Face, your beauty is such that all things to which are granted to behold it are not sufficient to admire it.[9]

According to Cusa, the image of God as represented by an inexhaustibly beautiful face that creates all beauty is permitted, as long as we realize God's awesome transcendence of all corporeal being. And yet, at the same time, Cusa follows the classical Christian notion that in the incarnation God did have a human face. This paradoxical position, of affirming the human face of God in the incarnation vis-à-vis the supreme transcendence of the Godhead, harkens back to an observation made in Chapter 2 between the concept of *totus Deus* (wholly God) and *totum Dei* (the whole of God). Christians affirm that Jesus was wholly God and human but not the whole of God. In this case, Cusa may be read as affirming that to see the face of Jesus of Nazareth would be to see the face of God, but the *totum Dei* remains beyond human powers to fathom.

In the next section, let us consider another artistic path to revealing the sacred, in this case the nature of our embodiment in God's world. The terrain will follow the *via positiva* in the visual arts.

REVEALING THE DIVINE IN VENICE

How can art reveal what it means to be embodied persons in God's world? Developments unique to Venetian painting, from the late medieval to late baroque period, open spectacular insight into what it means to be embodied. Looking at these pictorial and material developments in Venetian art, the viewer not only sees the bourgeoning interest throughout Europe in the observation and recording of the world and all that is visible, but also recognizes in paintings a growing interest in how to depict an understanding of embodiment itself. Painting grew to convey somatic knowledge of mind and body through ideas about the manipulation of the physicality of oil paint. The physicality of oil paint can function metaphorically for how you and we feel in our connections to ideas, emotional states, and our place in the larger world.

In Venice, all of the major religious and civic buildings are filled from floor to ceiling (that is, the ceilings are covered too) with tempera and oil paintings, often very large ones. The subject matter of Venetian painting is a towering mix of the sacred with the civic, histories of battles, myths, and legends.

One path through the vast collections of paintings in Venice is to ask: How and why did painting move from the kind of representation and expression found in Antonio Vivarini's painting *Virgin and Child Blessing* to Giovanni Battista Tiepolo's *Discovery of the True Cross* some three hundred years later?

[9] Ibid., p. 244.

FIGURE 6.3 Antonio Vivarini, *Virgin and Child Blessing*, tempera on panel, 56 × 41 cm, 1441, Gallerie dell'Accademia, Venice. Web Figure 2. Photo courtesy of Gallerie dell'Accademia.

This isn't a comparison of worth, or value, or even just style. Some changes involved very practical things (the introduction of oil paint and canvas, which became widely available due to the Venetian Navy). There were also changes in how artists thought about their role, but here we will look at how changes in composition and the handling of the physicality of paint itself came to carry a new psychological immediacy and intimacy.

In Vivarini's painting, the figures of Mary and the child Jesus are encased in gold leaf as if laid into the gold. Without a sense of a light source illuminating the figures, the light appears to emerge from the figures themselves. This is what gives the work life. The beautiful, still world Mary and Jesus live in has no shadows. The only shadows present are within folds of flesh and fabric. While this painting is not an icon, it reflects the influence of Byzantium in Venice. In the tradition of Eastern Orthodox Christianity, icons do not depict figures at a specific time of day, such as morning or evening; instead they suggest a timeless presence.

Revealing the Divine in Venice

FIGURE 6.4 Giovanni Battista Tiepolo, *Discovery of the True Cross,* oil on canvas, diameter: 192 inches, 1745, Gallerie dell'Accademia, Venice. Web Figure 3. Photo courtesy of Gallerie dell'Accademia.

In contrast, Tiepolo's depiction of figures in space is unmoored compared with Vivarini's work. We are introduced to a world where bodies are no longer bound by gold leaf. The people in this world are beholding angelic levitation while witnessing the true cross. Tiepolo uses ideas of gravity and propulsion. The horse gallops down the left side of the painting to upend the lowest cross, which in turn brings our eyes to the true cross raised in the middle and being celebrated with veneration and joy. There is an effusive, even ecstatic movement as angels venerate the cross, a cloud of incense rising from swinging thuribles.

Early Venetian painting was influenced by its Byzantine inheritance. At St. Mark's Basilica, the work at the high table, called the Pal'a'doro, or golden cloth, is considered one of the most exquisite works of Byzantine enamel. It is made of gold, silver, enamel plaques, pearls, garnets, emeralds, and many other gems. It measures 9.8 feet by 6.6 feet. It was commissioned in 976, expanded in 1105, and completed in 1345.

Well known by Venetian artists, this work of art – along with the vivid juxtapositions of color in the glass made by glass blowers on the nearby island of Murano – is believed to have had a huge influence on the rich color and surfaces that characterized early Venetian painting. In contrast to the art of Venice, the art of Florence was known for scholarship, theory, and the development of mathematical perspective to depict space.

Another phenomenon in Venice, which many believe has had an equal effect on Venetian painting's contribution to Western painting, is the ever-present movement of light. Light reflects off the canals and illuminates the built world from every direction, creating reflections and shadows that move as the water moves. So many Venetian works employ visual echoes, it might be that the percussive rhythms of sound, created by water and stone permeating the atmosphere of Venice day and night, helped shape ideas in painting.

FIGURE 6.5 Ca' d'Oro, Entrance Hall corner on the Grand Canal, Venice, Italy, built 1428–30. Photo by J. Evans

Revealing the Divine in Venice

In our account of art and embodiment in Venice, consider Carlo Crivelli, who was born into a family of painters well known in Venice.

FIGURE 6.6 Carlo Crivelli, *Madonna and Child*, tempera and gold leaf on wood, 14 7/8 inches × 10 inches, c.1480, Metropolitan Museum of Art. Photo courtesy of Metropolitan Museum of Art.

Crivelli developed highly ornate, detailed surfaces, revealing the growing interest in observation of the world. He depicts groves of trees in a landscape of undulating hills. At the same time, certain parts of the body, like Mary's fingers, are elongated in exaggeration. Her own body is standing in a world of bugs and cracked walls, while she and the child are unearthly in their pallor. Their flesh is less real-looking than the fruit hanging next to Mary's head. Mary holds Jesus on a wall in front of her. A scrim hanging behind her provides a separation from the landscape, suggesting her status as divine. The painting is a curious combination of attention to the natural world combined with an older, mannered depiction of the human body.

A major shift in representation occurs, in part, with the introduction of oil paint in Venetian painting. The art biographer and painter Vasari credits Antonello de Messina, a Sicilian painter, with bringing oil paint from Flanders to Italy. He only spent about a year in Venice, but his technique, adopted from Flemish painters, had a huge influence on Venetian painting. Oil paint can reflect light in a way that egg tempera cannot. Egg tempera, a water-based paint, dries quickly with a mat surface. It doesn't allow for blending of colors; they have to be laid in by separate strokes. Oil paint can be layered in various degrees of transparency that allow the light to pass through the layers and reflect back. Oil paint allows the painter to create many more atmospheric effects. Color can then be used to establish more subtle spatial relationships rather than relying on only drawing and mathematical perspectival systems. Oil does not dry quickly, allowing the painter to build a greater vocabulary over time.

Giovanni Bellini was the first Venetian painter to explore the greater freedom oil paint provides.

He painted the San Giobbe altarpiece. The theme of this altarpiece is *sacra conversazione*, or sacred conversation, gathering saints from different times and places. The work was modeled after Messina's altarpiece. Now, instead of depicting a completely separate world set apart from the viewer, as seen in earlier Venetian painting, Bellini is creating more lifelike figures. But they are still aloof. They exist in the same unified space, but they fulfill official roles in their separate, unique narratives. We see muscles, young and old flesh, but a curiously languid St. Sebastian and a distant-looking Mary. Bellini is preserving a sacred role for the image, while developing a greater naturalism for the figuration and space. He includes a fictive chapel that recalls the interior of St. Mark's with its ceiling mosaics. The saints lean on one leg or another, indicating bodies in a universe with gravity; but they don't interact with one another, so there is still a high degree of meditation and silence surrounding them.

The painter Titian, working a few decades later, came to dominate commissions for most of the sixteenth century in Venice.

FIGURE 6.7 Giovanni Bellini, San Giobbe altarpiece, oil on panel, 15.4 feet × 8.5 feet, c.1487, Gallerie dell'Accademia. Web Figure 4. Photo courtesy of Gallerie dell'Accademia.

FIGURE 6.8 Titian, *Assumption of the Virgin,* oil on panel, 22 feet × 11.6 feet, 1516–18, *Basilica di Santa Maria Gloriosa dei Frari or Frari Church in Venice.* Web Figure 5. Photo courtesy of Bridgeman Images.

Assumption of the Virgin is an early commission, for the largest altarpiece in Venice within the Friari, the city's largest Gothic church. One of Titian's recent biographers, Sheila Hale, claims that this painting was unlike "any seen in Venice or anywhere else. ... It unsettled his contemporaries and changed the direction in European Art in a way that was not repeated until Picasso 400 years later."[10]

[10] Sheila Hale, *Titian.* (New York: HarperCollins, 2012), pp. 157–158.

Revealing the Divine in Venice

What might lead Hale to make this claim? What did Titian introduce to European painting?

Titian's painting introduced a radical shift in energy, composition, and interaction between figures. He has painted Mary and those crowded below her as if existing in the Friari. The people on the ground are on the same level as the worshippers who approached the altar. The people are twisting around to witness Mary as she twists up into the heavens. Titian also originated a whole new way to think about color: He gave the painting an "overall" color. This painting is as if drenched in a rose hue that creates another unity. Before Titian, color was discreet in its placement: say, a blue robe for Mary, or a gold halo behind the head of a saint. While painters before Titian had developed unity with color, this overall atmosphere of color opened up a new experience for aesthetic feeling, or affectiveness.

Looking at *Assumption of the Virgin*, we find that our bodies experience an empathetic response to the twisting figures and the movement of Mary raising her arms, joining us more physically to a visual image with a great urgency. It is hard to recapture this for twenty-first-century eyes, because we are so used to large screens with actual moving images. But this new way of composing bodies in space was itself a new way for painting to engage with architecture, a place of worship, and the bodies and minds of those gathered to worship.

The Punishment of Marsyas is a painting Titian worked on for years. It has been said that the use of mythology is the only help we have in getting any distance from this image – to make it possible to look. In one version of the myth, the musician and satyr Marsyas boasts that he can make finer music on his double-pipe aulos than Apollo, the god of music, could play on his cithara (a stringed instrument similar to a lyre). They enter a contest to be judged by the Muses. Eventually, the Muses declare Apollo the winner, and he is given the right to have Marsyas punished in any way he chooses. His choice is to have Marsyas flayed alive. While Marsyas is being flayed, Apollo stands in the near distance playing his cithara. Here, Titian has used paint itself as a metaphor for suffering. The scale of the brushstrokes is not unlike the scale of the flayed skin fragments. Paint is physically present as something broken down into strokes of flickering light and flesh. We feel the weight of Marsyas, hanging upside down, helpless, while the shapes at the top of the painting are made with his satyr legs opening up and out. This creates the duration of time in the painting. We don't fall off the bottom of the painting with Marsyas; we keep ascending and descending, following the curvatures of working arms and the gazes of intent onlookers to the torture. Some four hundred years later, the Dutch painter Willem de Kooning said: "Flesh was the reason why oil paint was invented."[11]

The *Pietà* was Titian's last painting, meant for his tomb. Here, Christ is being held by Mary, while a figure, thought to be St. Jerome (as well as being

---

[11] Willem de Kooning, The Renaissance and Order, a talk delivered at Studio 35, 8th Street, New York City, Autumn 1949. From the Willam de Kooning Foundation.

FIGURE 6.9 Titian, *The Punishment of Marsyas*, oil on canvas, 83 inches × 81 inches, c.1570–6, Archdiocesan Museum Kroměříž, Archbishopric Castle Kroměříž, Kroměříž. Photo courtesy of Derek Bayes/Bridgeman Images.

a self-portrait of Titian) approaches Christ on his knees and reaches to touch Christ's hand. Mary Magdalene appears to run in front of the group, but it is unclear whether she is arriving or fleeing. Other figures include a statue of Moses and the Hellespontine Sibyl, their identities inscribed on their pedestals. A putto angel hovers over the group with a lit torch, the flame harshly lighting just aspects of the scene, creating a strong contrast between the cold of the stone and the vulnerability of human flesh and life. In the last years of his long life, Titian's palette was more somber, but still infused with light that flickers and moves. He invented a way to bring our sense of touch, of being touched, both physically and psychically, to the medium of oil paint. There is a kind of intentional hesitancy in the drawing in the painting – in the places where skin turns to stone, or where light disappears into shadow – which conveys emotion about the transient and our mortality.

Revealing the Divine in Venice

FIGURE 6.10 Titian, *Pietà*, oil on canvas, 12.75, feet × 11.5 feet, 1575, Gallerie dell' Accademia, Venice, Italy. Photo courtesy of Gallerie dell'Accademia.

While Titian developed ways to reveal the experience of embodiment, a very different painter named Tintoretto emerged. He was half Titian's age when he came on the scene.

The presentation of the Virgin to the temple in Jerusalem was a common theme in Venetian painting. It served several narratives, not the least portraying Mary ascending the steps of the temple to meet the priest, who played a dual role as the Doge of Venice and who often waited at the top of stairs to greet visitors. The painting begins, as it were, near the bottom of the stairs and takes us into the crowd where Mary appears. Tintoretto reimagines how pictorial space can function in painting, not so much as opening a window onto a world as throwing you through it. We are faced immediately with young Mary's back as she is ushered up the steps. There are strong diagonals, something Tintoretto

FIGURE 6.11 Tintoretto, *Presentation of the Virgin,* oil on canvas, 14 feet × 15.75 feet, 1553–6, Madonna dell'Orto, Venice. Photo courtesy of Cameraphoto Arte Venezia/ Bridgeman Images.

would use over and over again in his work to create drama and speed. The scale of the priest is huge, looming over the stairs, while other large figures on the stairs stand along the edges of the painting in darkness, framing the tunnel of light provided for Mary's ascent. This painting is an early indication of how Tintoretto would exploit compositional devices to create powerful drama in his paintings.

Prolific his entire life, Tintoretto had a reputation for never turning down a commission. French philosopher Jean-Paul Sartre wrote this about Tintoretto:

Left to himself, he would have covered every wall in the city with his paintings, no campo would have been too vast, no sotto-portico too obscure for him to illuminate. He would have covered the ceilings, people would have walked across his most beautiful images, his brush would have spared neither the facades of the palaces, nor the gondolas, or perhaps the gondoliers.[12]

---

[12] Jean-Paul Sartre, *Essays in Existentialism,* edited by Wade Baskin (New York: Citadel Press, 1993), p. 348.

Revealing the Divine in Venice 131

FIGURE 6.12 Tintoretto, *The Massacre of the Innocents,* oil on canvas, 13.85 feet × 17.91 feet, 1582–7, Scuola Grande di San Rocco, Venice. Web Figure 6. Photo courtesy of public domain.

In *The Massacre of the Innocents*, Tintoretto works with a narrative found in the Christian New Testament. After Jesus is born, King Herod is told that a child has been born who will become the king of the Jews. Herod then orders that all infant boys in Bethlehem are to be killed. In Tintoretto's depiction, women and their sons are in a horrendous struggle for survival, brutally assaulted and killed. The strong L-shaped area of the left side of the painting, moving along the foreground, holds bundles of bodies being pushed and pulled. A woman leaning over the wall clutching an infant's hand and wrist is either trying to pull the child up to her to save or to lower the child to another for saving. The inconclusiveness of our ability to read this contributes to the anxiety and trauma of the entire work. As you move further back into space, the massacre continues. The contrast between light areas and dark areas – each existing in distinct, yet connected geometric shapes – combined with extreme diagonal angles crossing the picture plane, creates some of the most dynamic and nearly inexhaustible worlds ever experienced in painting. As you look at this image, it's almost impossible to keep track of how many rooms are pictured or how many "outside" spaces there are. This is another theme Tintoretto explored – a way to picture simultaneity of events in different places without losing the unity of the image.

Tintoretto's paintings strike hard with their play of balance and imbalance.

Here, strong contrasts in darks and lights jump around the canvas, which causes our eyes to jump around, and mimics the chaos, confusion, and urgency of what we are looking at. We have a visceral experience of chaos and losing our way.

Our final Venetian painter to think about is Giovanni Battista Tiepolo, who worked in the eighteenth century. Like Titian, he received many commissions from royal families and the church. He made fresco paintings, altar paintings, ceiling paintings, and smaller sketches. His work can be found throughout northern Italy, especially in and around Venice, as well as in Spain. His most famous last works are in Germany in the Wurzburg Palace.

His world is big, crowded but never claustrophobic, and always in motion. He gives us a picture of spherical space – infinities. This spherical space is how rhythm establishes the notion we find in Tiepolo of everlastingness. In our view, Tiepolo brings together the saturated but subtle color of Titian with the urgency of Tintoretto's gesture.

Tiepolo engages our imagination all the time with figurative ambiguities and bizarre constructions, doubling and tripling limbs to make figures and creatures that break apart our expectations and habits of perception. In *The Apotheosis of the Spanish Monarchy*, a sketch for a larger work for King Charles III of Spain, he includes signs and symbols. The enthroned female in the center stands for Spain, the lions protecting her symbolizes the province of Leon, while Mercury flies in with her crown. Hercules, the traditional protector of Spain, is shown with a column representing Gibraltar. In the lower left, there appears to be a small elephant trunk making its way into the scene.

Tiepolo's paintings give the impression that they are being painted while you are looking at them. The speed of his line, as it describes a shape and then leaves the shape, seems to be almost a kind of automatic writing. The effect is exciting: you don't know what the line is going to do next; it is always ahead of you, a physical lure for the viewer into the inexhaustible spaces of his skies. This is the embodiment of Tiepolo. He isn't working with the intimacy of Titian's pathos, or the fierceness of Tintoretto's identification with suffering and human agency. Rather, he develops a way for the viewer to experience ecstatic habitation in his worlds.

French philosopher Gaston Bachelard offers a way to think about how painting can convey an idea of habitation. How does the painter create a world where what is in the painting wants to stay in the painting? How does the painter create a world that the viewer's mind wants to inhabit? In one of his last books, *The Poetics of Space*, Bachelard looks at images found in French poetry that call up "felicitous spaces" – spaces that we love. For Bachelard these poetic images are archetypal ones that answer some need in us, some fulfillment in us, which goes deeper than any psychological or psychoanalytical theory could account for. Bachelard wrote:

FIGURE 6.13 Giovanni Battista Tiepolo, *The Apotheosis of the Spanish Monarchy*, oil on canvas, 33 inches × 27 inches, 1760s, Metropolitan Museum of Art. Web Figure 7. Photo courtesy of Metropolitan Museum of Art.

The poetic image is an emergence from language, it is always a little above the language of signification. By living the poems we read, we then have a salutary experience of emerging.[13]

Bachelard goes on to examine images of the house, from the cellar to attic, drawers, chests and wardrobes, nests and shells, corners, miniatures and immensity as they occur in poetic images in poems, as a way to draw out how we inhabit these spaces both literally and in our imagination. He takes the image of the hut as one example. The hut is always by itself in our imagination, and the

---

[13] Gaston Bachelard, *The Poetics of Space*, translated by Maria Jolas (Boston: Beacon Press 1994), p. xxvi.

hut standing alone in the woods is the ultimate image of centralized solitude. Now how different from the world of the hut is the world of Tiepolo's sky?

Everyone is busy in Tiepolo's paintings: They are usually carrying something or someone, standing guard, or dispensing justice. But Tiepolo has given them all intimate immensity, to use Bachelard's phrase, to move around in. The world of Tiepolo is an ecstatic one. The ecstatic habitation in Tiepolo's paintings is grounded in real densities and physical weight. This is what gives his world veracity, and it is part of the tension in his work that makes it alive. Thinking about the paintings of Titian, Tintoretto, and Tiepolo, one wonders how much the weight of water – and its constant presence as a force of destruction as well as protection of Venice – led to a kind of ecstatic movement upward in their compositions, not unlike the upward movements in the music of Venice's famous composer Vivaldi.

THRESHOLDS

We can't see light; we see what light reveals.

FIGURE 6.14 Pieter de Hooch, *The Asparagus Vendor* 1675–80, oil on canvas, 30 × 40 in., Minneapolis Institute of Art. Gift of Charles and Margaret Sweatt. 82.46 Web Figure 8. Photo courtesy of Minneapolis Institute of Art.

Pieter de Hooch's *The Asparagus Vendor*, painted in Amsterdam (1675–80), depicts a popular theme in Dutch painting in the mid seventeenth century: celebrating the nuclear family and the role of orderly domestic duties as a priority for the good of society as a whole. The figure in the center of the painting, the mistress of the house, is oriented in two directions. From the shoulders down, she is turning to greet the asparagus seller at the open door, her hand held open with coins. But her head is turned toward the man descending the dark staircase in a deep vermillion red kimono (a detail to signal the Dutch trade with the East). It's a meeting of commerce with the home, a household moving in an ordinary day, everyone but the maidservant poised for personal acknowledgement.

The maidservant, tucked along the back wall between a window and cabinet, sits sewing. Her head, tilted slightly down, is brightly illuminated by the light streaming downward through the transform windows high above her; the wall above her head is the same color as the sky seen above the trees outside the door.

The brightness of the light brings us here, and this is true of many of De Hooch's paintings. There is considerable attention paid to the light and leaded partitions in the casement window closest to the maidservant. The light in this window is different in hue and value. The light on the wall coming through the transform windows is cool and fast on the white wall, as it is in the sky beyond. It has a violet tinge. The light in the window next to the maidservant fills a space more slowly with a yellow-rose color, a more intimate color that feels closer to her and to us as viewers.

There is a vividness in what is revealed here, this extremely careful attentive control of temperature and brightness. This is where the painter lives, at this threshold, calling attention to the intimate shelter of the family inside while reminding us, through glimpses, of a beautiful freedom we sometimes experience under the dome of the sky. Just as the mistress beholds and attends to the asparagus seller and her husband by means that can't be measured, only felt, so too the painter brings us to the light gathering at this window and to the light of the air outside, and we behold both beauties simultaneously.

But why is this threshold so moving? Light, without weight but which we turn to for its life-giving energies, gathers at the most vulnerable place – where the outside meets and either threatens or blesses what is inside. In this way, light gains weight. This material poetics reveal those places in the psyche where we are neither completely protected from the world nor restricted to the confinement of the known. The desire to live at this threshold is a religious impulse, what the philosopher Boethius called Insight. It is the desire to hold the particular with the universal simultaneously, without striving and perfectly whole.

In De Hooch's painting we find ourselves at the threshold of those forces, both material and mysterious, whose scale we cannot measure.

STEPPING BACK AND MOVING FORWARD

We have largely been concerned with the visual arts' power to reveal and conceal elements of the sacred, and with our relationship to the sacred. If it turns out that the world of Christian theism is true, or even more specifically, if the Roman Catholic teachings about Mary and Christ are true, then these religious paintings – of Mary and the Christ child, the wondrous nature of the cross, the assumption of Mary, the portrait of Jesus in a state of dereliction after the crucifixion – may all count as authentic disclosures of what they are depicting.

As we have observed earlier, a revelation need not be backed up by convincing evidence to count as a revelation. Moreover, we suggest that a work of art that accurately reflects some aspect of the sacred may be genuinely disclosive even if the artist does not herself believe in the disclosure. Christian theology has traditionally been quite open to how a divine disclosure can occur even if the agent involved has no conception of the divine. In the *Confessions*, Augustine writes about hearing a child singing "tolle lege" ("take up and read"), which he interprets as a message from Heaven. Without thinking that the child is intending to be a messenger from God, Augustine interprets the invocation as sacred and this leads him to take up and read Paul's Epistle to the Romans 13:13. Hearing that singing was the moment of his conversion.[14] In their fine book *Picturing the Apocalypse*, Natasha O'Hear and Anthony O'Hear write about St. John (according to tradition, the "beloved disciple," and author of The Book of Revelation). They write:

Although it may be difficult for a sceptical modern reader to accept that John was the recipient of visions from Heaven, all one has to accept in reading Revelation is that the man responsible for writing the text *felt* himself to be experiencing visions. In that sense he did have visions from some source or other – maybe from God, maybe not – but whichever way, visions which he then felt an overwhelming urge to record and to communicate. Far from distinguishing him as a madman, this capacity for visionary experience actually places John of Patmos within a long and distinguished visionary tradition which included the Jewish prophets Daniel and Ezekiel.[15]

---

[14] Some philosophers have contended that for a person to perceive some object, X, X itself must be causally involved in the perceiving (for example, to visually see the Statue of Liberty, the statue itself must play some causal role in the visual observation). In reply, religious experience may rightly be seen as more permeable than observing discrete physical objects; after all, the God of Abrahamic faiths, Brahman in Hinduism, and the Compassionate Buddha are not limited by circumscribable locations. In the case of Augustine, God may be understood as being able to use almost limitless channels to speak to the future Bishop of Hippo. See *Divine Discourse: Philosophical Reflection on the Claim That God Speaks* by Nicholas Wolterstorff (Cambridge: Cambridge University Press, 1995).

[15] Natasha O'Hear and Anthony O'Hear, *Picturing the Apocalypse: The Book of Revelation in the Arts over Two Millennia* (Oxford: Oxford University Press, 2017), p. 17.

Stepping Back and Moving Forward 137

Some Christian philosophers contend that for revelation to be credibly believed it needs confirmation by a miracle.[16] But this is not universal. Thomas Aquinas thought that no miracle was necessary.[17] John Henry Newman proposed that the reasons for accepting revelation may rest on a combination of factors, including an appreciation for its desirability:

> The Word of Life is offered to a man, and, on its being offered, he has Faith in it. Why? On these two grounds, the word of its human messenger, and the likelihood of the message. And why does he feel the message to be probable? Because he has a love for it, his love being strong, though the testimony is weak. He has a keen sense of the intrinsic excellence of the message, of its desirableness, of its likeness to what it is to him Divine Goodness would vouchsafe did He vouchsafe any, of the need of a Revelation and its probability.[18]

We suggest that traditions of revelation in the different world religions need not be exclusive. We see a deep complementarity between Christian revelation claims and the Hindu portrait of Krishna in the Gita and the Compassion of the Buddha. The portraits of Mary and Jesus would resonate with the Islamic understanding of Jesus and Mary.[19]

Our thesis, then, is that if one or more of the religious worlds is true (or contains important truths) then the works of art we have studied may carry authentic, revelatory content about the divine; they may function as that through which we may experience the sacred. It also needs to be ceded that if secular naturalism turns out to be true, then the visual arts in the Christian tradition and other nonnaturalistic traditions would not be revelations or divine disclosures. In that eventuality, Sigmund Freud's *Civilization and Its Discontents* (according to which the desire for the divine is regressive and distorting) would count as far more disclosive of the human condition than the best paintings of Tiepolo. From the standpoint of secular naturalism, the novella *Death in Venice* by Thomas Mann may be more revelatory than the Venetian paintings we have engaged in this chapter.

Our focus in this chapter has been the visual arts (partly because one of us is a painter), but of course there are other sensory mediums that can function with great power to conceal or reveal our identity and the sacred. In the Abrahamic faiths, Hinduism, and Buddhism, music is of overwhelming significance.[20] In

---

[16] Richard Swinburne, *Revelation* (Oxford: Oxford University Press, 2007), pp. 111–112.
[17] Aquinas, *Quodlibetal Questions*, Q.2, A.4.
[18] John Henry Newman, *Oxford University Sermons*, Sermon XI, "The Nature of Faith in Revelation to Reason" (London: Longmans, Green and Co., 1909), pp. 202–203.
[19] On the compatibility of many revelation traditions, see R. C. Zaehner's *At Sundry Times: An Essay in the Comparison of Religions* (London: Faber and Faber, 1958).
[20] In *The Oxford Handbook of Religion and the Arts*, edited by Frank Burch Brown (Oxford: Oxford University Press, 2014), see the "Musical Ways of Being Religious" by F. B. Brown, chapter 7; "Judaism and Music" by Mark Klegman, chapter 15; "Christianity and Music" by Paul Westermeyer, chapter 19; "Islam and Music" by Amon Shiloah, chapter 23; "Hinduism and Music" by Guy Beck, chapter 26. As Brown points out in chapter 7, while many religious

Christian tradition, St. Francis of Assisi, Gertrude More, and Richard Rolle stand out as fostering a musically mediated experience of the divine. In his book *The Fire of Love* (*Incendium Amoris*) Rolle, a fourteenth-century English mystic, identifies music as one of the three portals by which God was experienced. In her classic work, *Mysticism*, Evelyn Underhill offers this rich portrait of Rolle's spirituality:

> Rolle's own experience of mystic joy seems actually to have come to him in this form: the perceptions of his exalted consciousness presenting themselves to his understanding under musical conditions, as other mystics have received them in the form of pictures or words. I give in his own words the classic description of his passage from the first state of "burning love" to the second state of "songful love" ... when "into song of joy meditation is turned." "In the night, before supper, as I my psalms sung, as it were the sound of readers or rather singers about me I beheld. Whilst, also praying, to heaven with all desire I took heed, suddenly, in what manner I wot not, in me the sound of song I felt; and likeliest heavenly melody I took, with me dwelling in mind. Forsooth my thought continually to mirth of song was changed, and my meditation to praise turned; and my prayers and psalm-saying, in sound I showed."[21]

In Chapter 7 we revisit an essential element of aesthetic personalism, the essential reality of ourselves and our subjective, aesthetic experiences, and then consider how some works of art may be viewed through the lens of the relationship between the mental and physical, minds and bodies.

---

traditions teach about the danger of music (it can be used to arouse damaging emotions), few religious traditions have shunned music altogether, the exceptions being early Buddhism, some forms of radical Protestantism, and so on. For a Christian theology of music, see *The Extravagance of Music: An Art Open to God* by David Brown and Gavin Hopps (New York: Palgrave Macmillan, 2018) and *Theological Aesthetics: God in Imagination, Beauty, and Art* by Richard Viladesau (Oxford: Oxford University Press, 1999).

[21] Evelyn Underhill, *Mysticism*, p. 56. Rolle, along with Walter Hilton, the author of *The Cloud of Unknowing*, Julian of Norwich, and Margery Kemp, are often thought to have created the Golden Age of English mysticism.

7

Public Perception of Religious and Art Objects

> To know is thus ... to unveil and comprehend the beings in question and their world.
>
> Henry Corbin[1]

In Chapters 1 through 3, we compared the aesthetic visibility and invisibility of God and persons and introduced a substantial, high view of human persons as able to encounter the transcendent experientially. In Chapter 4 we undertook an aesthetic investigation into a series of religious worlds and their secular alternatives; in Chapter 5 we reflected on the religious significance of beauty; and in Chapter 6 we reflected on how works of art can conceal or reveal secular and sacred values.

In this chapter we begin by exploring how some religious artifacts can bring the visible and the invisible into concord. We then take two steps: affirming our substantial understanding of the self at the heart of aesthetic personalism and presenting the idea that some religious artifacts and artworks can function with a life of their own. The reason to take these two steps is that while we do not think that works of art are persons as you and I are, we think that some works of art can function as persons or have a personal presence. In our experience of the artworks, we are interested in this personal aspect of works of art, not because we propose that (like corporations) works of art should be granted rights, but because we think that some works of art can be understood in terms of a mind–body relationship. Some works of art display a fitting aesthetic integration of mind (purpose, intent, desire) and body (material or sensory constitution). This chapter concludes with an analysis of an exhibition of art that failed to bring a cohesive integration of the visible and the invisible, persons and a work of art;

---

[1] Henry Corbin, *The Voyage and the Messenger: Iran and Philosophy* (Berkeley, CA: North Atlantic Books, 1998), p. xix.

and we then highlight an exhibition of artwork we propose would gratify even an aesthetic ideal observer.

THE MARRIAGE OF THE INVISIBLE AND THE VISIBLE

There are at least three modes in which the mind, or person, may be made visible in works of art: the allegorical, the symbolic or sacramental, and embodiment. In *The Allegory of Love*, C. S. Lewis compares allegory and what he refers to as symbolism or sacramentalism. On allegory, Lewis writes:

> It is of the very nature of thought and language to represent what is immaterial in picturable terms. What is good or happy has always been high like the heavens and bright like the sun. Evil and misery were deep and dark from the first. ... To ask how these married pairs or sensible and insensibles first came together would be great folly; the real question is how they ever came apart. ... This fundamental equivalence between the immaterial and the material may be used by the mind in two ways. ... On the one hand you can start with an immaterial fact, such as the passions which you actually experience, and then can then invent *visibilia* to express them. ... This is allegory.[2]

Lewis himself composed an allegory called *The Pilgrim's Regress*, a 1933 novel depicting a journey to Christian faith through paganism, materialism, and idealism, modeled on the seventeenth-century work *The Pilgrim's Progress* by John Bunyan.[3] For Lewis, allegories can be illuminating and fitting (as in Edmund Spenser's *The Faerie Queene*), or they can be hampered when allegorical figures are mismatched. Lewis objected to the battle scenes in Prudentius' early fifth-century Latin work *Psychomachia*, in which Patience and Mercy engage in mortal combat with the vices.[4] Lewis seemed ready to accept that Courage might be allegorized as a warrior, but he had no love for picturing virtues using swords to kill vices as when Chastity kills Lust! Lewis praises a more synthesized representation of the visible and the invisible:

> But there is another way of using the equivalence, which is almost the opposite of allegory, and which I could call sacramentalism or symbolism. If our passions, being immaterial, can be copied by material inventions, then it is possible that our material world in turn is the copy of an invisible world, of something else. The attempt to read that something else through its sensible imitations, to see the archetype in the copy is what I mean by symbolism or sacramentalism. ... The allegorist leaves the given – his own passions – to talk of that which is confessedly less real ... a fiction. The symbolist leaves the given (the material world) to find that which is more real. Symbolism comes to us from Greece. It makes its first appearance ... with the dialogues of Plato. The Sun is the

---

[2] C. S. Lewis, *The Allegory of Love* (Oxford: Oxford University Press, 1936), pp. 44–45.
[3] There is a new annotated version of Lewis' work, *The Pilgrim's Regress: Wade Annotated Edition*, edited by David Downing (Grand Rapids: Eerdman, 2014).
[4] *The Allegory of Love*, pp. 68–69. For an analysis, see Aparajita Nanda's "The Battle Rages On: The Pyschomachia and the Faerie Queene, Book 1" in *Renaissance Essays*, edited by S. Chaudhuri (Oxford: Oxford University Press, 1995).

The Marriage of the Invisible and the Visible

copy of the Good. Time is the moving image of eternity. All visible things exist just insofar as they succeed in imitating the Forms.[5]

This symbolist aesthetic provides a material context or site for that which is transcendent. This form of representation goes beyond allegory. For example, Beatrice in Dante's fourteenth-century epic poem *The Divine Comedy* is not just an allegorical figure (love), but also a person who interceded for Dante and through whom (with the help of Virgil) Dante the pilgrim is able to experience the divine. The figure Beatrice is based on a real person whom Dante describes meeting in his *La Vita Nuova*. The work may rightly be seen as a Christian allegory. But it is not mere allegory (as in Bunyan's characters Giant Despair, Hopeful, Good-Will, Mr. Worldly Wiseman); many of Dante's figures were flesh-and-blood persons, from Beatrice, Paolo and Francesca to the host of named persons in Hell, Purgatory, and Paradise.[6]

A third option for integrating the visible and the invisible occurs when the visible is not just a representation or imitation or symbol of what is beyond, but when it is also an integrated embodiment of person (mind) and body. This is our own view of human embodiment (as noted in chapters two and three). When we are mentally healthy and function honestly as unified persons, then our bodies do not point to the invisible, but we ourselves become visible in healthy embodiment.

Unfortunately, those who share our view that there is more to persons than our bodies sometimes fail to stress the functional unity of integrated life. For example, in *Are We Bodies or Souls?* Richard Swinburne offers the following account of embodiment:

What is it to have a body? It is to have a chunk of matter through which one can make a difference to the physical world (for example, by opening a door by grasping it with one's hand and pulling), and through which one learns about the world (for example, by light impinging on one's eyes and sound waves impinging on one's ears, and one's nerves transmitting signals from eyes and ears to the brain).[7]

We do not deny that the two elements Swinburne identifies as agency and knowledge are vital for embodiment. But Swinburne does not stress that, under healthy conditions the union of mind (or person) and body form a whole, unified being. It would be useful to expand the above account by

---

[5] Ibid., pp. 45–46.
[6] Taliaferro addresses how religious experience or the perception of the divine can be mediated by symbolic representations in "Religious Rites" in *The Cambridge Companion to Christian Philosophical Theology*, edited by Charles Taliaferro and Chad Meister (Cambridge: Cambridge University Press, 2009), pp. 183–200. See especially "The virtues of symbolic reference," pp. 187–190.
[7] Richard Swinburne, *Are We Bodies or Souls?* (Oxford: Oxford University Press, 2019), pp. 73–74. While we register some reservation on Swinburne's view of embodiment, we enthusiastically support many of Swinburne's views on the soul and personal identity.

stressing that we suffer and rejoice, receive nourishment and undergo deprivation as embodied persons.

Although we were critical of Roger Scruton's philosophy of the self in Chapter 3, we commend his portrait of the way in which persons can come to be revealed to each other in sexual intimacy. In his book *Sexual Desire*, Scruton reflects on how healthy sexual embodiment involves a unity of person and body that is like the unity of God and flesh, as imaged in the Christian view of the incarnation.

> That, I believe, is the real mystery of incarnation. It is part of the genius of Christianity that it invites us to understand the relation between God and his creation in terms of a mystery that we have, so to speak, continually between our hands. The mystery that we confront in the sexual act, we can neither resolve nor abjure. No first-person perspective can bear the identity of a person, nor can it be united with the only thing – the body – in which individuality is revealed to us. And yet, so powerful is the paroxysm of desire that it seems to me as though the very transparency of your self is, for a moment, revealed on the surface of your body, in a mysterious union that can be touched but never comprehended. Those parts of the body which remain dark to me are dark only with the shadow cast by the flame of your self. This burning of the soul in the flesh – the llama de amor viva of St John of the Cross – is the symbol of all mystic unions, and the true reason for the identity of imagery between the poetry of desire and the poetry of worship. The unity which I endeavour to elicit from you is one which I seek also to enact in myself. We are engaged in an impossible but necessary enterprise. We are attempting to unite our bodies with a non-existent 'owner', who is unable to possess the individuality for which he craves, but who sustains the illusion of his own existence, as a reflection in the glass of another's eye. In this resides the true significance of the 'involuntary' self-expressions which, I argued, form the initial focus of desire. The smile that draws me on is of flesh and blood. The desire to kiss it is the desire to plant my lips, not to a mouth, but to a smile: to a portion of the body into which I have summoned the other's perspective. A smile is indeed the food of love, while a mouth can be the food of love only for someone whose rage has turned desire to appetite.[8]

We suggest that such an integrated, healthy wholeness or, under the opposite condition, a total lack of unification can be evident not just in sexual intimacy, but throughout one's personal life. Works of art can also be integrated or heavily conflicted in ways that are analogous to the way we persons can be integrated or conflicted.

PERSONS AND WORKS OF ART

Some philosophers have proposed that persons can or should be seen as works of art. We suggest that this may be helpful, but it comes with complex, sometimes unhelpful implications. For example, it may encourage taking an abstract, detached aesthetic approach to oneself and action. There may be

---

[8] Roger Scruton, *Sexual Desire: A Philosophical Investigation* (London: Continuum, 2006), p. 128.

times, though, when it is fitting to regard some relationships (such as marriage) or skills (excellence in cooking) as works of art or arts. But one view we oppose is a deflationary thesis, according to which persons are likened to works of art analogous to fictional characters in novels. Philosopher Daniel Dennett adopts such an approach.

According to Dennett, to be a self, you do not need to actually be a conscious, enduring, experiencing subject. Persons or selves are not so much substances or things, he says, but we are abstract interpretations of the behavior of ourselves and others. He assimilates being a self to the idea that physical objects have a center of gravity: While we all posit that ordinary physical objects have a center of gravity, he maintains, this is part of our interpretation of the behavior of such objects. Thus "the center of gravity" is not itself a thing or substance. It refers to the concentrated weight of a body and its being subject to gravitational forces. Dennett says we posit that objects have a center of gravity to account for how objects behave in a gravitational field. Similarly, according to Dennett, our concept of being a self is something posited to explain behavior rather than something that has an evident self-awareness. He writes:

A self is ... an abstract object, a theorist's fiction. The theory is not particle physics but what we might call a branch of people-physics: it is more soberly known as a phenomenology or hermeneutics, or soul-science. ... The physicist does an *interpretation*, if you like, of the chair and its behavior, and comes up with the theoretical abstraction of a center of gravity, which is then very useful in characterizing the behavior of the chair in the future, under a wide variety of conditions. The hermeneuticist or phenomenologist – or anthropologist – sees some rather more complicated things moving about in the world – human beings and animals – and is faced with a similar problem of interpretation. It turns out to be theoretically perspicuous to organize the interpretation around a central abstraction: each person has a *self* (in addition to a center of gravity). In fact we have to posit selves for *ourselves as well*. The theoretical problem of self-interpretation is at least as difficult and important as the problem of other-identification.[9]

Dennett understands us as narrative beings. Our individual lives have a narrative unity as we posit that we each have a self that helps us to explain our own and others' behavior. But for all that, a self is, like a center of gravity, not a substantial individual thing.

We propose not just that Dennett's proposal is counter to our bedrock experience of ourselves as individuals, but also that his framework of inquiry is flawed from the start. We are able to identify or interpret the behavior of others only if we know who we are as individuals. Imagine someone points to someone or something moving about in the world and claims, rhetorically, how would you explain *that* without positing some (perhaps invisible) self? How would you know what *that* refers to without knowing that *that* refers to *that which the speaker is drawing your attention to?* The meaning and reference of

---

[9] Daniel Dennett, "The Self as a Center of Narrative Gravity," in *Philosophia*, 15, pp. 275–288. 1986. Available online: https://ase.tufts.edu/cogstud/dennett/papers/selfctr.pdf

indexical terms like *this*, *that*, *here*, and *there* are only understandable if the speaker and hearer are distinct, conscious, individual, real (nonfictitious) subjects who can communicate what to attend to. Without being aware of yourself as a self, how would you even know when or if you are being addressed? For us to even understand Dennett's proposal that we should try to explain behavior of those animals or things roving about, we will need to have an antecedent awareness of who we are and who is proposing we explain what is occurring.

The fundamental primacy of our first-person awareness is evident when considering the implausibility of its denial by various philosophers. Antony Kenny writes, "The self ... is a mythical entity ... a piece of philosopher's nonsense consisting in a misunderstanding of the reflexive pronoun."[10] Elizabeth Anscombe claims that to treat the first person "I" as referring to a self is a "grammatical illusion."[11] Various philosophers have proposed that rather than Descartes being able to assert "I think, therefore I am," he should have claimed as a basic, first step: "This thing thinks."[12] David Armstrong has claimed that a mental state can no more be conscious of itself than a person can eat himself.[13]

We propose that each of these proposals may be seen to be false. How can there be a myth or illusion, unless there is a myth or illusion *for someone*? There cannot be some "grammatical illusion" floating abroad, so to speak, without it being *an illusion to persons*. The proposal that Descartes would be better off claiming "this thing thinks" faces the problem that without evident self-awareness no one would know what *this* refers to. (As an aside, we suggest that if someone in ordinary life started referring to oneself with an indexical "this thing" – saying, for example, "this thing is hungry" – that person would probably be understood as trying to make a joke or not understanding the language or suffering from some strange dissociative disorder). On Armstrong's rather colorful account about mental states and self-cannibalization, we respond that *mental states* are not the sorts of things that can be self-aware. *Persons* are aware of themselves. The mental state of awareness is not (and cannot be) self-aware because mental states are not selves. We conclude Armstrong's proposed analogy is wrong.[14]

If we are very different from fictional objects, can we make any sense of the idea that works of art might still be like persons?

---

[10] Antony Kenny, *The Self* (Marquette: Marquette University Press, 1988), p. 4.
[11] G. E. M. Anscombe, "The First Person" in *Mind and Language*, edited by S. Guttenplan (Oxford: Clarendon Press, 1975), p. 65.
[12] For an overview of these attempts to circumvent the evidence of first-person self-awareness, see Lynne Baker's *Naturalism and the First Person Perspective*.
[13] D. M. Armstrong, *A Materialist Theory of the Mind* (London: Routledge, 1993).
[14] For a compelling case for the reality of self-awareness, see Roderick Chilsholm's *Person and Object*, chapter 1, "The Direct Awareness of the Self" (La Salle: Open Court Publishing Company, 1976).

Persons and Works of Art

Recent philosophy of art and artifacts has been more open to the notion that some works of art can and should be thought of as persons or person-like beings. As Alfred Gell and others have argued, works of art can be experienced as though they are persons with desires, intentions, demands, and the like.[15] What sorts of desires and intentions? Very often, the desire for your attention, as W. J. T. Michell contends in *What Do Pictures Want? The Lives and Loves of Images*.[16] But more than that, intentions expressed in works of art may be distinctly religious, as Crispin Paine has proposed: a statue of the Buddha may invite persons to worship or meditate. Indeed, perhaps because of this animate aspect of religious objects, some museums have sought to accommodate religious devotion or at least have endeavored to cultivate respect for museum objects as religious or sacred objects.[17] As the art historian and Museum Studies scholar Carol Duncan has observed, some museums can function as temples in which visitors are sometimes invited to undertake a ritual act:

> [The ritual] is seen as transformative: it confers or renews identity or restores order in the self or to the world through sacrifice, ordeal, or enlightenment. The beneficial outcome that museum rituals are supposed to produce can sound very like claims made for traditional, religious rituals. According to their advocates, museum visitors come away with a sense of enlightenment, or a feeling of having been spiritually nourished or restored.[18]

This phenomenon suggests that persons can ritually interact with artifacts, which (either as themselves or as objects that mediate some sacred reality) can bring about personal change. Anthropologist Janet Hoskins rightly highlights the experience of art objects as having an agency of their own:

> Art is about doing things, that it is a system of social action – and that we have to look at how people act through objects by distributing parts of their personhood into things. These things have agency because they produce effects, they cause us to be happy, angry, fearful or lustful.[19]

---

[15] Alfred Gell, *Art and Agency: An Anthropological Theory* (Oxford: Clarendon Press, 1988). See also Randall Dipert's *Artifacts, Art Works, and Agency* (Philadelphia: Temple University Press, 1993) and Susan Pearce's *Museums, Objects, and Collections* (Washington, DC: Smithsonian Books, 1993).

[16] W. J. T. Michell, *What Do Pictures Want? The Lives and Loves of Images* (Chicago: University of Chicago Press, 2006).

[17] For background, see Crispin Paine's "Museums and Religion: A Quick Overview" in *Museums and Faith*, edited by Rosemarie Beir-de-Hahn and Marie-Paule Jungblut (Luxembourg: Musee d'Historire de la Ville de Luxembourg, 2010); "Sacred to Profane and Back Again," by Ivan Gaskell, in *Art and Its Public: Museum Studies at the Millennium*, edited by Andrew McClellan (Oxford: Blackwell, 2003); "Ritual," by Ronald Grimes, *Material Religion: The Journal of Objects: Art and Belief*, 7/1, 2011, pp. 77–83; "The Sacred and the Profane: The Need for Sensitivity in Using Ethnographic Resources in Education," by Moira Simpson, *Journal for Museum Ethnography*, 10, 1998.

[18] Carol Duncan, *Civilizing Rituals inside Public Art Museums* (London: Routledge, 1995), p. 13.

[19] Janet Hoskins, "Agency, Biography and Objects" in *Handbook of Material Cultures*, edited by D. Tilley et al. (Los Angeles: Sage Publications, 2006), p. 78.

Is this talk – of religious artifacts as sacred persons or person-like forces that can be enlightening – merely a metaphor? Perhaps it is indeed metaphorical usage, but if so the metaphor seems to be alive (as opposed to a dead metaphor) and has descriptive, referential content. Richard Davis observes:

> Objects have life-stories just as humans do. Many objects are born and live their entire lives without leaving their own villages – just as many humans do. But some objects experience lives of travel and change, disruption and transformation, influence and celebrity, and it is the lives of such mutable objects that make for the most interesting biographies.[20]

As Julian Thomas points out:

> A keystone of the phenomenological approach is the understanding that the "subjective" aspects of experience are not superficial elements constructed on the bedrock of invariant materiality, but are the means through which the material world reveals itself to us.[21]

And in his excellent book *Religious Objects in Museums: Private Lives and Public Duties*, Crispin Paine has articulated a convincing portrait of how some religious artifacts behave in museums: They make demands on visitors and curators, they call for respect, and they respond to other objects and persons. Moreover, Paine describes the way curators can subvert and redirect the intentions and the character of religious artifacts.

We readily admit that there are times in the history of art when artworks have been more widely recognized as person-like. In *The Lives of Paintings*, Elsje van Kessel explores the social lives of paintings in sixteenth-century Venice. In one example she follows the cult that forms around a portrait of a Venetian woman, Bianco Capello, who married the Florentine heir to the grand-ducal throne, Francesco de' Medici. The portrait, which she presents as a gift to her Venetian friend Francesco Bembo, was visited by hundreds of people at Bembo's house. It even made its way to the Doge's Palace where it was invited to dinner and then spent the night in the Doge's apartments. The real Bianco Capello in Florence comes to have a real presence and influence in Venice through her portrait. Van Kessel concludes:

> Paintings in sixteenth-century Venice often acted as living objects, in the sense that they participated in society. Notwithstanding official church dogma, they interacted with human beings in all kinds of ways: they received visitors and attracted pilgrims; they healed and saved people; they made money; they had people fall in love with them; they provoked aggression and were victims of violence; they worked as agents of artists, of

---

[20] Richard Davis, "The Dancing Shiva of Shivapuram: Cult and Exhibition in the Life of an Indian Icon" in *A Place for Meaning: Art, Faith and Museum Culture*, edited by Amanda Millay Hughes and Carolyn Wood (Chapel Hill, NC: Auckland Art Museum, 2009), p. 82. See also Davis' *Lives of Indian Images* (Princeton: Princeton University Press, 1997).

[21] Julian Thomas, "Phenomenology and Material Culture" in *Handbook of Material Culture*, edited by Chris Tilley et al. (Los Angeles: Sage Publications, 2006), p. 57.

noble families and princely courts; they were beaten; they were kissed and caressed. Therefore, we may consider them as person-like.[22]

We propose that the best case for treating religious artifacts as persons or person-like agents is phenomenological. That is, in experience. Sometimes with some objects, we experience them as subjects or agents.[23] In her museum studies, Susan Pearce cites a label in a Newfoundland museum: "When you look at an artifact, you are looking at a person's thought."[24] This may well be a way of proposing that you are seeing the manifestation or expression of the artist's thinking, but it also suggests that you can look at thought by looking at a work of art. The position we are advancing shares with Susanne Langer's philosophy of art the idea that some works of art can make subjective feeling visible. Langer writes about the appearance of a work of art:

> This image, though it is a created apparition, a pure appearance, is objective; it is charged with feeling because its form expresses the very nature of feeling. Therefore, it is as *objectification of subjective life*, and so is every other work of art.[25]

Some qualifications: We are not likening all works of art to persons or saying that they are all person-like. We are only claiming that in our experience some religious artifacts and artworks appear to have such a quality. This is a claim about ourselves and our experience. So, our view does not entail that the wrongful destruction of some person-like religious artifact is akin to murder – though we have some sympathy with the poet John Milton's admonition to the book-burners of his day that to burn a book is akin to burning the author.[26]

---

[22] Elsje van Kessel, *The Lives of Paintings: Presence, Agency and Likeness in Venetian Art of the Sixteenth Century* (Boston/Berlin/Leiden : Walter de Gruyter Inc. Copublished by Leiden University Press, 2017), p. 225.

[23] James Elkins records many contemporary cases of persons experiencing art works in terms of personal presence in *Pictures and Tears; A History of People Who Have Cried in Front of Paintings* (New York: Routledge, 2004).

[24] Cited by Crispin Paine, *Religious Objects in Museums: Private Lives and Public Duties* (London: Bloomsbury, 2013), p. 15.

[25] Susanne Langer, *Problems of Art* (New York: Charles Scribner's Sons, 1957), p. 9.
We are not committing ourselves here to Langer's philosophy of mind. For our appreciative but critical understanding of Langer, see our *The Image in Mind*.

[26] A reader of an earlier draft of our philosophy of art wondered whether we were advancing a superstitious animism ("a sort of voodoo") or whether our view would invite an absurd spectacle of works of art qua persons dying and being resurrected on a regular basis. One way to correct this macabre criticism is to align ourselves in the company of John Dewey's art as experience. We give more weight than Dewey does to the material reality of works of art, but we share his stress on *aesthetic experience*. We are not proposing, for example, that a statue of the Compassionate Buddha is literally hearing the petitions of the faithful, but that religious practitioners may experience the Compassionate Buddha in the course of experiencing the statue. In terms of the categories spelled out at the beginning of this chapter, the statue may be experienced akin to engaging an allegorical figure, or the statue may be experienced as a symbol or as an embodiment of Buddha's compassion. By way of a further clarification of our position, we do not accept the so-called Chicago school of criticism that

Still, the experience of the personhood of some religious artifacts and artworks may help explain our urgency to protect them from destruction.

Consider the two Buddha statues carved into a sandstone cliff during the fifth century in Bamiyan in central Afghanistan. At 174 and 115 feet tall, they were the largest Buddha statues in the world until their destruction by the Taliban in 2001. The predominant reason given for their destruction was that they were not Islamic (or were an insult to Islam), notwithstanding tolerance of the statues since the Islamic invasion in the seventh century. There are abundant reasons why the statues should not have been destroyed in terms of world heritage and respect for Buddhists, including the many Buddhists who once thrived in monasteries next to the statues. We submit that they also should not have been destroyed because they are experienced as persons or person-like beings. Just as we have a prima facie duty to rescue innocent persons, there was a prima facie duty to rescue these statues from destruction. In fact, as part of the evidence that the duty to rescue is operative in the minds of many, news of the impending destruction sparked worldwide protests (including protests from Islamic states such as Saudi Arabia, the United Arab Emirates, and India with its substantial Muslim population). The threat brought offers to transport the statues (to Japan, among other places) to prevent their demise. Since the dynamiting of the statues, there has been some dialogue about rebuilding or recreating these statues. The idea that the statues are themselves persons or person-like beings helps explain the desire to resurrect the statues.

Let us now consider two exhibitions of works of art and how the integration or failure of integration of person and artwork occurs.

Scaffold

In 2012 the American artist Sam Durant created *Scaffold*, a two-story, open-frame sculpture, built with 51,000 pounds of wood. He based its design on seven different gallows used in seven high-profile hanging executions in the United States between 1859 and 2006. It consisted of raised platforms, which could hold several people, with wooden staircases on each side. Only one staircase allowed access to the platforms; the others hovered several feet off the ground. The whole structure, supported by steel beams, created a feeling of levitation, further emphasizing the content of hanging. It was exhibited in Europe in three locations before being purchased by Walker Art Center in Minneapolis, Minnesota, in 2014. The disassembled sculpture was put in storage until it could be placed in Walker's collection in the redesigned eleven-acre Minneapolis Sculpture Garden.

One source for the design of the sculpture was the gallows used in the hanging of thirty-eight Dakota men in Mankato, Minnesota, in 1862 in the

---

rules out any role for an artist's intentions in assessing the meaning and value of works of art. See Colin Lyas' *Aesthetics* (New York: Taylor & Francis, 1997).

aftermath of the U.S.–Dakota War in Minnesota. After the war, 303 Dakota men were tried in military court and convicted of raping and murdering civilians. The Minnesota governor sent a letter to President Abraham Lincoln requesting the right to execute all of them. President Lincoln sanctioned the execution of thirty-eight men. The Mankato hanging remains the largest mass execution in United States history.

The public had been witnessing the construction of the sculpture for weeks. Days before the sculpture garden was to reopen, protests of *Scaffold*'s presence began. The director of Walker Art Center sent an open letter to *The Circle*, a Twin Cities newspaper that serves the Native American community. In the letter she apologized for not involving the Dakota community in the placement of the sculpture. The letter was then posted on Walker's website, which announced to the public that the work was based partly on the 1862 hanging of the Dakota men.

American Indians arriving to see the work, visible behind steel-mesh barricades until the sculpture garden would reopen, were flabbergasted by what they saw. Most of the Native American protesters interviewed said they didn't see art when they looked at the sculpture; they recognized the tall pole in the middle of the platform, a detail from the gallows built in 1862, and saw exactly that – the gallows where their ancestors had been hanged. Sheldon Wolfchild saw the sculpture. A filmmaker and descendent of Wakan Ozanzan (Medicine Bottle) who was one of two Dakota warriors hung at Fort Snelling in 1865, Wolfchild said:

Generational trauma comes directly back into yourself and what our young people face. … We have the highest suicide rate for our young people. What are our children going to say when they see that scaffold? They have no other place to go but to think about killing themselves.[27]

The protests of *Scaffold* by the Native American community had many layers that are still unresolved even as Native and non-Native artists and audiences have sought to understand what led up to the initial purchase and placement of *Scaffold*, its final dismantling, and the copyright ownership turned over from the artist to the Dakota tribe. Many protesters pointed to the ignorance of non-Natives of Native history and the genocides suffered through colonization and war. Some saw its placement in-between the pop art sculptures of a giant spoon and cherry[28] and a giant blue rooster,[29] where visitors also spend summer hours playing mini-golf in artist-designed courses, as trivializing and dishonoring the history and trauma of the 1862 execution.

"What's happening with *Scaffold* is that we are waking up to the fact that we need our own Native people to represent our own Native Art," said Graci Horne, artist and curator, who helped organize the protests.[30]

---

[27] Hyperallergic.com, Sheila Regan, May 29, 2017.
[28] *Spoonbridge and Cherry* (1985–8), by Claes Oldenburg and Coosje van Bruggen.
[29] *Hahn/Cock* (2013), by Katharina Fritsch.
[30] Hyperallergic.com, Sheila Regan, May 29, 2017.

Representatives of Dakota Spiritual and Traditional Elders and of the four federally recognized Dakota tribes met with museum staff, city officials, and the artist. The Native people expressed why the work was not "art" to them and why it felt like the 1862 gallows itself was being honored. What's more, the piece was being erected on the ancestral homeland of the Dakota people.

Before that meeting took place, the artist, Sam Durant, posted statements on Walker's website about the intention of his work:

> It has been my belief that white artists need to address issues of white supremacy and its institutional manifestations. Whites created the concept of race and have used it to maintain dominance for centuries, whites must be involved in its dismantling. However, your protests have shown me that I made a grave miscalculation in how my work can be received by those in a particular community. In focusing on my position as a white artist making work for that audience [white audience] I failed to understand what the inclusion of the Dakota 38 in the sculpture could mean for Dakota people. I offer my deepest apologies for my thoughtlessness. I should have reached out to the Dakota community the moment I knew that the sculpture would be exhibited at the Walker Art Center in proximity to Mankato.[31]

This letter of apology does not answer the question of how artists and institutions should work with subject matter of oppressed groups to which they do not belong. Nor does it address questions about works of art that are taken out of one context and put into another.

When *Scaffold* was shown first at Documenta 13 in Kassel, Germany, in 2012, and then later in Scotland at Jupiter Artland and at The Hague in the Netherlands, the content was identical to the content in Minneapolis; only the context had changed. Is proximity of an artwork to past events of trauma the only question for us to consider?

On May 29, 2017, Chief Arvol Looking Horse said in a letter he would like to see the scaffold taken down as soon as possible, so people could live in peace. He wrote:

> For many years we have been riding horseback, walking and running to carry a message of healing to the site of the 38 Dakota plus two, where our relatives hung in Mankato, Minnesota. We are still healing from this tragedy, which was the largest execution in the United States of America. ... After great thought of this issue, I know that this man who created this structure has a good heart, but does not know any better. I am aware his understanding is different than our own culture, and in his view was trying to bring awareness. So now we have become aware of one another's boundaries in what we create to memorialize our loved ones.[32]

We propose that the trauma caused by *Scaffold* may be understood as a kind of person–body fracture. The artist's intention to dismantle white supremacy and

---

[31] https://walkerart.org/magazine/a-statement-from-sam-durant-05-29-17
[32] "'Scaffold' sculpture offends viewers, delays Sculpture Garden reopening," Michelle Bruch / Mbruch@Southwestjournal.com, May 29, 2017.

expose past crimes against Native Americans was lost in the work's damning message to Native audiences. While the sculpture functioned as less of a person-like object than the two Buddha statues, it was experienced by Native Americans as profoundly linked to the persons who are their ancestors, leading Dakota representatives' decision to bury the bones of the gallows at Bdote, a sacred place of creation.

From the standpoint of aesthetic personalism, the work failed to take into account the persons immediately impacted by its aesthetic force.

HEARTS OF OUR PEOPLE

Before *Scaffold* appeared in the sculpture garden in 2017, an exhibition called *Hearts of Our People: Native Women Artists* was being organized by the Minneapolis Institute of Art (Mia). Opened in 2019, it brought together 117 objects of art made by Native American women from antiquity to the present. The exhibit had the support and sponsorship of the Shakopee Mdewakanton Sioux Community. The show challenged the representation of Native women's art as secular and decorative. The catalogue for the exhibition ably presents the works as stemming from a holistic spirituality:

> The denial of the deeply intellectual and spiritual basis of Native women's arts is nowhere more evident than in the false distinctions made between the "sacred" and "secular" in Native arts. Such Western distinctions fail utterly to recognize the holistic nature of Indigenous philosophies and artistic expression in which spiritual dimensions are omnipresent.[33]

Several aspects of this exhibition broke with common museum practices. The first break with curatorial practice was the decision of the two cocurators[34] to form an advisory committee of twenty leading Native women artists. This committee worked with the curators over months and years to build consensus, select the art, and secure the lending of works to the exhibit. The second break with tradition was to make a very clear statement that when possible, the curators and advising committee would choose works of art that could be identified with individual makers. This broke with centuries of presenting objects from Native communities as "types" that stand in for different Native cultures and peoples. Instead, in *Hearts of Our People*, individual artists and makers are identified and celebrated. In Native culture, these artists and masters are known by their community, but rarely are recognized outside of it. And while most Native art is made by women, this is rarely acknowledged by the art world.

---

[33] *Hearts of Our People: Native Women Artists*, edited by Jill Ahlberg Yohe and Teri Greeves (Minneapolis: Minneapolis Institute of Art, 2020), p. 47. The terms "religion" and "religious" do not appear in the catalogue, but references to "spiritual" and "spirituality" are plentiful. See especially p. 22, 25, 37, 38, 44, 47.

[34] Jill Ahlberg Yohe at Mia, and Teri Greeves, Kiowa artist and scholar.

Throughout the exhibit, old and new works were juxtaposed to create lineage and to display how creativity and imagination are in constant play in the exhibit's art. There was a common sense among the recorded voices of the living artists in the exhibit that they are part of a web. The Native artists on the committee were adamant that the artwork of their people is ALIVE: "We are related to it and it relates back."[35]

In summary, whether works of art make visible horrifying crimes, genocide, and oppression, or they bring to light collaborative aesthetic creativity, they involve an important person or mind–body relationship. In experiencing and assessing works of art, it is important to ask: Does the work of art link intent and meaning through allegory, symbols, or embodiment? Is this linkage illuminating? Does the work betray the artist's pacific, perhaps admirable goals and communicate instead a grotesque, demeaning message to those who have already suffered profound injustice?

The message of *Hearts of Our People* is an inspiring call to recognize the extraordinary artistic achievements of Native women. It is extraordinary, too, for its display of profound, personal collaboration, involving more than 115 artists from the United States and Canada.

In Chapter 8 we offer further reflection on the role and nature of museums and the aesthetic study of works of art.

---

[35] Jill Ahlberg Yohe and Teri Greeves, p. 22, Introduction, *Hearts of Our People, Native Women Artists*, published by Mia in association with University of Washington Press.

8

A Personal Guide to the Aesthetic Experience of Works of Art

> A work of art is an expressive form created for our perception through sense or imagination, and what it expresses is human feeling. The word *feeling* must be taken here in the broadest sense, meaning *everything that can be felt*, from physical sensation, pain and comfort, excitement and repose, to the most complex emotions, intellectual tensions, or the steady feeling-tones of a conscious human life.
>
> Suzanne Langer[1]

We began this book with a comparison of the visibility and invisibility of persons and God, stressing the importance of being available to others and the transcendent; we have reflected too on the importance of examining different, ever-expanding points of view when it comes to aesthetics and values. In this chapter we offer a personal guide to enhancing aesthetic experiences of and through works of art.

While this chapter pertains to works of art in almost any context, the focus is on the engagement of works of art in museums. Although we addressed two museum experiences in Chapter 7, we offer some further reflections on museums here, before presenting our guide to the aesthetic experience of works of art.

There are, of course, museums dedicated to science, natural history, agriculture, the military, whaling, and so on; some museums are commercial, some are not. Our interest in this chapter is noncommercial fine arts museums that include paintings. Elsewhere, in other published work, we have defended what we call the Philosophical Culture Model of museums, in which museums not only provide exhibitions but also provide sites where people can gather to engage in philosophical reflection on values and history.[2] We believe that

---

[1] Suzanne Langer, *Problems of Art* (New York: Scribners, 1957), p. 15.
[2] See "The Open Museum and its Enemies: An Essay in the Philosophy of Museums," by Charles Taliaferro in *Philosophy and Museums: Essays on the Philosophy of Museums*, edited by V. Harrison, A. Bergqvist, and G. Kemp (Cambridge: Cambridge University Press, 2016), pp. 35–53. The article advocates a strong role for museums in what Karl Popper called open societies. See Popper's *The Open Society and Its Enemies*, which is a strident defense of democratic culture over

museums serve not just the purpose of entertainment (a role we appreciate), but they can also play a role in promoting healthy public debate on matters that are vital to the functioning of a democratic republic. Obviously, there are many places for engaging in philosophical reflection – colleges and universities, coffee shops, pubs, parks, town halls, convention centers, religious sites, restaurants. What can make a public museum especially valuable is that it can create an educational setting with objects and events that can stimulate and inform important exchanges. Particularly in cases where museums are free and open to the public, they can be sites in which the elite are not favored. Unlike restaurants, coffee houses, and so on, (ideally) there should be no barrier to the economically disadvantaged.[3] A shining example of this free access occurred in Glasgow, Scotland, during the 1980s economic destitution under Prime Minister Margaret Thatcher. While Glasgow had the lowest employment in Europe, the city's museums remained open to all; they served as sanctuaries for people to find solidarity, mutual support, and opportunities to organize for political action.[4]

We believe that responsible museum practices can be vital in terms of providing a historical context for informing decision-making in a democracy or a site for developing democratic thinking in states that are not democratic. In a telling essay called "Reverence Is All," the New York City art critic Harold Rosenberg praised the role of museums in American culture as providing some protection from an American susceptibility to accept false historical narratives. Evidently, Joseph Goebbels, the Third Reich minister of propaganda in Nazi Germany, who studied American advertising, thought Americans could be controlled by controlling their understanding of history.

In America especially, a place had to be set aside to instruct people that there is such a thing as Time, beyond timeclocks and timetables and snobberies based on who Arrived When. Goebbels envied the Americans their skill in turning the past into a tool or weapon of the present. A museum is an institution designed to retard that talent. ... With regard to public education, the museum has one paramount function: to inseminate a sense of the reverence in regard to the past.[5]

By "the past" Rosenberg is not recommending we revere false histories that have been used to oppress and marginalize; museums instead have a mission to expose false narratives and represent and engage the many persons and cultures that have been ignored or falsely maligned in canonical histories.

---

against totalitarian regimes, theocracies, and tribal societies. He wrote this important work during World War II; it was published in London in 1945.

[3] This is not to deny that elites can still use free public access museums to their advantage, for example, by sponsoring shows that privilege works of art they might own or control.

[4] We owe this observation to Mark O'Neill (personal communication) who has worked with Glasgow museums for over 20 years. His many projects include his setting up the Open Museum and the St. Mungo Museum of Religious Life and Art.

[5] Harold Rosenberg, "Reverence Is All." In *Discovering the Present: Three Decades in Art, Culture, and Politics* (Chicago: The University of Chicago Press, 1973), p. 135.

Museums have not always been praised by philosophers. Let us consider three objections to museum practices.

The first objection may be conceded straight away. When museums are used to advance and support powerful oppressive forces (exhibiting artwork stolen from other persons, for example), they are highly objectionable. There are over fifty thousand museums today in over two hundred countries, and there would not be a field called Museum Ethics if each of the museums functioned with great virtue.[6] There is nothing about the concept of a museum per se that would rule out establishing an institution that displayed art based on monstrous falsehoods, distorted values, and perverse aesthetics. Adolf Hitler had designs to build a museum in Linz, Austria, the Führermuseum, to display works of art that were stolen or confiscated throughout Europe. Had Hitler been successful, the Führermuseum would still have been deemed a museum, just as a library of white supremacy literature would still be a library. The term *museum* is derived from the Greek for "the seat of the muses," suggesting that museums may be thought of as sites for creativity; sadly, institutions classified as museums may aim at stifling creative independence. So, we conclude that a defense of any and all museums would not just be futile, it would also be profoundly objectionable.

Consider a second objection to museums from the viewpoint of American pragmatism. John Dewey developed an important account of aesthetic experience in his book *Art as Experience*. According to Dewey, the aesthetic consists in our finding valuable, affectively vivid unities in our experience. Dewey sought to ground aesthetics first and foremost in everyday activity and popular culture: the sight and sound of a fire engine, a baseball player's grace, the satisfaction in domestic life, jazz, movies, sensational news stories, the comics, the art of car repair. Out of this affirmation of the aesthetic throughout our lives, Dewey lamented the ways in which museums of fine art seem to move the aesthetic "to a separate realm."[7] We wind up with what Dewey called "the museum conception of art" and "the esoteric idea of fine art" that overshadows the natural, aesthetic art in ordinary life.[8] Dewey linked the emergence of museums in the modern world with the rise of imperialism and nationalism.

Continuing this second objection to museum practices, philosopher Richard Shusterman has defended Dewey's critique of the museum as setting up a stifling dualism with the result of lowering our appreciation of nonmuseum experience. This dualism harms both our appreciation of works of art themselves and our personal values, Shusterman argues:

More than art suffers from its spiritualized sequestration [in museums] nor was this compartmentalization established simply by and for aesthetics to secure and purify their pleasures. The idea of art and the aesthetic as a separate realm distinguished by its

---

[6] See, for example, *The Routledge Companion to Museum Ethics*, edited by Janet Marstine (London: Routledge, 2011) and *A Practical Guide to Museum Ethics*, by Sally Verkovich (New York: Rowman & Littlefield, 2016).
[7] John Dewey, *Art as Experience* (New York: Perigee Books, 1980), p. 9.   [8] Ibid., pp. 19, 90.

freedom, imagination, and pleasure has as its underlying correlative the dismal assumption that ordinary life is necessarily one of joyless, unimaginative coercion. This provides the powers and institutions structuring our everyday life with the best excuse for their increasingly brutal indifference to natural human needs for the pleasures of beauty and imaginative freedom. These are not to be sought in real life, but in fine art, an escape that gives temporary relief.[9]

We offer three replies.

First, it should be conceded that there have been times when museum culture has been experienced as an ethereal realm, an escape from the dull world of the everyday. Here is an over-the-top account of a visit to the National Gallery in London by William Hazlitt in the early nineteenth century:

> [The National Gallery] is a cure (for the time at least) for low-thoughted cares and uneasy passions. We are abstracted to another sphere: we breathe empyrean air; we enter into the minds of Raphael, of Titian, of Poussin, of the Carracci, and look at nature with their eyes; we live in time past, and seem identified with the permanent forms of things. The business of the world at large, and even its pleasures, appear like a vanity and an impertinence.[10]

It should also be appreciated that one of the most important early modern museums, the Louvre, was used by Napoleon to promote his nationalist and imperial ambitions, displaying art acquired throughout Europe by the French military or coerced by way of treaties.

Today much of museum culture is very different from the Napoleonic imperial practices, Hazlitt's exalted view of the museum experience, and the Dewey–Shusterman portrait of museums compartmentalized from everyday life or as arenas for purified pleasures. Increasingly, artists have become bolder in employing everyday objects in their art – from the *Brillo Box*[11] to pop art's use of comic graphics to the use of urine, fecal material, blood, and so on in "shock art." Today, it is not uncommon to be confronted in museums with art addressing racism, sexism, and the horrors of war.[12] It is hard to see how the

---

[9] Richard Shusterman, "Pragmatism: Dewey" in *The Routledge Companion to Aesthetics*, edited by Berys Gaut and D. M. Lopes (London: Routledge, 2001), p. 102.

[10] William Hazlitt, cited by Carol Duncan, *Civilizing Rituals: Inside Public Art Museums* (London: Routledge, 1995), p. 15.

[11] See Andy Warhol's *Brillo Box* (Soap Pads), silkscreen and house paint on plywood, 13 ½ × 16 × 11 ½ inches, 1963–4.

[12] Examples of exhibits: *Artists Respond: American Art and the Vietnam War, 1965–1975* (Minneapolis Institute of Arts, 2019–20); Kara Walker's commissioned *Fons Americanus*, 2019, a thirteen-meter-tall working fountain installed at Tate Modern's Turbine Hall (London, England), whose themes explore the transatlantic slave trade and interconnected histories of Africa, America, and Europe; *Ravaged – Art and Culture in Times of Conflict*, 2014, at M Museum in Leuven, Belgium, an exhibit that juxtaposed international contemporary artists commemorating the centennial of the beginning of WWI with artworks in the permanent collection, addressing the ways in which culture and art are victims of war.

exhibit of such art provides a pleasant escape from the ordinary or the opportunity to avert our gaze from human needs.

Second, we think all experience has aesthetic dimensions. So, while there are different experiences to be had listening to jazz rather than listening to poetry or looking at paintings by Titian, they each involve aesthetics. We see no reason to rank the experience of the ordinary as any less or more aesthetic than the experience of works of art in a museum. To be sure, some settings may be more directly oriented to aesthetic experience (museums) than others are (a routine bus ride), but it is possible for any occasion to be a site for transforming aesthetic experience. Both C. S. Lewis and John Hick reported aesthetically charged conversion experiences while riding a bus.

Third, Dewey and Shusterman valorize the aesthetic experiences to be found in jazz clubs and popular culture. Insofar as art museums do not charge an admission fee, the museum would be a more democratic forum than any number of ordinary everyday sites noted by Dewey and Shusterman. Ordinarily, it costs money to go to jazz clubs, to acquire popular artwork and recorded music; whereas it may cost an individual nothing to enter a museum (except insofar as the individual is a taxpayer and the state sustains the museum).

Consider a third objection to museums. The philosopher Michel Foucault contends that museums play a dangerous role in shaping what we take to be cultural knowledge. The museum object is presented in an ostensibly objective format with accurate didactic texts offering us a neat guide to what we are experiencing. But while visitors may think that they are freely exploring an exhibit, he says, in practice their experience is being subtly controlled by the object's position, lighting, and texts. Most important, the museum creates an illusion of timelessness or a sense of the totality of history. Objects are placed in the same building from remote time periods and yet all of them appear to the museum visitor simultaneously or sequentially as she walks through the exhibits. Foucault uses the word *heterotopia* (utopia of many things) to refer to the museum's insatiable appetite and ability to endlessly collect objects from different times. He writes:

Museums and libraries are heterotopias in which time never ceases to pile up and perch on its own summit, whereas in the seventeenth century, and up to the end of the seventeenth century still, museums and libraries were the expression of an individual choice. By contrast, the idea of accumulating everything, the idea of constituting a sort of general archive, the desire to contain all times, all ages, all forms, all tastes in one place, the idea of constituting a place of all times that is itself outside time and protected from its erosion, the project of thus organizing a kind of perpetual and indefinite accumulation of time in a place that will not move – well, in fact, all this belongs to our modernity. The museum and the library are heterotopias that are characteristic of Western culture in the nineteenth century.[13]

---

[13] Michel Foucault, "Different Spaces," translated by R. Hurley in *Essential Works of Foucault* (London: Penguin, 1998), volume 2, p. 182.

Foucault's overall position merits serious attention. Museums in the past, and some today, enhance canonical pictures of the past that absolve or airbrush crimes from history. Founded in New York City in 1985, the Guerilla Girls, a group of feminist activist artists have (with good reason) repeatedly exposed and challenged the pervasive gender and racial inequality in contemporary museums. Moreover, the so-called Enlightenment did offer a variety of "objective" accounts of human development and progress that we can readily now see (looking back) as advancing the "power politics" of the past. We propose that any defensible philosophy of museums must recognize that they can be instruments of false narratives, of promoting damaging, oppressive frameworks. One also needs to appreciate that the ambition of a museum to achieve a maximal exhibition of all points of view, all events, and so on would be an unattainable goal. But recognizing these limitations should not undermine a real, vital contribution that museums can make in helping us come to terms with facts and values.

As for the charge of museums being unreal because they exhibit objects that are assumed to be in separate times (or the objects from different times create a false sense of simultaneity or presence), it is hard to see why such an objection might not be made against the reality of one's grandmother's collection of the notes you sent her at different times or even the reality of a grocery store with goods that were harvested at different times and places.

We now turn to the project of engaging works of art.

HOW DO YOU GET INTO A WORK OF ART?

This question implies at least two things: Some works of art offer a place to abide, to occupy; and inhabiting that place is not a passive activity or event – it is something you do.[14] It sounds very basic, but we think that in order to experience art as something we can inhabit, and which in turn inhabits us, we have to attend to the artwork. How someone attends to an artwork is as particular and specific as the person attending.

What does it mean to attend – to give your attention? At the very least, it means suspending initial reactions regarding what you like, don't like, are attracted to, or not attracted to. It means suspending judgments, at least for a while, regarding aesthetic values such as the beautiful, the grotesque, or the indifferent. When a viewer can suspend the impulse to categorize, then there is liberty to ask oneself, what do I observe? This simple beginning, reflecting on everything you can about what you observe, is the necessary stepping back from yourself to allow for the possibility of a threshold into a rich experience. It is the

---

[14] The works of art addressed in this chapter may be described as presenting us a world or spatial environment. Some works of art do not. Often sculptures are made to inhabit or aesthetically affect a space rather than to create a distinct space of their own. For example, the British sculptor Andy Goldsworthy makes site-specific and land art, designed to interact with their natural and urban settings.

beginning of meeting the work halfway. You leave yourself long enough to acknowledge all of the ways in which the work is presenting itself.

In *An Experiment in Criticism*,[15] C. S. Lewis draws a useful distinction between "using" pictures and receiving or being open to them:

> While you retain this attitude [of using pictures] you treat the picture – or rather a hasty and unconscious selection of elements in the picture – as a self-starter for certain imaginative and emotional activities of your own. In other words, you "do things with it." You don't lay yourself open to what it, by being in its totality precisely the thing it is, can do for you.

Lewis notes how a child may use a toy, a religious practitioner may use a crucifix, or someone may use the painting of a nude for prurient purposes. This is in contrast with "real appreciation." He continues:

> Real appreciation demands the opposite process. We must not let loose our own subjectivity upon the pictures and make them its vehicles. We must begin by laying aside as completely as we can all our own preconceptions, interests, and associations. We must make room, for Botticelli's *Mars and Venus,* or Cimabue's *Crucifixion,* by emptying out our own. After the negative effort, the positive. We must use our eyes. We must look, and go on looking until we have certainly seen exactly what is there. We sit down before the picture in order to have something done to us, not that we may do things with it. The first demand any art makes upon us is surrender. Look. Listen. Receive. Get yourself out of the way. (There is no good asking first whether the work before you deserves such a surrender, for until you have surrendered you cannot possibly find out.)[16]

The art historian T. J. Clark offers an excellent example of such attending in his book *The Sight of Death: An Experiment in Art Writing*.[17] Clark was awarded a six-month research fellowship at the Getty Museum in early 2000. After arriving, he found himself in the company of two Nicolas Poussin paintings, *Landscape with a Calm*[18] and *Landscape with a Man Killed by a Snake*.[19] Known for his scholarship developing ideas about art in and through sociopolitical contexts, Clark surprised himself when he began to write down his observations about the paintings; he could not stop.

He wrote in the style of diary entries, noting changing light conditions due to how much natural light was present through the ceiling louvers, or how intense the interior museum lighting was or was not on a particular day. Every day the paintings presented themselves differently, depending on time of day and the condition of light. Not setting out to write a book about Poussin, Clark made the diary entries that became a record of his attending to Poussin's paintings, of

---

[15] C. S. Lewis, *An Experiment in Criticism*, pp. 16–17. [16] Ibid., pp. 18–19.
[17] T. J. Clark, *The Sight of Death: An Experiment in Art Writing* (New Haven and London: Yale University Press, 2006).
[18] Nicolas Poussin, *Landscape with a Calm,* oil on canvas, 97 × 131.5 cm. 1650–1 (J. Paul Getty Museum, Los Angeles).
[19] Nicolas Poussin, *Landscape with a Man Killed by a Snake,* oil on canvas, 118 × 198 cm. 1648 (National Gallery, London).

looking. It was only after several weeks of writing that he began to see it might be a worthwhile exercise to share what he was discovering with others.

In his book on art writing, Clark explains that he begins most diary entries with what he sees first, or is thinking about, when he starts looking. Early on in his experiment, he questions his own motives and why he is drawn to do this repeated looking:

I know there is something excessive, and maybe ludicrous, to entering this closely into someone else's imagined world. But these diary entries are partly meant as an argument in favor of such entry. They are meant as an apology for (a glorification of) painting's stasis and smallness and meticulousness – for the way a painter like Poussin does not know when to stop. Time and again, writing these entries, I imagine a viewer asking what Poussin could have thought was the point of this degree of barely perceptible detail, or this pushing and pushing till every coordinate is locked into place for eternity. ... Perhaps I imagine such a viewer especially now, in our current circumstances of image production, when stasis and smallness and meticulous coordination are by and large the opposites of the qualities – the kinds of world-making – that visualizations [today] are involved with.[20]

FIGURE 8.1 Nicolas Poussin, *Landscape with a Calm*, oil on canvas, 97 × 131.5 cm, 1650–1 J. Paul Getty Museum, Los Angeles. Photo courtesy of J. Paul Getty Museum.

[20] Ibid., pp. 42–43.

How Do You Get into a Work of Art? 161

In entering Poussin's worlds in these two paintings, over and over again, Clark writes about decisions Poussin made involving scale, human activities, and what he calls the "overall" tone of the paintings, the balance and distribution of lights and darks, that he believes affects him, the viewer, most of all.

What is so promising for the reader of Clark's book is that the longer he stays in the two paintings, the richer the paintings become as we look with him. The paintings do not get "figured out." They become more complicated; they raise more questions; they reveal layers of invention in each encounter. Sometimes they withhold.

Poussin was a painter highly educated in humanist philosophy and contemporary Catholic thought. The tensions one feels in Poussin's work – between his philosophical interest in our place in the larger cosmos, philosophical Stoicism, classical literature, ancient mythology, poetry, and a contemporary Catholic theology reviving an interest in the classics – makes Poussin's work complexly layered in its sources.

Throughout the book, Clark comes back again and again to questions about point of view. Where is the viewer in relationship to the various planes of space in each painting? He comes to the gallery one morning with this question in mind about *Landscape with a Man Killed by a Snake*.

FIGURE 8.2 Nicolas Poussin, *Landscape with a Man Killed by a Snake*, oil on canvas, 118 × 198 cm, c.1648 National Gallery, London. Photo courtesy of National Gallery.

Having spent many hours before this painting in its normal location in London, Clark is familiar with it; but looking at it in the Getty, he begins to ask new questions about his experiences. It is a landscape distilled from Poussin's years living and working in Rome. In the composition, figures are placed in a staggered fashion, moving back into deep space following a zigzag pattern initiated in the foreground. In the lower left, a man is lying in a pool of water with a snake wrapped around his body. The man nearest him flees from the sight of him (the sight of death), his outstretched arm pulling him into the center of the painting up a path where a woman sits, both of her arms stretched out in surprise at seeing the man running toward her with a look of terror on his face. As you follow the pattern going back and forth into the distant hills and sky, you encounter classical forms of architecture layered into the scene, solid enough but also remote in feeling and atmosphere because they lack the detail of the foliage surrounding them. These areas can "suddenly become charged – touching in their next-to-nothingness."[21] Clark describes the content imbued with Poussin's different treatment of representational detail, mirroring how our minds create and hold on to different aspects of an event, a locale, or even persons, as laden with values:

Poussin is among other things the painter of the unnoticeable; and the ethics of this has to do with precisely not using the unnoticeable as a place in the picture where mere illusionism can stop and a demonstration of power or facility take over. ... The hillside is insignificant, and that's what has to be painted. An accurate likeness of the unnoticeable is a testing, as dignified, a task as getting "mirroring" right, for instance, or the balance of light before dusk sets in – these obviously ethically charged subjects, in other words, on which the picture turns, these reflexive and metaphysical props.[22]

Thinking about point of view, Clark goes to several places in the painting to ask if "this" is the place offered for him to identify as his place to look at the composition. Maybe it is the seated woman in the center of the painting with her outstretched arms, or the onlookers on the hill, or the snake's red eye, or the empty eye socket of the man running from the snake coiled around a dead body.[23] Clark decides that all of the places he identifies as potential locations, while not wrong, do not address the moment the viewer experiences in that first leap into the imaginary world of the painting. He writes:

We are outside the picture, then, aware of it as a finite rectangle, but all the same set down in a space that strikes us as being provided by the scene we are looking at – conjured up by it, implied (ideally) by it. This above all is what a spectator, once hooked, feels the need to experience again in front of the real thing. Ah yes! This is where the painting puts me – at this imaginary distance from its action, in this sort of touch with its manufacture, at this level, in this continuation of its atmosphere, feeling my own size (in relation to the miniature sizes running and agonizing inside the frame) altered like this. The effect is involuntary.[24]

[21] Ibid., p. 39.   [22] Ibid., p. 39.   [23] Ibid., p. 133.   [24] Ibid., p. 134.

Drawing Your Way into a Work of Art 163

What this effect elicits in the viewer is discovered by the painter in the making of the painting as well. The kind of painting Poussin does is developed over time with the same kind of back-and-forth positioning in front of the work, feeling for the relationships of scale, tone, degree of abstraction, that will be true to the understanding the painter wants to see realized – and in this way of painting, what the painter wants to see realized is discovered in the process of making. Clark writes about the phenomena of making and looking that happens in Poussin's painting:

> But painting for them [Poussin and one of his patrons, Pointel] was about overall organization being arrived at in front of one's eyes, being fragile as well as strong, being sometimes truly disturbed – held in suspension by the play of events.[25]

This is an experience of unity arrived at over time, after adopting different points of view, after placing oneself in different relationships within the painting as a living phenomenon that in turn creates new knowledge of consequence.

The human desire to experience imaginary worlds, different points of view, and create connections between what one finds there and one's own life experiences is very simply put by Clark near the end of his book:

> When I am in front of a picture, the thing I most want is to enter the picture's world: it is the possibility of doing so that makes pictures worth looking at for me.[26]

Clark used writing to help him enter the worlds of Poussin's two paintings; and in doing so, he was also able to examine his own reactions to what he was experiencing. Of course, the amount of time he was able to devote to this was a rare privilege of both time and financial support, which he acknowledges. But even without such support, writing your responses while looking at any work of art can help bring your mind to an awareness of what you are experiencing.

Another approach to inhabiting artworks is to draw them. In the following section, we will be using first person in the prose, as an example of one person's (Evans') experience drawing artworks as a means to inhabit works of art. And, coincidentally, it is another story about attending artworks that begins with Poussin and then moves on to works by other artists.

DRAWING YOUR WAY INTO A WORK OF ART

My particular practice of drawing works of art grew out of following someone else's enthusiasm for a particular painter. It is natural to be drawn to investigate a work of art that someone you love or trust, or are inspired by, is excited about.

Years ago, reading the book *Painting as an Art* by Richard Wollheim,[27] I discovered the many pages he devoted to Nicolas Poussin. I knew nothing about

---

[25] Ibid., p. 84.   [26] Ibid., p. 222.
[27] Richard Wollheim, *Painting as an Art* (Princeton, NJ: Princeton University Press, 1987).

Poussin at the time. What caught my attention was Wollheim's psychological reading of Poussin's paint application, color, compositions, and subject matter.

But in reading Wollheim, I was in a quandary, because I liked what he was saying about Poussin, but I couldn't make sense of the language he was using. He described figures that exuded luxurious sensuousness, voluptuousness, and desire. This was language of immediate and heightened awareness. There is a stillness in Poussin's paintings that I initially took, looking at reproductions of his work, for frozen stiltedness. That first impression was about to change forever when I decided to follow Wollheim's enthusiasm to the National Gallery in London and the Ashmolean Museum in Oxford to see what all the excitement was about. I decided to *sketch* Poussin's paintings, and that is when Poussin's worlds began to open up to me.

FIGURE 8.3 J. Evans, *After Landscape with Man Killed by a Snake* by Nicolas Poussin, pencil on paper, 8 × 11 in. Photo courtesy of J. Evans.

It was only when I began to *draw* Poussin's paintings, following his placement and contours of bodies, land, sky, and architecture, that I experienced a kind of interlocking roundness of things growing out of the center of every place on the canvas and endlessly expanding. These infinities of spherical space are what led Wollheim to read Poussin's compositions as giving form to ideas about time.

This sense that the past survives within the present, or that the present is heavy with the future, fosters in a general way that nothing is just what it appears to be. Disturbing forces, not fully assimilated, not fully anticipated, lurk within the most placid settings.[28]

Another way in which Poussin achieves this is in his windows in the architecture tucked back in the landscapes. In Poussin the windows are not eyes to be drawn into; rather they are eyes that look beyond the action of the depicted story, beyond the picture plane. Following these "eyes," the viewer is led to imagine other places. This is an opportunity for reverie for the viewer, initiated by the artist's reverie.

Drawing Poussin gave me an intimate experience with his painting. By holding my pencil and touching it to the page, finding my way through Poussin's shapes and patterns and darks and lights, his art began to inhabit my body and my mind. It deepened my understanding of how a human mind, the mind I encountered in Poussin, apprehends itself being surrounded by forces that can't be measured and by the timeless myths we have imagined as mirrors we carry in our psyches.

While Poussin's body of work addressed mythology, Christianity, and the role of Stoicism for life's contingencies, there was an effort by the Roman Catholic Church to use explicitly Baroque pictorial devices to persuade its followers to remain faithful to the main tenets of Catholicism during this period of the Counter-Reformation. The Jesuits played a significant role in establishing large baroque churches in Rome. One was dedicated to the founder of the order, the sixteenth-century Spanish priest St. Ignazio of Loyola, also known as St. Ignatius. The internal artworks of that church, including the vaulted ceiling painting, were completed by Andrea Pozzo, a Jesuit brother, in 1685. The vault is a trompe l'oeil depiction of the heavens painted on a flat ceiling; it celebrates St. Ignazio and St. Francis Xavier, who was a missionary in Asia. It is widely considered the apex of High Roman Baroque on a grandiose scale.

One of St. Ignazio's main accomplishments was his introduction of Spiritual Exercises, a method of meditation to lead one out of unexamined assumptions and mental habits into greater awareness, empathy, and compassion through a path of guided visualizations that engage the imagination. While the meditations are focused on internal discernment, the ceiling of the church dedicated to St. Ignazio is a wild swirl of saints, animals, columns, light, and movement, all appearing to viewers in three-dimensional, illusionistic space. Light emanates from the Father to the Son to Ignazio and then bursts forth to the Earth's four continents, which are depicted in the four corners of the ceiling.

The scale of the ceiling painting is overwhelming. Unlike Poussin's paintings that are relatively close to our scale, Pozzo's painting soars several stories above the viewer. Its "heavenliness" is further emphasized by the fact that you have to

---

[28] Ibid., p. 224.

FIGURE 8.4 Andrea Pozzo, fresco ceiling painting at Church of St. Ignatius, 17 meters diameter, Rome, Italy, 1685–94. Photo courtesy of Saiko.

view it with your head tilted back as if lying down, inviting the pull of gravity to induce feeling the weight of your own head, no longer balanced at the top of your spine. In this position, the viewer sees sharply defined figures and cloudy amorphous forms, saturated colors and misty greys, move in and out of focus, complicating the viewer's ability to focus and follow any narrative in a sequential way.

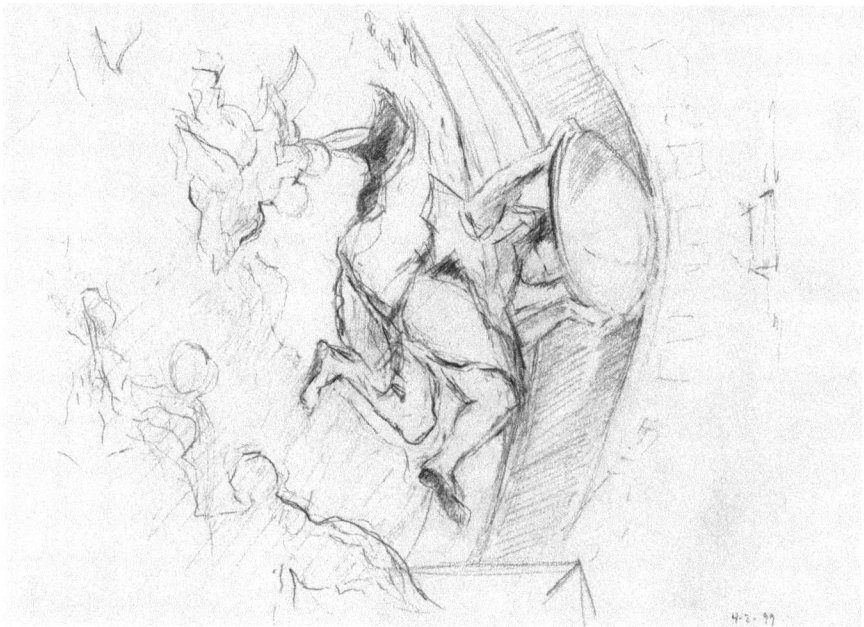

FIGURE 8.5 J. Evans, *St. Ignazio no. 2*, pencil on paper, 11 × 8 in. Photo courtesy of J. Evans.

Returning to the church daily to sketch the composition in sections, I began to bring the ecstatic vision of another time into an embodiment of drawings, translating this vision into my own. I sketched the swirling, intermixing of animals, columns, saints, and painted architecture as a way both to study Pozzo's work and to produce studies that I later used in larger oil paintings on canvas.

There is another way to get into a work of art, and that is to pay attention to what you don't like, or what you think is unavailable to you. Living in Oxford, England, one summer, I spent a great deal of time in the Ashmolean Museum on rainy days when I couldn't paint outside. The museum has a collection of paintings, the Daisy Linda Ward bequest, which consists of ninety-four Dutch and Flemish still-life pictures, primarily from the seventeenth century, or the Golden Age of Dutch art. While flower paintings in the late medieval period were highly symbolic and meant to aid devotion in meditation on Scripture and prayer life, the proliferation of still-life and flower paintings in Holland had as much to do with commerce and the intense interest in representing what the eye and other lenses could record.[29]

FIGURE 8.6 Jan Weenix, *A Vase of Flowers,* oil on canvas, 62 × 50 cm, 1680. Bequeathed by Daisy Linda Ward, 1939. Ashmolean Museum, University of Oxford. Web Figure 9. Photo courtesy of Ashmolean Museum.

I decided one day to try to draw one of the still lifes. The paintings seemed unavailable to me, closed down and sealed behind the meticulous articulation of every petal, leaf, and insect wing. I could appreciate their craft, but they felt remote, which is odd, because they are very intimate paintings in size and

---

[29] See *Still Life,* by Norbert Schneider (Cologne, Germany: Taschen, 2003). See also *The Art of Describing,* by Svetlana Alpers (Chicago: University of Chicago Press, 1983).

subject matter. I began to draw different works, looking for an underlying geometry and structure.

As I began to break through over time, I began to draw more quickly. I found in these small, dark, intensely colored works the ecstatic energy that is part of all Baroque art.

FIGURE 8.7 J. Evans, *After Van Aelst no. 3*, pencil on paper, 10 × 8 in. Photo courtesy of J. Evans.

It was almost as if the artists had wound and coiled that energy of their age into these exquisitely rendered bouquets, coiled it up so tight that it would last centuries and never dissipate.

For me to experience this, I had to suspend my skepticism about the subject matter, the seamless surfaces, only long enough to begin drawing the works.

There is play in drawing, and when you draw, you put something into play, taking you places you can't predict.

When you draw a work of art, you are touching someone else's decisions. Your eyes and hand work together to grasp the structure, the scale, and the form made by another body and mind, and in doing so, you experience mind in art. Mind is revealed in the aesthetic dimension. It is sensuous cognition or knowing, which in turn becomes the foundation of your interpretations and values.

The activity of drawing is an act of interrogation that enables you to see more and helps order your sensations and judgments over time. The kind of drawing I am talking about is not about trying to make a good drawing or to copy someone's work. It is instead using a pencil or pen or anything you can find to move around as a tool for engaging with the work to get inside it. The impulse to make marks is part of our nature, and we have thousands of years that testify to that. But somewhere along the line, many of us decided to associate drawing with talent, art with a capital A, something that just artists do. But it is something we can all do, and it rewards our attempts to connect ourselves with works of art, religious and secular.

Epilogue

The question that started our project, "Is God invisible?" took us into theological reflection on what might be meant by God being invisible and, just as importantly, what might be meant for our being invisible or visible to one another. We explored the religious worldviews of Judaism, Christianity, Islam, Hinduism, and Buddhism, and their secular alternatives in the three areas of aesthetics: aesthetic experience itself, the philosophy of beauty and ugliness, and the philosophy of art. In advancing aesthetic personalism, we have argued for the reality of embodied persons as enduring individuals with our distinctive aesthetic experiences and values. We have argued against defining persons and the transcendent so as to make it impossible for persons to have symmetrical experiences of God or the sacred. We propose that an omniscient or God's-eye point of view (as we find in the Abrahamic idea of God, the omniscience of Brahman, and the Compassionate Buddha) provides an important challenge to oppressive, false narratives and supports a realist view of the good, the true, and the beautiful. We have observed how some works of art can be concealing or revealing of values and minds, and how some religious artifacts and works of art can be viewed in terms of personal embodiment. Finally, we provided a personal guide on enhancing the aesthetic experience of works of art, religious and secular.

Index

Abrahamic faiths/traditions, 4, 18–46, 72, 76–77, 79, 110
   God of, 4, 12, 16
   music and, 137
Advanta Vedanta, 74, 104
aesthetic, *See also* philosophy of art
aesthetic emotions, 1, 99
aesthetic evaluation, 104
aesthetic experiences, 83, 101, 147, 171
   and beauty, 1
   and human experiences, 10–11
   and the divine, 7, 57
   cognitive nature of, 10
   Dewey and, 155
   Dewy and Shusterman on, 157
   of works of art, 171
   religious experience and, 26
aesthetic judgment, 98
aesthetic life, identification of, 8
aesthetic personalism, 3, 7, 42, 139, 151, 171
   and naturalism, 68
   and personalism, 10
   overview of, 9–12
aesthetic, cognitive apertures, 56
aesthetically complex experiences, 1
aesthetics, 7–8
   and religion, 1
   areas of, 2
   ideal observer theory and, 110
   point of view, 8
   relationship with religion, 9, 42
   ugliness and beauty, 1, 7
African religions, 9, 92, 112
   and omniscience, 112
Al-Biruni, 5

Alcibiades, 92
alienation, 112
Allah, 2, 24–25, 65, 77, 112
   and the shahada, 66
Amida, 106
analytical philosophy, 3
Anderson, Hans Christian, 58
Anderson, Pamela Sue, 110–112
   feminist and God's-eye point of view, 107
aniconism, 25
animism, superstitious, 147
annihilation, 69–70, 75, 78, 80
Anscombe, Elizabeth, 144
Anselm of Canterbury, 79
anthropomorphism, 73
anthropophobia, 73
anti-Semitism, and Christianity, 86
apophatic theology (*via negativa*), 117
Aquinas, St. Thomas, 35, 137
   worlds/worldviews, 65
Arendt, Hannah, 65
Arjuna/Krishna dialogue, 40–41, 56
Armstrong, David, 144
art
   and assessing of religious worlds, 65
   as being religious, 145
   as persons, 139–140
   being invisible and the visible in, 140–142
   monetary investment in, 82
   persons as, 142–148
   philosophy of, 2, 7–8, 145, 147, 171
art objects, 145
art, works of, 171
   and personal embodiment, 171
   what they reveal, 171

Index

asceticism, 8
Avalokiteshvara (Sanskrit), 106
Ayer, A. J., 4, 14, 19, 20, 28, 30, 33–34, 101, 103
  and the invisibility of God, 18

Bachelard, Gaston, 132–133
Balthasar, Hans Urs von, 90
beauty, 7, 101
  aesthetic experiences and, 99–100
  aesthetics of, 97
  and the eye of the beholder, 100–112
  and perfection, 22, 99
  concept of in early cultures, 93
  Diotima and, 91
  Diotima's ladder of, 93–99
  ideal observer theory and, 110
  overview of, 91–93
  philosophy of, 171
behaviorist/materialist approach, the, 14
beholder, beauty and, 100–112
Bellini, Giovanni, 124–125
Bembo, Francesco, 146
Berman, Morris, 64, 66
Bertocci, Peter, 10
Bhagavad Gita, 40–42, 56, 61, 64, 85, 137
Bible, 56
  Galileo's claim and, 12
Bitbol, Michel, 36
Blackburn, Simon, 70–71, 77, 81, 86
Bodhisattva Inexhaustible Intent, 106
Bodhisattva of Compassion, 106
Boethius, 79, 135
Book of Ezekiel, 63
Brahman, 2, 65, 74–75, 77, 104, 110
  belief in, 45
  omniscience of, 171
  the transcendent, 42
  translation of, 75
brahmavidya (extreme science), 58
Brown, David, 5
Buber, Martin, 60
Buddha
  Compassionate, 29, 171
  destruction of statues of, 148
Buddha of Infinite Light and Life, 106
Buddhism, 4, 8, 75, 80, 171
  and annihilation, 75
  and omniscience, 72
  challenges faced by, 83
  consciousness and, 58–59
  focus of, 59
  glory and, 72

meaning of life and, 81
music and, 137
the Bodhisattva of Compassion, 106
Bunyan, John, 102, 140, 141

Cahill, Thomas, 72
Cambridge Platonists, 38
Camus, Albert, 11
Capello, Bianco, 146
cataphatic theology (*via positiva*), 117
Catholic theology, 161
causes and reasons, 51–56
charity, principle of, 65, 82, 84–86
Chastity vs. Lust, 140
Chief Arvol Looking Horse, 150
Christian Bible, 56, 87
Christian tenet, 12
Christian theism, 136
Christianity, 8, 171, *See also* God of the
  Abrahamic traditions
  and nature of the world view, 79
Christians, and praying, 20
Clark, T. J., 159–163
classical theism, 4
communion, 26, 35, 52, 66, 101
Compassionate Buddha, 29, 74, 110–111, 147, 171
concealment, 116–119
Confucianism, 9
conscious subjectivity, 10
consciousness, 6
consciousness, primacy of, 58–59
Copleston, Frederick, 19, 34
Cottingham, John, 61
Counter-Reformation, 165
Craig, William, 47
Crane, Tim, 11, 37, 44
  theism and, 43–45
  transcendent God concept and, 42
creative productivity, 94
Crivelli, Carlo, 123–124
Cudworth, Ralph, 38
Cusa, Nicholas of, 117–119

d'Hondecoeter, Melchior, 114
Dakota peoples/tribes, 150
Dakota Spiritual and Traditional Elders, 150
Dalai Lama, 106
Dante, Alighieri, 141
Daoism, 9, 93
dark night of the soul, the, 8

Darwin, Charles
  and Darwinian origin, 83
  as a naturalist, 68–69
Davis, Richard, 146
Day, Dorothy, 69
de Hooch, Pieter, 135
de' Medici, Francesco, 146
Dennett, Daniel, 143–144
Deus absconditus, 8
Dewey, John, 155, 157
  and Shusterman view of museums, 156
Dionysius the Areopagite, 79
Diotima
  and beauty, 91
  ladder of beauty, 93–99
disembodiment, 35
divine invisibility, 24–35, *See also* invisibility of God
Divine Names (Dionysius the Areopagite), 79
divine omnipresence, 24
divine omniscience, 1
divine presence, 29, 33
divine revelation, pictures of, 56
divine, the, 15
  anthropomorphic imagery of, 80
  face-to-face disclosure, 56
  revealing in Venice, 119–134
  revealing the presence of, 22
Divine-Thought, 101
Dominican Roman Catholic religious order, 20
dualism, 155
DuBois, W. E. B., 29, 103
Duncan, Carol, 145
Durkheim, Emile, 37
Durant, Sam, 148, 150
Dutch painting, golden age of, 114–116
Dworkin, Ronald, 70–71, 77, 81, 86

Eastern Orthodox Christianity, and icons, 120
Easwaran, Eknath, 29, 38, 41, 81, 105
  beauty and, 104
Ecke, Dianne, 87
Ellis, Fiona, 54
Ellison, Ralph, 14
embodied conscious awareness, 56
embodied conscious life, 59
embodied knowledge, 45
embodied persons, 14
embodiment, 140
emptiness, 72, 76
Emptiness (sunyata), 75
Enlightenment, 158

Eros, 95
  desire and, 79, 95
ethical evaluations, 110
evil, problem of, 83
experience, 2–3, 10
  and aesthetic dimension, 9
  religious constraints, 13
experiential apertures, 59
experientialism, 2
exploitation, in art, 116

face-to-face disclosure, 56–62
Fadiman, Anne, 48
Felix, Marcus Minucius, 88
feminist point of view, 111
Fischer, John, 11–12
Flew, Antony, 14, 30, 33
  and the invisibility of God, 18–20
Foucault, Michel, 157–158
Freud, Sigmund, 81, 137
Fumerton, Richard, 2, 54

Galileo, 11–12
Gallagher, S., 36
Gandhi, Mahatma, 29, 41, 69, 85
  and satyagraha, 8
Guatama, Siddhartha, 72
Gell, Alfred, 145
Gellman, Jerome, 50
genocide, 87
glory, 72
God, 2, 65, 77
  of Abrahamic traditions, 12, 16, 18, 171
  as a hypothesis, 43–44
  being invisible, 8, 171
  natural or nonnatural, 12–15
  passionate presence of, 51
  presence of, 21–22, 26, 50, 52, 57, 77, 81
  supernatural or nonnatural, 35–39
  transcendent, 42–43, 51, 54
  Trinitarian understanding of, 74
God of Abrahamic faith, 27
God's-eye point of view, 2, 109–111, 171
  Anderson's feminist critique of, 107
  beauty and, 91
  feminist ethics and, 111
  ideal, 104, 112
  Klemke and, 108
  meaning of life and, 107
  objections to, 107–112
  Putman and, 107, 109
  self-alienation and, 112

Index

Graham, Gordon, 5
Griffith-Dickens, Gwen, 5

Hale, Sheila, 126–127
Harper, Ralph, 100
Harrison, Victoria, 5
Hazlitt, William, 156
Hebblethwaite, Brian, 57
Hebrew Bible, 16, 56, 63–64, 88, *See also* Bible
Hedley, Douglas, 5
hell, 77, 79
  Abrahamic traditions of, 87
  creating for others, 81
  naming of persons in, 141
  portrayals of, 88
  reality and, 81
Hellespontine Sibyl, 128
Heschel, Abraham Joshua, 49, 51
Hick, John, 87, 157
Hinduism, 4, 8, 75, 80, 85, 105, 171
  and omniscience, 105
  forms of, 74
  music and, 137
Homer, 72
  and Homeric desire, 95
  and Homeric literature, 78
homesickness and nostalgia, 100
Hoskins, Janet, 145
Hume, David, 4, 14, 17–18, 30, 33, 66, 78, 101–103

iconoclastic movements, Christian, 25
Iddrisu, Abdulai, 112
ideal aesthetic observer theory, 1, 91, 98, 102–112
idolatry, 25
immanent goods, 81, 86
Inge, W. R., 87
intelligent power, invisible, 17
invisibility of God, 12–13, 19–21
  Abrahamic traditions and, 16
  and of people, 171
  Ayer and, 18
  Flew and, 18–20
  Hume and, 17–18
  Moore and, 18, 20
  omniscience and, 24
invisibility of persons, 12, 15, 171
  criticism of, 18
  disguising goals and ideas and, 14
  embodied persons and, 14
  mental life and, 14

invisible intelligent power, 17
Inwagen, Peter van, 109
Isaac of Nineveh, 88–89
Islam, 8, 80, 171
  and rejection of the Trinity, 77
  images and, 25
Islamic invasion, 148

James, Henry, 84
James, William, 43
Jantzen, Grace, 27
Jayatilleke, K. N., 76
Judaism, 8, 171, *See also* God of the Abrahamic traditions
  as a monotheistic religion, 77
  Greco-Roman world and, 72

Kant, Immanuel, 98
karma, 75
Kenny, Anthony, 36, 83–84, 144
Kessel, van Elsje, 146
Kierkegaard, Sören, 8
Kitcher, Philip, 37, 77
Klemke, E. D., 108–109, 111–112
knowledge argument, the, 14, 30, 67
Kongzi, 93
Kwan, Kai-man, 48

Langer, Susanne, 147, 153
Langland, William, 79–80
Lash, Nicholas, 12, 73
Law, William, 81
Leeuw, Geradus Vendler, 46
Levinas, Emmanuel, 61
Lewis, C. S., 65, 140, 157, 159
Lewis, David, 88
Lewis, H. D., 32
liberal naturalism, 68
Lincoln, Abraham, 149
literature, 49, 65, 73, 161
  Lewis on, 65
  on religious experience, 22–23
  scriptural sources of religious experiences, 22–23
  white supremacy, 155
liturgy, God apprehended through, 26
logical positivism, 19
Lotus Sutra, The, 106
  Watson's translation of, 106
Louvre, 156
Loux, Michael, 109

Mackie, J. L., 46–47
Madhyamika, 75
Madhyamika school, 76
Mahabharata, 40, See also *Bhagavad Gita*
Maitri Upanishads, 104
Mankato hangings, 148
Mann, Thomas, 137
Marcel, Gabriel, 1, 6, 61
Maritain, Jacque, 99
Marxism, 10
Maslow, Abraham, 38
material world
   sensory experience, 45
McCabe, Herbert, 12, 73
McGinn, Colin, 68
McNamara, Patrick, 54
Melville, Herman, 16
menagerie paintings, 114–116
mental life/lives, 14–15, 31
   of nonhuman animals, 33
   of persons and animals, 53
mental operations, 18
Merleau-Ponty, Maurice, 112
Merton, Thomas, 116–117
Messina, Antonello de, 124
metaphysics, 49, 76
Metz, Thaddeus, 73
Michell, W. J. T., 145
Miles, Margaret, 5, 100
Milton, John, 102, 147
mind–body relationship, 14, 139, 152
minds and bodies, approach to, 14
Minneapolis Institute of Art (Mia), 151
Minneapolis Sculpture Garden, 148
mirror image, 102
Mohammad, 56
Moore, Gareth, 14, 28, 30, 32–33, 35, 55, 88
   and mental life, 31
   and the invisibility of God, 18, 20–21
Mothersill, Mary, 97
motives, unobserved, 14
Mt. Sinai, 16, 38
Mundaka Upanishad, 60
Murdoch, Iris, 96, 100, 103
museum rituals, 145
museums, 155
   and Dewey–Shusterman, 156
   as unreal, 158
   inequality in, 158
   objection to, 157
   Philosophical Culture Model of, 153
   religious devotion and, 145
   role of, 154–158
music, 137–138, 157
   Apollo and, 127
myth of Sisyphus, 77

Nagarjuna, 75–76
Nagel, Thomas, 11, 31, 58
Native American
   art, 8
   experience, 8
Native American community
   and Durrant's *Scaffold*, 149
Native American spirituality, 9
naturalism, 49, 68
   robust, 36
   secular, 3
Nazianzus, Gregory, 23
negation (*via negativa*), 114, 117
Nehamas, Alexander, 97–98
Neoplatonists, 23
Newman, John Henry, 137
Newton, Isaac, 59
Nicene Creed, 23
nihilism, 11
Nineveh, Isaac of, 88–89
nirguna Brahman, 74
Nirvana, 45, 75–76
nostalgia and homesickness, 100

O'Connor, Flannery, 65
O'Hear, Anthony, 5, 83, 136
O'Hear, Natasha, 136
Omniscience, 171, See God's-eye point of view
Origen, 39
other minds, problem of, 14

Paine, Crispin, 145–146
Pearce, Susan, 147
perfect being tradition, the, 45
perfection, 76, 96
   and beauty, 22, 99
personal embodiment, and art and religious
   artifacts, 171
personalism, aesthetic, 171
personalist movement, 9
personalist perspective, of aesthetics, 9–12
personalists, and treatment of persons, 9–10
personhood
   of art objects, 3, 145
persons
   as perspective, 54, 56, 103, 142
   treatment of and personalism, 9–12

Index

phenomenology, 2–3, 143
  and treatment of persons, 10
  of experience, 13, 18
  of face-to-face encounter, 56–62
  religious experience and, 22
Phillips, D. Z., 4
Philosophical Culture Model of museums, 153
philosophy, 2
  analytical, 3
  of art, 2, 7–8, 145, 147, 171
  classic problem in, 14
  of religion, 4–5, 18, 38
Piranesi, Giovanni Battista, 18
Plato, 60, 93
  and Socrates, 100
  on love and beauty, 95–96
  view of desire and, 95
Platonic Christian tradition, 90
Platonic heritage, 96
Platonists, 95
  Cambridge, 38
Plotinus, 33, 100–101
Plutarch, 92
Poe, Edgar Allan, 14, 100
point of view
  God's-eye, 2, 91, 104, 107, 171
positivism, logical, 19
Poussin, Nicolas, 159–163
Pozzo, Andrea, 166
presence
  of God, 21–22, 26, 50, 52, 57, 77, 81
primacy of consciousness, 56
principle of charity, 84
Protagoras, 100
Prothero, Stephen, 85
public perception of art, 140, *See also* art
  Hearts of Our People, 151–152
  integration of invisible and the visible, 140–142
  persons as art and, 142–148
  Scaffold (Durrant), 148–151
Putnam, Hilary, 109
  and realism, 107

quantum dynamics, laws of, 43
quantum energy, fluctuating, 47
Quanyin (Chinese), 106
Qur'an, 16, 56, 80, 85
  acknowledgement of Jesus, 76
  and divine omnipresence, 25
  and idolatry, 25
  and invisibility, 24
  as a scriptural source, 22

Ramakrishna, Sri, 29, 85
Ramanuja, 74, 104
Ramayana, 7, 47, 53
Rand, Ayn, 81
realism, 107
reasons vs. causes
  Scruton, 52
rebirth, 106
reincarnation, 75
Reinhardt, Ad, 116–117
religion
  definition of, 8–9
  philosophy of, 4–5, 18, 38
  relationship of aesthetics and, 9
  relationship with aesthetics, 42
  worlds/worldviews, 6
religious and ethical attunement, 59–62
religious art objects
  personhoods of, 3
religious artifacts, 3
  and personal embodiment, 171
  and the visible and invisible world, 139
  personhood of, 146
religious devotion, 145
religious dimension
  and aesthetics, 2
religious experiences
  as apertures to encountering the divine, 58
  philosophy of, 51
religious objects, 3, 8, 15, 145
religious rituals, 145
Rijksmuseum, 114
rituals, 145
robust naturalism, 36
Rolle, Richard, 137–138
Roman Catholic, 9
Rosenberg, Harold, 154
Ross, Stephen David, 93
Rowling, J. K., 103
  and Harry Potter imaginarium, 19
Rudd, Anthony, 5
Russell, Bertrand, 4, 14, 16, 33, 38, 46, 69
  and Jews, 84
  despair and, 70, 80

sacramentalism, 140, *See* symbolism/sacramentalism
sacraments, 45, 66
saguna Brahman, 74

Saint Catherine's Monastery, 39
Sartre, Jean-Paul, 130
satyagraha, practice of, 8
Scarry, Elaine, 97
  and Kant's early theory of aesthetics, 98
  philosophy beauty and, 98
Scruton, Roger, 52, 90
  cognitive apertures, 56
  natural sciences and, 43, 53
  philosophy of self of, 142
  primacy of naturalism and, 57
  self as a perspective and, 54
  sexual intimacy, 142
  transcendent God concept of, 42, 51
Searle, John, 82
secular naturalism, 3, 67–71, 137
  aesthetics and, 67
self-alienation, 112
self-awareness, 53, 55, 83, 143–144
  absence of, 15
  and consciousness, 84
selfishness
  secret, 116
  virtue of, 81
sensory experiences, 18, 27, 38, 45
shahada, 66
Shankara, 74
Shintoism, 9
Shusterman, Richard, 155–157
  and Dewey's view of museums, 156
Sikhism, 9
Sircello, Guy, 97
slavery, 87–88, 115
  Darwin and, 69
  Harriet Tubman and, 27
Smart, Ninian, 87
Smith, Huston, 87
Socrates, 91–93
Solomon, 72
Solon, 65
Song of Songs, 22
soul,
  as invisible, 23
  rightful order of, 90
  the dark night of, 8
Spenser, Edmund, 140
Sprigge, T. L. S., 31
Spurgeon, Charles, 88
St. Catherine of Sienna, 35
St. Denis, Abbot Sugar of, 97
St. Francis of Assisi, 29
St. Francis Xavier, 165

St. Ignatius, 165
St. Ignazio, 165
St. Irenaeus, 24
Stowe, Harriet Beecher, 88
strict naturalism, 68
Stump, Eleonore, 30
Sugar, Abbot of St. Denis, 97
superstitious animism, 147
Swinburne, Richard, 141–142
symbolism/sacramentalism, 140–141
symbolist aesthetic, 141

Taylor, A. E., 89
Teresa of Avila, 29
test of time, 65, 82, 87
theism, 4, 8, 12, 26
  as a hypothesis, 44
  Christian, 136
  classical, 4
  Crane on, 43–45
  critics of, 17, 22
  God of the Abrahamic traditions and, 38
Theravada Buddhism, 76
Thomas, Julian, 146
thought experiments, 59
Tiepolo, Giovanni Battista, 119, 121, 132–134, 137
Tintoretto, Jacopo Robusti, 129–132, 134
Titian, Vicello, 126, 128, 132, 134, 157
Tolkien, J. R. R., 9, 65
transcendent God concept, 42, 54
  aesthetic, cognitive apertures, 56
  Crane and, 42–43
  Crane and Scruton, 51
  face-to-face disclosure and, 56–62
  primacy of consciousness and, 58–59
  religious and ethical attunement, 59–62
  Scruton and, 42
  Wettstein and, 42
Trigg, Roger, 109
Trinity, 35, 77
truth, 11
  desire for, 17
  everlasting, 70
  holding on to, 8
  love of, 17
  making sense of, 2
  of theism, 26
  scientific, 11
Truth, Sojourner, 88
Tubman, Harriet, 27

Index

ugliness, 7, 45, 70
  affective nature of experience and, 2
  philosophy of, 7, 171
Ultimate Reality, 9, 45, 75
Underhill, Evelyn, 6, 138
unselfing, 103
unselfing process, 100
Upanishads, 41, 60, 72, 74–75, 104

values
  being void of, 9
  significant, 72
van Gogh, Vincent, 103
Velleman, David, 78
Venetian painting, and the divine, 119–134
via negativa (apophatic theology), 117–118
via positiva (cataphatic theology), 117
  and visual arts, 119
virtue, and religious change, 87
Vishishtadvaita, 74
Vishnu, 40
visibility/invisibility, 7, 14
  of God, 1
  of persons, 1, 14
visual arts, and *via positiva*, 119
Vivaldi, 134
Vivarini, Antonio, 119–120
Vivekananda, 85

wabi-sabi, 99
Waismann, Friedrich, 42–43
Walker Art Center, 148–150
Wallace, Alan, 59
Ward, Keith, 88
Watson, Burton, 106

Waugh, Evelyn, 57
Weenix, Jan, 168
Weil, Simone, 27
  experience of beauty, 57–58
Wells, H. G., 20, 33, 84
Wesley, John, 88
Wettstein, Howard, 42, 48–51, 65
Weyden, Rogier van der, 118
Wilberforce, William, 88
Wiman, Christian, 71
Wolfchild, Sheldon, 149
Wollheim, Richard, 163–164
Wolterstorff, Nicholas, 5
Woolf, Virginia, 65
  on T. S. Eliot, 85
world religions, and living in different worlds, 64
worlds/worldviews, 26
  assessing, 82–89
  eliminating consciousness from, 58
  meaning of live and, 81
  religious, 5, 15, 67, 171
  scientific, 109
  theistic, 111
Wynn, Mark, 5

Xenophanes, 73

Yahweh, 16
Yoruba discourse/people, 92, 112

Zaehner, R. C., 87
Zahavi, Dan, 35–36, 101–102, 112
Zoroastrianism, 5, 9

Lightning Source UK Ltd.
Milton Keynes UK
UKHW010635091021
391745UK00008B/100